AQA Economics

Exclusively endorsed by AQA

A2

Jim Lawrence
Steve Stoddard

Nelson Thornes

Published in 2009 by:
Nelson Thornes Ltd
Delta Place
27 Bath Road
CHELTENHAM
GL53 7TH
United Kingdom

11 12 13 / 10 9 8 7 6 5 4 3

A catalogue record for this book is available from the British Library

ISBN 978 0 7487 9965 7

Cover photograph by Martin Sookias Photography
Illustrations by eMC design
Page make-up by eMC design

Printed in China by 1010 Printing International Ltd

Photograph acknowledgements

The authors and publishers wish to thank the following for permission to use photographs:

p10 Photolibrary/Mark & Audrey Gibson; p22 Alamy/i love images; p26 Photolibrary; p29 Science Photo Library/Ian Hooton; p42 Alamy/Adrian Sherratt; p46 Topfoto; p52 Alamy/Justin Kase zsixz; p57 Rex Features/Sipa Press; p78 Photolibrary/Denkou Images; p79 Corbis/Charles O'Rear; p81 Ronald Grant Archive; p90 Getty/Wesley; p92(l) Science Photo Library/ Mark Thomas,(r) Rex Features/Mark Leech; p97 Alamy/Danny Clifford; p103 Alamy/Ashley Cooper; p111 RexFeatures/Anthony Upton; p112 Rex Features/John Callan; p124 Alamy/ Photofusion Picture Library; p126 iStockphoto/David H. Lewis; p142 Corbis/Bihop Asare; p146 Alamy/S and J Photography; p148 Superstock; p152 Fotolia; p158 Rex Features/Jason Bye; p161 Alamy/Richard Sheppard; p167 Topfoto; p171 Rex Features/Anthony Upton; p176 Governor and Company of the Bank of England; p180 Corbis/Bettmann; p183 Alamy/Jenny Matthews; p198 Corbis/Sherwin Crasto; p199 Alamy/PSL Images; p218 Corbis/Frithjof Hirdes.

Every effort has been made to contact the copyright holders and we apologise if any have been overlooked. Should copyright have been unwittingly infringed in this book, the owners should contact the publishers, who will make the corrections at reprint.

The authors and publisher would like to thank Tutor2u Limited for their kind permission to reproduce copyright material throughout this book.

Contents

AQA Introduction

Nelson Thornes has worked in partnership with AQA to ensure this book and the accompanying online resources offer you the best support for your A2 course.

All resources have been approved by senior AQA examiners so you can feel assured that they closely match the specification for this subject and provide you with everything you need to prepare successfully for your exams.

These print and online resources together **unlock blended learning**; this means that the links between the activities in the book and the activities online blend together to maximise your understanding of a topic and help you achieve your potential.

These online resources are available on **kerboodle!** which can be accessed via the internet at **www.kerboodle.com/live**, anytime, anywhere. If your school or college subscribes to this service you will be provided with your own personal login details. Once logged in, access your course and locate the required activity.

For more information and help visit **www.kerboodle.com**

Icons in this book indicate where there is material online related to that topic. The following icons are used:

💡 Learning activity

These resources include a variety of interactive and non-interactive activities to support your learning, such as Simulations, Data response activities and Worksheets.

☑ Progress tracking

These resources include a variety of tests that you can use to check and expand your knowledge (Revision quizzes) and a range of resources that enable you to analyse and understand examination questions (On your marks...).

How to use this book

This book covers the specification for your course and is arranged in a sequence approved by AQA.

The book content is divided into chapters that match the AQA Economics specification for Units 3 and 4 – Business economics and the distribution of income and The national and international economy. Chapters 1–10 cover Unit 3 and Chapters 11–19 cover Unit 4

The features in this book include:

Learning objectives

At the beginning of each chapter you will find a list of learning objectives that contain targets linked to the requirements of the specification.

Key terms

Terms that you will need to be able to define and understand.

■ Case study

A mixture of real-life and devised case studies contextualising and exemplifying the core concepts.

■ Activity

Activities that will help you to test your knowledge and understanding.

■ Links

This highlights any areas where topics relate to another part of this book, or to the AS textbook and specification.

AQA Examiner's tip

Hints from AQA examiners to help you with your study and to prepare for your exam.

AQA Examination-style questions

Questions in the style that you can expect in your exam appear at the end of each chapter.

AQA examination questions are reproduced by permission of the Assessment and Qualifications Alliance.

Learning outcomes

A bulleted list at the end of each topic or chapter summarising the content in an easy-to-follow way.

■ Web links in the book

As Nelson Thornes is not responsible for third party content online, there may be some changes to this material that are beyond our control. In order for us to ensure that the links referred to in the book are as up to date and stable as possible, the websites provided are usually homepages with supporting instructions on how to reach the relevant pages if necessary.

Please let us know at **kerboodle@nelsonthornes.com** if you find a link that doesn't work and we will do our best to correct this at reprint, or to list an alternative site.

Acknowledgements

The authors and publishers wish to thank the following for permission to use copyright material:

p9 Diminishing returns case study adapted from Robert Shiel 'Improving Soil Fertility in the Pre-Fertiliser Era,' in Bruce M. S. Campbell and Mark Overton (eds.), Land, Labour, Livestock: Historical Studies in European Agricultural Productivity, Manchester University Press, 1991; p12 The new face of hunger, 17 April 2007 © The Economist Newspaper Limited, London 2007, reprinted with permission; p13 Article by Kathy Fong, 21 November 2007, http://sites.thestar.com; p16 'The economics of nuclear power' Briefing paper 8, www.uic.au/nip08.htm. World Nuclear Association, reprinted with permission; p21 'Nike admits to Mistakes over Child Labour' by Steve Boggan The Independent, 20 October 2001, reprinted with permission; p28 'A diamond mine changes hands', 29 November 2007 © The Economist Newspaper Limited, London 2007, reprinted with permission; p34 Susanne Huttner, 'The Internet economy: Towards a better future', OECD Observer No. 268, June 2008, © OECD 2008, www.oecdobserver.org; p36 'BT Becomes First Foreign Firm Entering China's Telecom Market', People's Daily, http://english.peopledaily.com.cn; p38 'Cheap no more', 6 December 2007© The Economist Newspaper Limited, London 2007, reprinted with permission; p47 Recent Developments in the Economics of Price Discrimination by Mark Armstrong 2006, reprinted with permission from the author and Cambridge University Press; p50 Vivendi Diagrams, from 'Water as a Public Service' by David Hall and Emanuele Lobina. Public Services International Research Unit www.world-psi.org; p50–1 Why do companies need to make profits? OFWAT © Crown Copyright reprinted under Crown Copyright PSI License C2008000256; p59 Antitrust: Commission imposes €38 million fine on E.ON for breach of a seal during an inspection. http://europa.eu © European Communities 1995–2009; p61–62 'Bananas to UK via the Channel islands?' by Ian Griffiths and Felicity Lawrence, The Guardian, 6 November 2007, www.Guardian.co.uk copyright Guardian News & Media Ltd 2007; p63 'Fingers pointed at credit rating agency monopoly', The Telegraph 20 August 2007, reprinted with permission; p63 'A beleaguered industry looks to reform itself', 9 February 2008 © The Economist Newspaper Limited, London 2008, reprinted with permission; p63 Who are the stakeholders? adapted from an article by Michael Mainelli, Z/Yen Limited, reprinted with permission; p73 'Irish Outlook – If only we could harness hot air', adapted from Michael Casey, Sunday Times, 8 October 2006, reprinted with permission from © NI Syndication, London (2006); p85 'Army offers bursaries to boost recruitment' by Audrey Gillan, The Guardian, 29 March 2008© Guardian News & Media Ltd 2008; p94 'NHS consultants given 27 per cent pay increase' by Jeremy Laurance, The Independent, 22 November 2007, reprinted with permission; p106 Minimum wage set to rise by 21p by Deborah Summers, The Guardian, 5 March 2008 copyright Guardian News & Media Ltd 2008;p107 Market failure and income and wealth inequality by Geoff Riley from http://tutor2u.net reprinted with permission – see www.tutor2u.net; p108 'Young people face "pensions time bomb"', The Press Association, published in The Guardian, 11 June 2004; p127 Human Development Report 2007/08 © United Nations Development Programme, reprinted with permission from Palgrave Macmillan; p129 'Quality of life gets a higher profile' by Lucy Ward, The Guardian, 24 November 1998, copyright Guardian News & Media Ltd 2008; p134 Actual and forecast growth of GDP, UK 1997–2006 (annual % change), adapted from the Pre-Budget Report, HM Treasury, December 2003 HM Treasury © Crown Copyright reprinted under Crown Copyright PSI License C2008000256; p134-5 British is best – adapted from the Pre-Budget Report, HM Treasury © Crown Copyright reprinted under Crown Copyright PSI License C2008000256; p137 The shopping crunch table, see www.mysupermarket.co.uk, accessed on 15 April 2008, reprinted with permission; p145 'Household energy bills forcing up inflation' by Grainne Gilmore and Gary Duncan, Timesonline, 19 March 2008, reprinted with permission from © NI Syndication, London (2008); p148 The Benefits of a Flexible Economy, HM Treasury, © Crown Copyright reprinted under Crown Copyright PSI License C2008000256; p150 Labour Market Trends, Office for National Statistics © Crown Copyright reprinted under Crown Copyright PSI License C2008000256; p154 The disappearing Phillips Curve. Charles Bean, Chief Economist of the Bank of England, in a speech given in November 2004; p156 'Qualms over unemployment among young' by Andrew Taylor, 14 February 2008, Financial Times http://www.ft.com reprinted with permission from the Financial Times; p160 Income tax payable by income bracket, 2006. Office for National Statistics © Crown Copyright reprinted under Crown Copyright PSI License C2008000256; p164–5 National debt hits record £500bn mark by Ashley Seager, The Guardian, 19 January 2007, copyright Guardian News & Media Ltd 2008; p169 Pre-Budget Report December 2003© Crown Copyright reprinted under Crown Copyright PSI License C2008000256; p170 'Take the politics out of fiscal policy' by John Kay, Financial Times, 27 February 2003, reprinted with permission from the Financial Times; p172 Broad money supply, 10 May 2008 © The Economist Newspaper Limited, London 2008; p179 'Bank's inflation controllers leave the NICE decade to enter the not-so-nice' by Ashley Seager and Larry Elliott, The Guardian, 3 May 2007, copyright Guardian News & Media Ltd 2007; p183 'The Influence of Globalisation' by Chun Lie, 21 February 2005 Chun Liew www.globalenvision.org; p191 'China slams EU anti-dumping charges on shoes', 24 February 2006, www.chinadaily.com.cn; p194 'Davos meet urges new push for Doha deal, amidst economic uncertainty' adapted from Bridges Weekly Trade News Digest, 27 January 2008, reprinted with permission; p200–202 'The golden gateway' adapted from an article by John Arlidge, Sunday Times, 3 December 2006, reprinted with permission from © NI Syndication, London (2006); p210 'Does the Bank of England want the pound to weaken?' adapted from an article by Jeremy Batstone-Carr, 12 December 2007, www.moneyweek.com reprinted with permission from Moneyweek www.moneyweek.com; p215 'Fixed or Flexible? Getting the exchange rate in the 1990s', Economic Issues 13, by Francesco Caramazza and Jahangir Aziz, 1998, International Monetary Fund; p216 'China is allowing its currency to rise more rapidly', 10 January 2008 © The Economist Newspaper Limited, London 2008, reprinted with permission; p222 'EU services package is approved, but delivery uncertain' by Anthony Browne, adapted from The Times,17 February 2006, reprinted with permission from © NI Syndication, London (2006); p226 'Enlargement troubles' 13 December 2006 © The Economist Newspaper Limited, London 2006 reprinted with permission; p231 'A turning point?' 5 July 2007 © The Economist Newspaper Limited, London 2007, reprinted with permission.

Every effort has been made to contact the copyright holders and we apologise if any have been overlooked. Should copyright have been unwittingly infringed in this book, the owners should contact the publishers, who will make the corrections at reprint.

Business economics and the distribution of income

Introduction

In Chapter 1 we will start our advanced study of microeconomics by building on your knowledge from AS. We will look at the costs of production faced by the individual firm and we will analyse them in more depth than you experienced at AS. We will look at marginal and average costs and revenues and use numerical examples to explain firms' behaviour. You will become aware of the diagrammatic presentation of costs curves which we use at A2 level and the effect of time on the firms' costs in terms of short-run and long-run behaviour.

In Chapter 2 you will study the firms' revenue curves in greater detail and you will appreciate that economists are interested in marginal amounts – both marginal costs and marginal revenue. You will learn how to handle the calculations and the importance of the profit-maximising concept of marginal costs equalling marginal revenue and the difference between normal and supernormal profit. In short you will become familiar with the economists' terms in the theory of the firm. Moving on in the chapter we will challenge the concept that firms exist to maximise their profits and we will use other terms such as 'satisficing' to try to explain the real-world behaviour of firms. It is in this area that economists are able to draw on the empirical evidence that is more the prerogative of business and management studies. We will conclude the chapter by considering the growth of firms and how such growth might come about, allowing us to explore the costs and benefits of mergers and similar activities.

In Chapter 3 we look at the economists' model of perfect competition where there are a very large number of firms comprising the industry. Some of you, on reading the assumptions of the model, will no doubt feel that the operations which are described in the model are somewhat unrealistic. While this may be true the model is used by economists as a benchmark as it does exhibit certain efficiencies which are not found elsewhere. It should also allow you to appreciate why under most conditions economists will argue that competition is beneficial. You will revisit the ideas of allocative and productive efficiency that were introduced at AS but in greater detail and will see how these relate to the individual firm in different circumstances.

In Chapter 4 we introduce the first chapter on concentrated markets and move to the other end of the market structure spectrum and consider the effects of one firm accounting for the whole industry. This is known as a monopoly. We will look at the conditions required to create monopoly and how monopolists are likely to act – how their structure is likely to influence their conduct and performance and how this will differ to perfect competition. We will look at the advantages and disadvantages of monopolies and introduce a new concept of efficiency called dynamic efficiency. You will be introduced to the monopoly diagram and will learn how to interpret it, and learn that monopolists can indulge in a practice called price discrimination where under certain conditions they can sell the same good or service to different consumers at different prices.

Chapter 5 represents the second chapter on concentrated markets and is the theory of oligopoly. This relates to how the market is likely to operate when it is dominated by a small number of large firms. You will learn about how the number of firms will affect how the market behaves and how the firms are interdependent and likely to react to changes in their competitors' behaviour. You will see the techniques that such firms use to keep new entrants out of the industry and appreciate the conditions under which they are more likely to collude with each other than compete. You will find that, unlike perfect competition and monopoly, there is no one theory of oligopoly but rather an analysis of different situations and why firms may behave in different ways. One of these 'theories' is that firms do not compete on price, and you will study not only the pricing techniques of firms but also their methods of non-price competition. You will experience the latest tool that economists use to analyse oligopoly, game theory and come to understand 'the Prisoners' Dilemma'.

In Chapter 6 we consider that concentrated markets are able to make supernormal profits at the consumers' expense and what can be done about it. With this in mind we consider competition policy in both the UK and the European Union (EU) and the remedies that the authorities might employ against overwhelming market power including breaking up the firm, imposing price controls and nationalisation. The theory of contestable markets, put forward by an American economist, is introduced at this point and allows students to compare it with present policies used by the authorities.

Chapter 7 is the first of two chapters on the labour market and commences by considering the factors that affect the demand for labour and then moves on to look at the factors that affect the supply of labour to the economy and to particular activities. We will also look at the relationship between wages and labour supply and consider the idea of the backward bending supply curve for labour.

Chapter 8 is all about wage determination and why labour in some areas is more highly paid than others. We look at the concepts of economic rent and transfer earnings and the effect of trade unions on the labour market. This chapter contains some important diagrams relating to different labour market conditions and you will need to become familiar with these diagrams. This chapter also considers discrimination in the labour market and how some groups are negatively affected by labour market operation.

The distribution of income and wealth is the content of Chapter 9 and we look more closely at this market failure that you were introduced to at AS level. We look at the differences between income and wealth and how wealth is created, distributed and accumulated. With income we consider both causes of and the degree of inequality of distribution both regionally and nationally and throughout the European Union. Government activity to reduce income and wealth inequalities is analysed. Poverty is a major concern to any economy and the causes, consequences and measures to reduce it are the closing concerns of this chapter.

The final chapter of Unit 3 concerns government intervention in the market and looks again at the causes of market failure, possible remedies that the authorities might apply and the possible outcomes.

The chapter concludes with an examination of a technique used to establish whether a government funded programme into, for example, a major infrastructure project will lead to greater costs and benefits. This is known as cost-benefit analysis and forms an important part of your analytical tool kit.

Throughout these chapters which cover Unit 3 you will come across diagrams that you will need to use when answering examination questions. As stressed earlier you need to work at these diagrams to ensure that you understand them and can both replicate and explain them when required.

1 The theory of production

Link

See *AQA Economics AS*, Chapter 7, p81 to remind you about a firm's costs.

Key terms

Total costs: fixed costs + variable costs.

Fixed costs: costs of production that do not vary as output changes.

Variable costs: costs of production that vary with output.

Short run: period during which fixed costs and the scale of production remain fixed.

Long run: period of time during which all factors become variable and the scale of output can change.

Marginal product: the output added by the extra worker or unit of a factor.

Covered in *AQA Economics AS* is the make up of a firm's costs, **total costs, fixed costs** and **variable costs**. These are the costs to the individual firm that it incurs as a result of production. This chapter aims to briefly revise the definitions before developing them further.

Production in the short run

In this chapter we will start by looking at a fictional firm that has been set up to produce reproduction furniture and has hired a factory unit and machinery in order to carry out production.

Initially the firm has incurred some fixed costs in terms of the factory unit and the machinery, and the owners of these will expect to be paid for their use from the outset, even though production has not yet started.

Economists study costs over different time periods. These are the **short run** and the **long run**.

As the firm commences production of furniture we assume that it is in a short-run situation where at least one factor remains fixed, for example, the size of the premises. To increase its output it will take on extra workers and as it does so it will find, up to a point, that each worker will add more to the total output than the previous workers. In the table below showing the output of worker number 3, the **marginal product** is 9 units whereas the marginal product of worker number 4 is 12 units. We refer to this as **increasing marginal returns**, where increasing the amount of the variable factor increases output more than proportionately. This has nothing to do with the quality of the workers as we are assuming they are all equally capable.

Table 1.1 *How levels of output change in the short run as more workers are employed*

No. of workers	Total product	Average product	Marginal product
1	3	3	3
2	7	3.5	4
3	16	5.3	9
4	28	7	12
5	45	9	17
6	60	10	15
7	63	9	3

As the firm grows and orders increase it will continue to employ more workers and purchase more raw materials. However, there will come a point where the premises cannot accommodate extra workers and their presence will reduce the output of the existing workers. As you can see from the table, marginal product rises up to five workers – each successive worker adds more output than the previous worker, but with worker number 6 marginal product begins to fall. However, **average product** rises and as the marginal is above the average it pulls the average up. Employment of the seventh worker only adds three units of output as the fixed factors (the size of the factory unit and the number of machines) are now becoming overloaded as there are too many variable factors for the size of the fixed factor.

In the short run the firm can only change its rate of output by combining more or less of the variable factors with the fixed factor and the table indicates that:

■ initially there are increasing returns to the variable factor so that output rises more than proportionately to the increase in the variable input

■ subsequently the firm experiences **diminishing marginal returns** to the variable input as the increase in output is less than proportional to the increase in labour input.

This sequence of events occurs because the plant is of a fixed size and must eventually become overloaded, and this is referred to as the law of diminishing returns. This is the 'law' that economists use to explain the short run.

While Table 1.1 indicates the amount produced, the pattern of costs can be inferred from it. Figure 1.1 illustrates both diminishing and increasing short-run costs where the average total cost curve is at its lowest point with the employment of six workers. This is known as the **optimal output**, the point where the firm has achieved the lowest cost combination between fixed and variable factors. This is also the point of **productive efficiency** in the short run as the firm is operating at the minimum average cost.

If the firm decides to increase its output and needs to employ extra workers, beyond six it will face increasing costs and will no longer be productively efficient.

Figure 1.2 indicates the revenues of the firm (output × price) and average revenue will be at a maximum at an output of 60 units where, as you can see from Figure 1.1, six workers are employed. If the firm produces more output its average revenue starts to fall.

In the short run we have encountered a number of costs: fixed, variable and marginal. We will now consider each of these in more detail.

Fixed costs

Fixed costs will not vary with output in the short run and they are sometimes called overhead or indirect costs. They are looked upon as contractual, that is, enforceable in a court of law, and usually consist of payments on buildings and machinery.

Fixed costs have to be paid whether the firm produces nothing or runs the plant 24 hours per day, and as a result, in a cost table fixed costs will be shown even when the firm is not producing any output, for example, at £180 at zero output in Table 1.2.

In addition to those mentioned, typical examples of fixed costs are rents, salaries of permanent employees and **depreciation**.

Key terms

Increasing marginal returns: where the addition of an extra variable factor adds more output than the previous variable factor.

Average product: the total product divided by the number of workers.

Law of diminishing marginal returns: where increasing amounts of a variable factor are added to a fixed factor and the amount added to total product by each additional unit of the variable factor eventually decreases.

Optimal output: the ideal combination of fixed and variable factors to produce the lowest average cost.

Productive efficiency: when a firm operates at minimum average total cost, producing the maximum possible output from inputs into the production process.

Depreciation: in relation to fixed assets, a fall in the value of an asset during its working life.

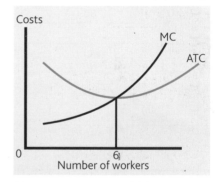

Figure 1.1 *Increasing and decreasing short-run costs*

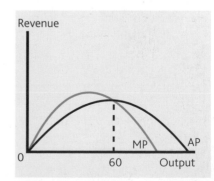

Figure 1.2 *The firm's revenues*

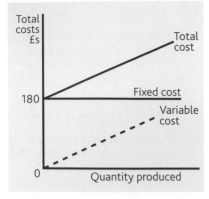

Figure 1.3 *Total costs*

■ **Key terms**

Semi-variable costs: costs which have both a fixed and variable element, e.g. landline telephone usage.

Variable costs

In contrast with fixed costs, variable costs vary directly with output. Increasing output will require an increase in such things as raw materials, power and labour. The variable costs of a firm are zero when there is no output, and increase and decrease as output rises and falls. When the firm is closed due to, for example, a holiday period, variable costs will be zero as production is not taking place. Variable costs are sometimes called unit-level costs as they vary with the number of units produced.

Semi-variable costs

As you are probably well aware by now, one of the great fascinations of economics is that it is infrequently clear cut, and costs are a good example of this as we have a category which is known as **semi-variable costs**. These are costs which have both a fixed cost and variable cost element; an electricity bill may include elements that are fixed (such as the fixed, or standing, charge for supplying the service) and elements that are variable (such as the amount of electricity used by machinery during the production process).

Figure 1.3 shows the total cost curves for a particular firm. Fixed cost remains at £180 over the range of output produced while variable costs increase as output increases. The addition of fixed and variable costs gives the total cost.

Information regarding cost curves can be portrayed in tabular form.

Table 1.2 *A firm's costs – All costs shown in £s*

Quantity	Total fixed cost (TFC)	Total variable cost (TVC)	Total cost fixed + variable (TC)	Average fixed cost (AFC)	Average variable cost (AVC)	Average total cost (ATC)	Marginal cost (MC)
0	180	–	180	–	–	–	
							195
1	180	15	195	180	15	195	
							35
2	180	50	230	90	25	115	
							175
3	180	225	405	60	75	135	
							75
4	180	300	480	45	75	120	
							165
5	180	465	645	36	93	129	
							183
6	180	648	828	30	108	138	
							243
7	180	891	1,071	26	127	153	
							369
8	180	1,260	1,440	23	158	180	
							450
9	180	1,710	1,890	20	190	210	

The first three columns of the table indicate the total costs; the second three columns are average costs; and the last column shows the marginal cost, which is the cost of producing the extra unit of output.

Total costs comprise total fixed costs and total variable costs. **Average fixed cost** (AFC) can be found by dividing the total fixed costs by the number produced, and diminishes quite rapidly as the cost is spread over an increasing number of units. Thus the AFC of unit 2 is TFC (180) ÷ 2 = 90 whereas by the time output has increased to nine units AFC has fallen to 20.

In contrast, **average variable cost** (AVC), TVC divided by the number produced, increases as output increases as variable costs increase with output. Thus the AVC of unit 1 is 15 but has increased to 190 by unit 9.

Average total cost (ATC) is total cost divided by the number produced and declines as the fixed cost is spread over more units but then increases as the growth in variable costs is greater than the fall in fixed costs. For unit 1 ATC is 195, falling to 120 for unit 4 but then rising as output increases and reaches 210 by unit 9.

Marginal cost (MC) is the amount added to the total cost of production by the next unit of output – the cost of producing one more unit. The marginal cost is calculated by taking the total cost and deducting the total cost of the previous unit, for example, the total cost of producing six units is £828; the total cost of producing five units is £645. The MC is therefore the difference between them, £183, and the actual cost of producing the sixth unit.

This information can be produced in diagrammatic form and Figure 1.4 shows three average cost curves: total, variable and fixed, as well as the marginal cost curve. The relationship between them is explained below.

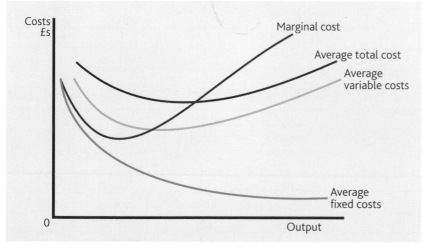

Figure 1.4 *A firm's cost curves*

The average fixed costs fall as output rises and in the table the fall is from £180 to £20 over nine units of output. The fall is very rapid as the fixed cost is spread over more units and this will reduce the cost of producing the extra unit. The falling average fixed costs pull the marginal cost curve downwards as the costs of producing each unit will fall. But the firm will be taking on labour and, after some point, the falling fixed cost will be unable to compensate for the increased labour cost and marginal cost will begin to increase. The marginal cost is shown as cutting the average costs at their lowest point and you need to understand this relationship.

The relationship between average and marginal costs

In order to appreciate the relationship, students should consider the problem from the perspective of a range of essay marks. Imagine that the average mark for essays is 15. In the next essay, the marginal essay, students get 10 marks – this will pull the average down. In the essay after this, students get 18 marks which will pull their average up. The relationship can be expressed as follows and can be clearly seen in Figure 1.1:

- If the marginal cost is below the average then it will pull the average down and the average cost will be falling.

- If the marginal cost is above the average then it will pull the average up.

- The marginal cost will cut the average cost at its lowest point.

Activity

Using the cost curves showing the output of firm x:

- Calculate the firm's costs and complete the table.
- Plot the average and marginal cost curves on graph paper. (Plot the marginal values midway between the units of output 0.5 to 5.5)
- At what level of output is the firm productively efficient?
- Explain why productive efficiency occurs at this level of output.

Table 1.3

Output	Total fixed cost	Total variable cost	Total fixed + variable	Average fixed cost	Average variable cost	Average total cost	Marginal cost
0	70		70		0		
1	70	120					
2	70	150					
3	70	175					
4	70	222					
5	70	295					
6	70	400					

Activities

1. Draw a diagram showing the relationship between the marginal costs and the average total cost.

2. Explain why the marginal cost can be rising when average cost is falling.

3. Outline the relationship between average fixed, average variable and marginal costs.

Case study

Diminishing returns

When land is initially under-utilised, when population is small and sparse, production is inefficient because of inadequate labour to work that land. With a sparse population, specialization is difficult or impossible; and fixed overheads (including protection costs) have to be divided amongst and borne by few people. Some forms of physical capital cannot be used effectively until more people are available and thus efficiency is in fact improved by adding more labour to that land. As more units of labour are added to that land/capital, the result is not only rising total output, but also rising output per extra unit of labour: that is, the extra or marginal product of labour is rising; the extra output produced by that last unit of labour is greater than that added by his immediate predecessor. These are, in part, the fruits of labour specialization: that is, the division of labour by specialized tasks.

Finally, after adding more and more labour to that land we reach a point of maximum or optimum efficiency; and then, as we add more labour, we encounter one of the most famous and important of all economic laws – The Law of Diminishing Returns, which should really be called the Law of Eventually Diminishing Marginal Returns. Thus, after that point of maximum efficiency, each additional or marginal unit of labour added to that fixed stock of land and capital (technology still constant) will produce smaller and smaller additional, or extra, or marginal units of output – smaller than that produced by the unit of labour previously added.

Note that we are talking about changes in that extra or marginal product, and not changes in total output or total product, or even average product, which will continue to rise for some time after marginal product begins to fall.

*Adapted from **Robert Shiel** 'Improving Soil Fertility in the Pre-Fertiliser Era,' in **Bruce M. S. Campbell** and **Mark Overton** (eds.), Land, Labour, Livestock. Historical Studies in European Agricultural Productivity, 1991*

■ Production in the long run

In the long run the firm can temporarily overcome the problem of diminishing returns as it can vary its fixed factors. In the case of the furniture manufacturer it could move to larger premises. But the problem of diminishing returns re-emerges as soon as the fixed factor becomes overloaded, and though specialisation can delay diminishing returns setting in, they will eventually reappear as the firm increases output beyond optimal output – the ideal combination of fixed and variable factors.

In Table 1.1 on page 4 the average total cost per unit is at its lowest at 6 workers where 60 units are produced (ATL must be at its lowest point as the average product is at its maximum). If the firm wants to produce 63 units without diminishing returns setting in, it will need a different combination of fixed and variable factors and this will be true of all different levels of output. This can be shown in Figure 1.5 where there is a separate short-run ATC curve for every level of output.

The firm producing the output 0A is producing at the lowest point on the curve labelled ATC, while the firm with the higher level of output faces a cost structure which is shown by curve ATC3. Each short-run average total cost (SRATC) represents the particular short-run size or the scale of the firm and we assume that **increasing returns to scale** are taking place as the trend of the costs is downwards as output increases.

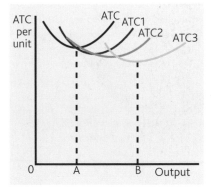

Figure 1.5 *The optimal output*

Figure 1.6 *Workers chopping trees*

We have seen that in the short run the firm's productively efficient level occurs at the lowest point of the average total cost curve and output below or above that level increases the firm's costs. In the long run we assume that firms can vary the scale of production and that it can vary all of its factors of production. In the long run the furniture manufacturer will be able to increase the size of, or move to, larger premises and employ more capital equipment in terms of a greater number of, and more sophisticated, machinery. Thus in the long run there are no fixed factors and we expect that increasing size will lead to economies of scale. The long-run average total cost curve is constructed from the optimum output levels of the short-run curves as shown in Figure 1.7.

Figure 1.7 shows the long-run average total cost (LRATC) facing the firm and we assume that as the firm's scale of operations increases it will face falling costs as it receives increasing returns to scale. The LRATC reflects that due to economies of scale an increase in factor inputs will result in a more than proportionate increase in output. However, as covered in *AQA Economics AS*, pages 83–4, this can only continue up to a certain level of output and then diseconomies of scale set in. This can be illustrated in Table 1.4 below:

Table 1.4 *Returns to scale*

Year	Inputs	Total product (£s)	Total costs of inputs (£s)	Average cost (£s)
1	50	10,000	10,000	1
2	100	25,000	20,000	80p
3	150	45,000	30,000	67p
4	200	58,000	38,860	67p
5	250	68,000	46,920	69p

Table 1.4 shows that the change in total output increases by a greater percentage as the firm increases its scale of production in years one to three. The firm is experiencing increasing returns to scale and so its average cost per unit falls, indicating economies of scale.

In years three and four outputs rise by the same percentage when inputs rise from 150 to 200. The firm has experienced constant returns to scale and average costs remain unchanged. In year five, output rises by a smaller percentage than inputs and the firm experiences **decreasing returns to scale** and the average cost per unit increases, which indicates diseconomies of scale. These differing returns to scale are shown in Figures 1.7 and 1.8.

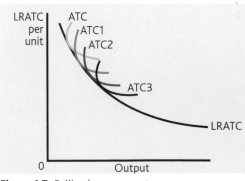

Figure 1.7 *Falling long-run costs*

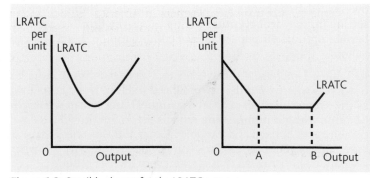

Figure 1.8 *Possible shapes for the LRATC curve*

In Figure 1.8 both diagrams show a situation where unit costs fall as output increases and the firm receives increasing returns to scale. But beyond a certain level of output costs begin to increase and the firm suffers decreasing returns to scale. Both diagrams tend to be stylised as different industries will have different cost structures. In some, all economies of scale will be reached very quickly, while in others the level of output required to exploit all available economies of scale may be huge.

In Figure 1.8 left diagram, cost savings are exhausted quickly and unit costs rise rapidly after a certain level of output. Firms in this industry do not have a great deal of choice about their level of output and are likely to be of similar size. The right diagram shows another possible shape of the LRATC – over the range of output 0 to A the LRATC falls and the firm receives increasing returns to scale. Over the range of output A to B, the curve is flat, and the firm experiences **constant returns to scale**. When output exceeds 0B decreasing returns to scale set in. Firms in this industry are more likely to be of different sizes as once they have reached 0A they may have the opportunity to be able to produce thousands more units of output before decreasing returns to scale set in at B. This flat part of the curve shows constant returns to scale.

The optimum level of long-run production for a firm occurs at the point of productive efficiency – at the lowest part of the LRATC. If the LRATC is saucer shaped, as in the Figure 1.8 right diagram, this will occur at the bottom of the curve, between A and B, where constant returns to scale exist.

Both diagrams also indicate diseconomies of scale where a less than proportionate increase in output occurs as a result of factor inputs. The LRATC shows the cheapest possible cost of producing any level of output.

Key terms

Constant returns to scale: where an increase in factor inputs leads to a proportional increase in factor outputs.

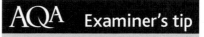

AQA Examiner's tip

- Do not confuse the short-run and the long-run when explaining a firm's behaviour.
- Do not use the long-run concept of economies of scale when explaining short-run cost curves.

Case study

The new face of hunger

On a conservative estimate, food-price rises may reduce the spending power of the urban poor and country people who buy their own food by 20 per cent (in some regions, prices are rising by far more). Just over 1 billion people live on $1 a day, the benchmark of absolute poverty; 1.5 billion live on $1 to $2 a day. Bob Zoellick, the president of the World Bank, reckons that food inflation could push at least 100m people into poverty, wiping out all the gains the poorest billion have made during almost a decade of economic growth.

In the short run, humanitarian aid, social-protection programmes and trade policies will determine how well the world copes with these problems. But in the medium term the question is different: where does the world get more food from? If the extra supplies come mainly from large farmers in America, Europe and other big producers, then the new equilibrium may end up looking much like the old one, with world food depending on a small number of suppliers and – possibly – trade distortions and food dumping. So far, farmers in rich countries have indeed responded. America's winter wheat plantings are up 4 per cent and the spring-sown area is likely to rise more. The Food and Agriculture Organization forecasts that the wheat harvest in the European Union will rise 13 per cent.

Ideally, a big part of the supply response would come from the world's 450m smallholders in developing countries, people who farm just a few acres. There are three reasons why this would be desirable. First, it would reduce poverty: three-quarters of those making do on $1 a day live in the countryside and depend on the health of smallholder farming. Next, it might help the environment: those smallholders manage a disproportionate share of the world's water and vegetation cover, so raising their productivity on existing land would be environmentally friendlier than cutting down the rainforest. And it should be efficient: in terms of returns on investment, it would be easier to boost grain yields in Africa from two tonnes per hectare to four than it would be to raise yields in Europe from eight tonnes to ten. The opportunities are greater and the law of diminishing returns has not set in.

Adapted from 'The new face of hunger', The Economist, 17 April 2008

The minimum efficient scale

In Figure 1.9 at output 0A the firm has grown large enough to have exploited all the benefits of the internal economies of scale – it has reached the **minimum efficient scale** (MES). This corresponds to the lowest point on the long-run average total cost curve and is also known as the output of long-run productive efficiency. While the minimum efficient scale is defined to be the first, lowest, point on the LRATC, in reality there is unlikely to be a single level of output; rather there will be a range of outputs, as indicated in Figure 1.9 between 0A and 0B, where costs are minimised. Firms that are unable to reach the minimum efficient scale are unlikely to be competitive with other firms. If it produces an output below 0A its unit costs will increase and render it uncompetitive with larger firms whose unit costs are lower as they have reached the MES. The output required to reach the MES will depend on the nature of the industry and its costs structure, and when fixed costs are extremely large compared to variable costs, expanding output will lead to decreasing average costs. The relationship between the MES and the size of the domestic market may mean that an economy may only be able to support one firm in the industry if the MES is to be achieved. A domestic firm wanting to reach the MES with only a small home market may need to export its products to increase the size of the potential market and the authorities may have to accept that a monopolistic structure is likely to be the most efficient.

Scherer (1975) calculated the minimum efficient scale for a number of industries and compared market size with the minimum efficient scale for the USA, Canada and Sweden. For example, if the market size allowed it to absorb say £200,000 worth of goods and the minimum efficient scale is £50,000 then four plants could operate at the minimum efficient scale.

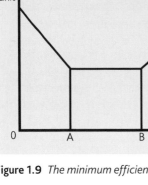

Figure 1.9 *The minimum efficient scale*

Key terms

Minimum efficient scale: this corresponds to the lowest point on the long-run average total cost curve and is also known as the output of long-run productive efficiency.

Table 1.5 *The minimum efficient scale in selected industries*

Country	Cigarettes	Steel	Weaving	Shoes
USA	16	35	447	493
Canada	1	3	12	48
Sweden	1	1	6	13

In the USA, for example, there is only room for 16 firms producing cigarettes at the MES, while in the industry producing shoes there is room for 493 firms and this pattern is broadly similar for all three countries.

Case study

No economies of scale for Proton without global partner

Although Proton Holding seems to be turning around, without a strong global partner the national carmaker will find it hard to achieve economies of scale and develop new technologies, said analysts.

The Government's move to end talks with Volkswagen and General Motors was a disappointment. But analysts said it might not be the end of the world yet if Proton was still on the look-out for alliances.

Analysts concurred that Proton's new management had made several right moves to revamp the national carmaker but a partnership with a foreign giant would have been even more beneficial to Proton for its long-term survival.

They noted that management efforts were bearing fruit with sales volume and market share on an uptrend since May.

Nonetheless, Proton needed to have production volume and economies of scale to survive the intensive competition locally and worldwide, they added.

After all, volume is the name of the game in car manufacturing; a firm must achieve the minimum efficient scale.

Given the saturating domestic passenger car market, Proton has to broaden its market abroad via exports to boost production volume at its Tanjung Malim plant.

It is indeed a vicious circle: when a carmaker fails to make good profits, it will not have the financial strength to invest in research and development (R&D) and that would delay the roll-out of new models to capture sales, consequently it would lose market share. 'Car manufacturers' competitiveness is very much dependent on R&D investments,' said Mr Khoo an analyst.

He opined that it might be difficult for Proton to finance the hefty R&D costs required to sustain the engineering and styling demanded by consumers in future launches, without some significant form of strategic or technological tie-up with a foreign partner.

*Adapted from an article by **Kathy Fong**, 21 November 2007*

Activities

1 Construct a diagram to show what will happen to a firm's level of unit costs as it expands its scale of operations.

2 Indicate on the diagram the minimum efficient scale (MES).

3 Explain why the MES is likely to vary between different industries.

Relationship between short-run and long-run costs

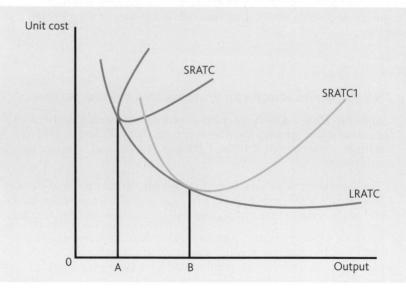

Figure 1.10 *The relationship between short- and long-run costs*

In Figure 1.7 we saw that any firm that is producing at the lowest point of the short-run average total cost curve is on its LRATC and as its scale of production increases its unit costs are likely to fall.

In Figure 1.10 a firm is producing at 0A where it is at the lowest point of its short-run cost curve. If the firm decides to increase its output rapidly to 0B, perhaps in response to an unexpected order, its unit costs will increase up the SRATC as it overworks its fixed factors and departs from the optimum factor combination.

If the firm decides to increase its scale of production then, as the fixed factors increase and are brought into use, the firm moves down SRATC1 until it reaches the LRATC at the output 0B where once again it has achieved the optimum factor combination and productive efficiency.

However some firms, typically smaller ones, may decide that expansion is not an option and will remain at their present size and overwork their fixed factors. This may be for reasons such as a lack of available finance, little likelihood of a planning application being granted, or fears that market growth may be temporary. Such firms are not reducing their costs to the lowest level but may ignore this fact as long as profits are adequate.

After completing this chapter you should:

■ understand the difference between the short and long run and the theories that underpin them

■ be able to use short-run and long-run concepts to answer questions

■ be able to explain the relationships between average and marginal costs both in words and graphically

■ understand the importance of firms achieving the minimum efficient scale and what it implies.

Extract A

The economics of nuclear power

The relative costs of generating electricity from coal, gas and nuclear plants vary considerably depending on location. Coal is, and will probably remain, economically attractive in countries such as China, the USA and Australia with abundant and accessible domestic coal resources as long as carbon emissions are cost-free. Gas is also competitive for base-load power in many places, particularly using combined-cycle plants, though rising gas prices have removed much of the advantage.

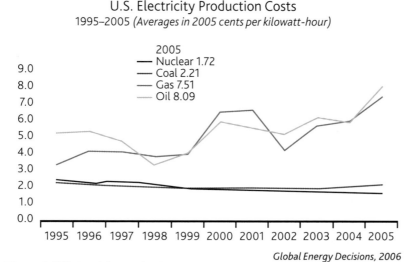

U.S. Electricity Production Costs
1995–2005 *(Averages in 2005 cents per kilowatt-hour)*

2005
— Nuclear 1.72
— Coal 2.21
— Gas 7.51
— Oil 8.09

Global Energy Decisions, 2006

Figure 1 *US electricity production costs*

Nuclear energy is, in many places, competitive with fossil fuel for electricity generation, despite relatively high capital costs and the need to internalise all waste disposal and decommissioning costs. If the social, health and environmental costs of fossil fuels are also taken into account, nuclear is outstanding.

Fuel costs are one area of steadily increasing efficiency and cost reduction. For instance, in Spain nuclear electricity cost has been reduced by 29 per cent over 1995–2001. This involved boosting enrichment levels and burn-up to reach the minimum efficient scale and achieve 40 per cent fuel cost reduction. Prospectively, a further 8 per cent increase in burn-up will give another 5 per cent reduction in fuel cost.

From the outset the basic attraction of nuclear energy has been its low fuel costs compared with coal, oil and gas-fired plants. Uranium, however, has to be processed, enriched and fabricated into fuel elements, and about half of the cost is due to enrichment and fabrication. Allowances must also be made for the management of radioactive spent fuel and the ultimate disposal of this spent fuel or the wastes separated from it.

But even with these included, the total fuel costs of a nuclear power plant in the Organization for Economic Cooperation and Development (OECD) are typically about a third of those for a coal-fired plant and between a quarter and a fifth of those for a gas combined-cycle plant.

French figures published in 2002 show (EUR cents/kWh): nuclear 3.20, gas 3.05–4.26, coal 3.81–4.57. Nuclear is favourable because of the large, standardised plants used.

In general the construction costs of nuclear power plants are significantly higher than for coal- or gas-fired plants because of the need to use special materials, and to incorporate sophisticated safety features and back-up control equipment. These contribute much of the nuclear generation cost, but once the plant is built the cost variables are minor.

Long construction periods will push up financing costs, and in the past they have done so spectacularly. In Asia construction times have tended to be shorter, for instance the new-generation 1300 MWe Japanese reactors which began operating in 1996 and 1997 were built in a little over four years, and 48 to 54 months is typical projection for plants today.

Note: the above data refer to fuel plus operation and maintenance costs only, they exclude capital, since this varies greatly among utilities and states, as well as with the age of the plant.

Adapted from 'The economics of nuclear power' – Briefing paper 8 – www.uic.au/nip08.htm. World Nuclear Association

1   (a)   Compare the costs of generating electricity by nuclear power with the other methods throughout the period 1995–2005.   *(5 marks)*

     (b)   The extract states Spain reduced costs by reaching the minimum efficient scale. Using the information, and with the help of a cost curve diagram, explain how both the firm and its customers may be affected by production at the minimum efficient scale.   *(10 marks)*

     (c)   Assess the view that diminishing returns can always be eliminated by a firm by increasing its levels of output.   *(25 marks)*

2   (a)   Using economic theory and current real-world examples analyse the factors that are likely to affect a firm's total costs.   *(15 marks)*

     (b)   Evaluate the view that 'Firms in the same industry have very similar unit (average) costs of production'.   *(25 marks)*

2 The objectives of firms

Key terms

Profits: when total income or revenue for a firm is greater than total costs.

Total revenue: what the firm receives for the sale of its product = price × number sold.

Average revenue: total revenue ÷ number sold.

Marginal revenue: the addition to total revenue from the production of one extra unit.

In the previous chapter, the issue of a firm's costs was dealt with; this chapter turns to an examination of a firm's revenue and its ability to make **profits**. The traditional view of a firm minimising its costs and maximising its revenue in order to maximise its profits is considered, along with later views that take a wider perspective of the firm's motivation. The aims of firms and how they are affected by technical change and innovation are also considered.

The firm's revenues

In a perfectly competitive market

We calculate a firm's **total revenue** by multiplying the units of output sold by the price. If all units are sold at the same price the revenues are as shown in Table 2.1 below.

Table 2.1 *Firm's revenue in a competitive market*

Output	Price per unit £s	Total revenue £s	Average revenue £s	Marginal revenue £s
0	500	–	–	–
				500
1	500	500	500	
				500
2	500	1,000	500	
				500
3	500	1,500	500	
				500
4	500	2,000	500	
				500
5	500	2,500	500	

Both the **average revenue** and the **marginal revenue** are constant as the same price is charged for the product. As the total revenue is either price multiplied by units sold or average revenue multiplied by units sold then price and average revenue are one and the same. The marginal revenue is the addition to total revenue from the production of one extra unit, so, in Table 2.1, unit 2 adds £500 to the firm's revenue making the total revenue £1,000.

In an imperfect market

If price per unit changes the marginal revenue changes, as shown in Table 2.2 below.

Table 2.2 *Firm's revenue in an imperfect market*

Output	Price per unit £s	Total revenue £s	Average revenue £s	Marginal revenue £s
0	500	–	–	–
				500
1	500	500	500	
				400
2	450	900	450	
				330
3	410	1,230	410	
				270
4	375	1,500	375	
				250
5	350	1,750	350	

In the table above, the firm is facing a downward sloping demand curve where more units are sold as the price falls. Average revenue and price remain the same but the marginal revenue is less than the average revenue. The explanation of this is that as more units are sold the price of all units has to be reduced.

Tables 2.1 and 2.2 are shown in Figure 2.1 below.

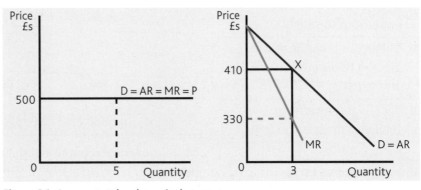

Figure 2.1 *Average total and marginal revenue*

The left-hand diagram in Figure 2.1 shows the situation in Table 2.1 where the firm sells all the quantity produced at the same price. The demand curve is shown as horizontal at a price of £500, which means that all units produced by the firm can be sold at this price. The demand curve also represents the average and marginal revenues as they are also equal to £500. The rectangle indicated by the area £500 × 5 shows the total revenue for the sale of five units, £2,500. Note that average revenue equals total revenue divided by the number sold, (£2,500 ÷ 5 = £500), so price and average revenue are one and the same, that is, the price is the average revenue. Total revenue is shown in the diagram by an area whereas average revenue is indicated by any point on the demand curve.

The right-hand diagram shows the second of the tables where the marginal revenue is shown as sloping downward beneath the average revenue. At unit 3 the price or average revenue is £410 but the marginal revenue is £330 (£1230 − £900) as the sale of the third unit has added £330 to the total revenue. The rectangle indicated by the area £410 × 3 shows the total revenue for the sale of three units while average revenue for three units is shown by point 'X' on the demand curve.

Figure 2.2 indicates the relationship between total, average and marginal revenue:

■ At a price of £60 the total revenue is £12,000 (AR × units sold = £60 × 200) while the marginal revenue is £40.

■ At a price of £40 the total revenue is £16,000 (£40 × 400). Total revenue is maximised at this point as marginal revenue is zero.

■ At a price of £30 total revenue has fallen to £15,000 as marginal revenue is negative and extra units produced beyond 400 have reduced total revenue.

In Figure 2.2, as price falls between A and B, the total revenue increases, which indicates that demand over this part of the curve is elastic. If price is reduced below B, total revenue falls indicating that demand over this part of the curve is inelastic.

■ Profit – maximising output

In the traditional theory of the firm, the models of which shall be explored in the next few chapters, the assumption is made that firms will always try to maximise profits and the theory suggests that firms will use the marginal quantity as a guide to where this is achieved.

Figure 2.3 brings together the marginal costs curve from Chapter 1 and the marginal revenue curve.

From Figure 2.3 we can see that:

■ If one unit is produced then the marginal cost of that unit is £20, while the marginal revenue is £50. This unit adds more to revenue than to cost and should be produced.

■ With two units produced, the marginal cost increases to £30, while marginal revenue remains at £50, but as it adds more to revenue than cost it should be produced.

■ Unit 4 adds £80 more to cost and £50 to revenue; the firm will not produce it as it would add more to costs than it does to revenue.

Units up to number three add more to revenue than cost and it pays the firm to produce them as the extra output adds to **total profits**, but output beyond the third unit adds more to costs than revenue and will cause profits to fall.

With the production of the third unit marginal revenue and marginal cost are equal but included in cost is what economists refer to as normal profit, and so it pays the firm to produce unit 3.

Normal profit

Normal profit is a return to the firm, which is just sufficient to ensure that it will continue to supply its good or service. In market theory firms' cost curves include normal profit as part of the cost of supplying the good. Economists differ from accountants in that they include in costs the opportunity cost of using any factor of production.

If the level of profit earned is below that of markets with equal risk the firm will transfer the use of its resources to another market where normal

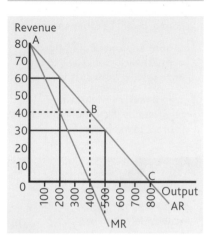

AQA Examiner's tip

Remember that price equals average revenue and that the terms may be used interchangeably.

Figure 2.2 *Revenue curves*

Link

See *AQA Economics AS*, Chapter 5 for information on elasticity.

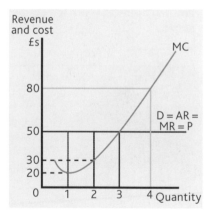

Figure 2.3 *How many to produce*

Link

See Chapter 1, p7 for the marginal cost curve.

Key terms

Total profit: total revenue minus total costs.

Normal profit: the amount required to keep a factor employed in its present activity in the long run.

Profit maximisation: where a firm chooses a level of output where marginal revenue equals marginal costs.

Supernormal profit: a return above normal profit – a surplus payment.

Sub-normal profit: profit below normal which should lead to the firms leaving the industry.

Entrepreneur: individual who organises the factors of production in order to make a profit.

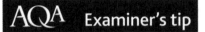

Examiner's tip

Remember that when revenue equals costs firms are making normal profit.

Activities

A firm faces a horizontal demand curve where the market price is £25. The table below indicates the firm's total costs at each level of output.

Table 2.3 *Table for activity*

Output	Total costs
0	3
1	15
2	25
3	33
4	40
5	55
6	78
7	105

1 Redraw the table and calculate the marginal costs.

2 Construct a graph to indicate the profit-maximising output.

3 Explain under what circumstances the firm would produce six units.

profit can be obtained. In terms of Figure 2.3, if the resources used to generate unit 3 are equal to £50 they have earned as much for the firm as they could in any other use. So any firm wanting **profit maximisation** will produce up to the point where marginal revenue equals marginal cost where the marginal cost is rising.

Depending on actual market conditions firms may earn **supernormal profit** (more than that required to ensure supply of the good) normal profit (just sufficient to ensure supply of the good) or **sub-normal profit** (less than that required to ensure supply of the good).

Thus an electrician wiring new houses may be prepared to work for, say, £25 per hour and may regard this as his normal profit and would not be prepared to continue doing his present job for less per hour and, if no longer able to achieve this rate of pay, would seek to use his skills elsewhere, for example, in the industrial sector. On the other hand, increased demand for houses and a shortage of electricians may mean that he is able to earn £30 per hour, in which case the extra £5 per hour would represent supernormal profit.

The economist's view of profits

■ Normal profit is a return that covers the opportunity cost of all factors used in the process; the amount necessary to keep a factor in its present occupation.

■ Supernormal or abnormal profit implies a return over and above normal profit.

■ Supernormal profits can be seen as providing an incentive to firms to enter an industry. They signal entrepreneurs to allocate more factors and therefore are important in allocating scarce resources to areas where they are required.

■ Supernormal profits may also indicate a lack of competition in the industry.

■ Negative or falling profits may indicate that oversupply is taking place and firms will leave the industry and reallocate their factors elsewhere.

Profits are used by accountants, investors and the media to judge the success of a firm. In the accounting sense of the term, net profit (before tax) is the sales of the firm less costs such as wages, rent, fuel, raw materials, interest on loans and depreciation.

■ A firm's objectives

The traditional theory of the firm argues that the firm's sole objective is to maximise its levels of profits and suggests that an **entrepreneur** will change levels of output every time there is a change in the level of prices or costs. However, in a world concerned about negative externalities and the destruction of the environment, a firm that ignored these considerations in order to increase its profit levels would be likely to lose custom and receive heavy censure. Thus is shown in the case study below.

Case study

'We Blew It' – Nike admits to mistakes over child labour

The multi-billion dollar sportswear company Nike admitted yesterday that it 'blew it' by employing children in Third World countries but added that ending the practice might be difficult.

The mere fact that Nike has produced such a report was welcomed in some quarters, but its main detractors, including labour groups such as Oxfam's NikeWatch and the Clean Clothes Campaign, said they were not convinced.

Philip Knight, the company chairman, clearly stung by reports of children as young as 10 making shoes, clothing and footballs in Pakistan and Cambodia, attempted to convince Nike's critics that it had only ever employed children accidentally. 'Of all the issues facing Nike in workplace standards, child labour is the most vexing,' he said in the report. 'Our age standards are the highest in the world.'

Even when records keeping is more advanced, and hiring is carefully done, one mistake can brand a company like Nike as a purveyor of child labour.

The report said Nike imposed strict conditions on the age of employees taken on by contract factories abroad, but admitted there had been instances when those conditions were ignored or bypassed.

Full article published in The Independent, *20 October 2001*

The theory of profit maximisation can be criticised and challenged on a number of grounds and a number of competing alternatives have been advanced.

The divorce of ownership and control

It is easy to see that individuals who own their own firms may be extremely keen on profit maximisation and it is likely to be one of the original reasons for the formation of the firm, but in larger firms there is a gap between ownership and control. The growth of the **Public Limited Company (PLC)** has led to vast amounts of financial capital being raised to fund a modern **corporation** which has led to a growth in the number of shareholders who have put their money into the firm and who presumably want to maximise their returns – their profits. Shareholders who own the firm, will gain from profit maximisation and will want costs kept as low as possible, are not in a position to run the firm. Shareholders appoint **directors** to represent their interests and directors appoint managers to run the company. Professional managers are given control and the interests of the managers may be different from that of the shareholders.

Directors and managers may be more concerned with job security and remuneration in terms of salary and other **'perks'** than in maximising the level of the firm's profits. In the UK, all company directors have to be shareholders and so receive **dividends** and possibly **share options**, but for some, their income from the directorship will make a larger contribution to their income than their dividends. As their salaries are determined more by the size of the business than the profitability of the firm this may colour their actions and they may seek market size in terms of its output, sales and employment rather than profitability. This would suggest that the sales growth will be an important objective of boards of directors. However mindful of the fact that shareholders have to be faced at the **Annual General Meeting (AGM)** and that **activist shareholders** are becoming more common, directors are unable to ignore profitability entirely. A sufficient level of profit to keep shareholders quiet, and to remove the likelihood of a **hostile bid** is an imperative and so, while the goal of profit maximisation may not be an appropriate assumption, firms may indulge in **satisficing.**

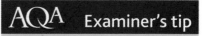

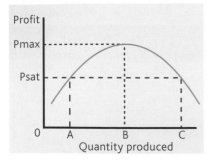

Figure 2.4 *A possible range of outputs*

■ Key terms

Stakeholders: firms, organisations or individuals with an interest in the firm.

Carbon footprint: the amount of greenhouse gases produced measured in terms of carbon dioxide.

Corporate citizenship: indicates that organisations embrace sustainable development.

Market share: percentage of the total market held by the company.

Market power: when a firm has the ability to exert significant influence over the quantity of goods traded or the price at which they are sold.

Rational choice theory: where all costs and benefits are considered before a decision is taken.

Figure 2.5 *Making the most of his perks*

Satisficing

A firm that is satisficing may produce a range of outputs that are within its target level of profits rather than the specific profit-maximising output. Figure 2.4 illustrates this possibility as it shows the relationship between output and profits. A profit maximising firm will produce at the output that maximises profits, Pmax, giving an output of 0B. A satisficing firm that does not want to make a smaller profit than that of Psat has a range of possible outputs between 0A and 0C.

Some large businesses now include 'social responsibility' among their objectives, which means they pay due regard to the needs of the **stakeholders** of the business – employees, customers and even national targets, such as reducing their **carbon footprint**. These so-called activities of **corporate citizenship** are likely to increase the firm's costs and so reduce its level of profits. This is, however, not always the case and those who argue for greater recognition of stakeholder requirements argue that such caring activities do not always conflict with profit maximisation. For example, good staff are easier to attract and retain by firms that are seen as socially responsible, and this reduces the costs of staff turnover.

■ Sales maximisation theory

This theory suggests that managers want the firms they work for to be as large as possible, as working as a high level manager for a very large corporation is an extremely prestigious position. Often the highest salaries, share options as well as prestige and 'perks' come from working for large companies. The manager of a large, moderately profitable corporation is likely to earn considerably more and have a much better package than the manager of a small but highly profitable corporation. On this basis a manager might be happier working for a large, averagely profitable, corporation rather than a smaller one that is maximising its profits. Managers may be receiving sales-related bonuses and, in this case, the manager might increase sales up to the point where marginal revenue is zero and total revenue is maximised. This would be at the output of 400 units in Figure 2.2. Under such circumstances, and as marginal costs are more likely to be positive than zero, the firm will not be maximising its profits by producing where marginal revenue equals marginal costs but maximising its sales revenue, and this will reward managers rather than shareholders who would benefit from profit maximisation. A further argument is that sales are the key to **market share** and possibly **market power**, and that growth is the key to future profits and managerial security. Managers may be reluctant to undertake short-term risky ventures, even if the profits are large as failure to achieve success could terminate their careers.

Inability to profit maximise

One of the problems faced by a profit-maximising firm is the assumption that firms have complete information about the costs and benefits of each option and they compare the options and then make a rational choice. There is considerable evidence to suggest that **rational choice theory** is unrealistic and that firms lack the information to make the choices that profit maximisation suggests. In order to set prices, a firm needs to know its marginal cost of producing the good, as well as the elasticity of demand – how responsive customers will be to changes in prices. In practice, real-world firms are typically very complex, produce multiple goods, and detailed information on marginal cost is rarely available. Firms would also need to experiment and to vary their prices until they achieve profit maximisation, which would lead to a loss of custom to other firms. These factors combine to make it almost impossible for a firm to make an accurate assessment of whether it is profit maximising. In addition, there is likely to be a natural time lag between accumulating and processing information, which means that important decisions may be made too late to maximise profits.

Firms are more likely to satisfice than maximise, that is, they will make what is acceptable and satisfactory rather than achieve the optimal solution. This means that the firm will make sufficient profits in order to keep shareholders happy but will not waste time and resources seeking the optimal solution. The firm's goals may be fairly diverse as the separation of ownership and control allows a number of stakeholders to exercise an influence over the firm. According to the group that it is trying to satisfy, the firm may try to achieve a certain level or rate of profit, provide excellent after-sales service and advice, or aim to reduce its carbon footprint within a certain period of time.

Organisational theory

According to profit-maximising theory, firms will choose an output and price that is the most profitable. Organisational theory stresses that in large firms, decisions are made after much discussion by groups and committees and once they are agreed and adopted they are changed only reluctantly. This contrasts with the dynamic firm seeking to maximise its profits. Organisational theorists suggest that satisficing will take place as the organisation pursues a number of goals, such as increasing their market share or level of sales. Profit maximisation is not then the major driving force of the firm, so an output could be chosen that ensures that the product will achieve market penetration rather than maximum profits.

Cost plus pricing

This approach argues that firms follow a policy of non-maximisation by choice. They pursue a policy which is known as full cost pricing. In this theory the firm sets its price equal to average cost, at normal capacity output, plus a conventional mark up. So the level of prices is the level of average costs plus, for example, 25 per cent, which is the conventional mark up (level of profits) for the industry.

Figure 2.6 shows the long-run average variable cost with the minimum efficient scale at 0A. Between 0A and 0B the firm experiences constant returns to scale. The cost plus view is that firms will produce somewhere between 0A and 0B and add a mark up when LRAVC changes. In this situation firms only change their prices when their average costs change substantially as the result, for example, of an increase in the cost of raw materials, but do not adjust their output to maximise profits along the lines suggested by the traditional theory.

This view of firms' actions does not have to conflict with profit maximisation as firms may set the mark up to maximise profits. However, some economists argue that firms that employ this technique do not typically set their prices at the profit-maximising level but rather are creatures of habit that, at most, make profit-oriented changes at infrequent intervals.

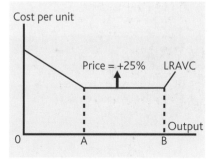

Figure 2.6 *Cost plus pricing*

Long-run profit maximisation

The neo-classical theory of the firm suggests that firms will react to every shift in market and alter their price and output accordingly. In reality this is unlikely to happen for a number of reasons, not the least of which is that if supply falls firms may avoid increasing prices too rapidly for fear of losing some brand loyalty due to their perceived avaricious behaviour. For large firms the costs of continually changing brochures and price lists

Key terms

Capital market discipline: where firms may be taken over by other firms if they appear to be making lower profits than their assets would suggest.

Delisting: refers to the practice of removing the stock of a company from a stock exchange so that investors can no longer trade shares of the stock on that exchange.

Innovation: turning invention into commercial use; introducing a new product or process.

Activities

1 Give two reasons why firms may choose not to pursue profit maximisation.

2 Explain, with the aid of a diagram, why maximising total revenue is not likely to maximise profits.

3 Why is a PLC unlikely to minimise its costs?

AQA Examiner's tip

Make sure that you keep up with real-world examples by reading a quality newspaper.

is likely to outweigh the benefits, and adjustments are likely to only take place annually or bi-annually unless large changes in market conditions occur.

This has led to the development of the concept of long-run profit maximisation as an attempt to explain firms' behaviour. The suggestion is that sales are the key to growth and growth is the key to future profits and managerial security. Firms will not attempt to increase short-term profits by undertaking risky, even if profitable ventures, as long-run profitability requires survival and survival may require caution. Firms are likely to be risk averse.

Company size

Profit maximisation suggests that all companies will react in the same way and this is not borne out by observations in the real world. We have to accept that a small entrepreneurial company is likely to respond differently to a huge multinational that has a range of different objectives.

In conclusion

Profits are very important to a firm and firms are strongly motivated in the search for profits and prefer to make more profits rather than less profit. A listen to the business news on Radio 4's *Today* programme or a look at the headlines on the financial pages, when firms are reporting their profits for the period, will give you an indication of the importance of profits. There is pressure to make large profits in the short run to keep shareholders happy and to maintain the price of the company shares. At present any acceptable theory is likely to be profit oriented, especially in the short run, because if the firms' managers fail to make the profit their assets can achieve, they will be subject to a takeover bid by other firms that think they can use the assets more successfully. This possible outcome is an example of **capital market discipline** and the pressure of takeovers is likely to limit the discretion of the managers to pursue other goals than profits. Such short-term behaviour may be to the detriment of the company's long-run aims as it may preclude capital investment, which, in the short run, would be extremely expensive and reduce profits but could prove to be extremely profitable in the long run. Some companies like Virgin have **delisted** their shares in order to remove such short-run pressures.

■ The growth of firms

Increasing profit requires either the reduction of costs, which can be achieved by reaching the minimum efficient scale and exploiting the economies of scale, or increasing revenue by increasing market share or obtaining a dominant position in the market. Both of these may occur as a result of a firm's growth. Growth may occur in one of two ways – internal and external growth.

Internal/organic growth

This process requires the use of profits or loans to finance expansion over a period of time by increasing the number of both fixed and variable factors within the firm. There is consensus in the academic literature that **innovation** and creativity, which increase the customer base, are central to organic growth. There are two ways in which internal growth can occur – extending an organisation's geographic reach, and expanding into new products in order to increase the size of its available market.

Organic growth may be a fairly slow process as the market may be saturated or the strength of the competition may mean the firm is unable to raise or even maintain prices. Lack of profit may also impede organic growth.

External growth

This can be a rapid way for a firm to expand by acquisitions and mergers. Firms merge amicably with other firms or a hostile takeover may occur in which the management of the target firm resists the advances of the buyer but is eventually forced to accept a deal by its current owners. However, in a majority of cases mergers have failed to deliver the benefits that were expected and have not justified their costs. This is due to diseconomies of scale in terms of 'people issues' such as cultural fit, leadership, poor communications and the company's ability to change.

There are four main types of mergers:

1 **Horizontal integration** is where two firms in the same stage of production combine their operations, for example, two breweries combining.

2 **Vertical integration** where two firms at different stages in the supply chain come together.

   ■ Vertical backward integration is where a firm combines with a firm in the previous process, for example, a brewery integrating with hop growers.

   ■ Vertical forward integration is combining with the next process, for example, a brewery taking over public houses.

3 A **conglomerate merger** is one where the firms have no obvious relationship but may decide to merge to increase their market size to satisfy managerial ambitions or to diversify and reduce their risk exposure.

4 A **lateral merger** is a type of horizontal integration in that there are some similarities between the businesses. For example, a brewery may merge with a restaurant chain to increase the market for its product.

The diagram below may help you understand the reasons for integration.

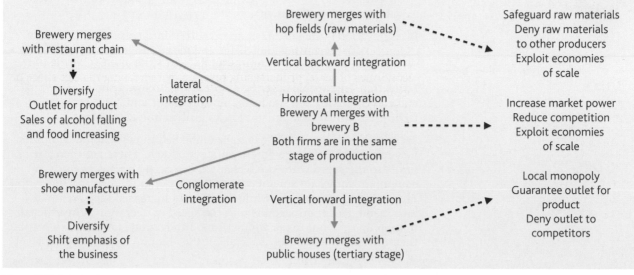

Figure 2.7 *Integration*

Examiner's tip

You should be aware of the growth of firms and the reasons for it.

Activities

1 Justify the view that Apple Inc. has grown organically.

2 Briefly list the advantages of external, as opposed to internal, growth.

3 What would you consider to be the advantages of backward vertical integration?

Figure 2.8 *Oh dear, this feels like a takeover!*

When considering external, as opposed to internal growth, companies may consider:

- Time constraints – external expansion is more rapid than internal growth.
- Cost – it may be cheaper to buy out another firm than to undertake new investment.
- The acquisition of a brand which is only available through external takeover.
- Asset stripping – the predator may be able to sell the firm's assets for more than it paid for them.

When it comes to efficiency the firms usually talk of synergies, where the combination of two firms is likely to lead to lower costs than they can achieve as separate firms. There is no agreement that this is actually the case and integration may be undertaken more to fulfil the ambitions of managers rather than achieving efficiency. Managers who have successfully taken over another firm gain in prestige and are in a better position to increase their incomes as they have successfully increased the size of the company and its market share.

■ Firms and technological change

Technical progress appears to have three key components:

- More output can be produced with the same inputs.
- Existing outputs undergo an improvement in quality.
- Completely new goods or services become available.

Technological progress enhances production and consumption possibilities by raising the productivity of capital – greater output can be obtained for the same inputs. Technical progress allows us to do more with less and this improves the quality of life compared to previous generations.

There are two terms that that need to be differentiated:

- Invention – coming up with a completely new idea or concept that can be patented. The UK is high up on the list of countries that invent and come up with patents.
- Innovation – the putting of an invention into commercial use, the process of converting knowledge and ideas into better ways of doing business or into new or improved products and services.

Firms that are capable of innovation are able to lower their costs and come up with new products, new processes and new production techniques which economists refer to as dynamic efficiency.

Technical progress usually has to be embodied in new capital equipment, new human skills or new intermediate products. There are therefore limits to the speed with which changes can occur, because new equipment comes on stream only at the rate of gross investment. Broadband is an example; while the UK has increased the take up of broadband, recent criticism is that the speed of operation is insufficient to keep up with our major competitors. Innovations take time to become the norm in all industries especially if they require extremely high levels of investment.

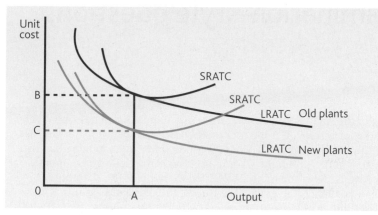

Figure 2.9 *The effect of innovation on the firm's costs*

Activities

1 Construct a diagram to show the effect of innovation on firms.

2 Explain why both invention and innovation are likely to shorten product lifecycles.

3 What is the likely effect on the consumer surplus of innovation over time?

Figure 2.9 shows a firm using existing technology facing increasing returns to scale as the LRATC labelled 'Old plants' is downward sloping. The firm is producing the output 0A at a unit cost of 0B. Now assume that some technological development lowers the costs curves of newly built plants and that the technology cannot be used by old plants because it must be embodied in new plants and equipment.

This is shown in Figure 2.9 by the LRATC labelled 'New plants' where at the same level of output it shows a unit cost saving of BC. New plants will now be able to earn profits and they will be built immediately. This will shift the industry's supply curve to the right and prices will fall. Firms that have not invested in new plants will find it difficult to compete as their costs will be higher than firms that have exploited the innovation.

Some industries experience virtually constant technical change where new innovations continually force costs down, for example, consumer electronics. Firms in such an industry experience very short lifecycles of their products. For example when DVD players were first introduced the retail price was about £450 but are now selling in Tesco for £19.99. An explanation of the high price is that with shorter lifecycles firms try to recoup as much of their initial investment costs as rapidly as possible before imitators enter the industry and force down prices. The original innovators, for example, Sony will be likely to discontinue producing solely players and concentrate on the newer technology which combine play and record functions. Less well known firms, perhaps from emerging economies, will be left to concentrate on the older models until they are no longer profitable and are discontinued, for example, video cassette recorders (VCRs).

After completing this chapter you should:

■ understand the difference between average, total and marginal revenue

■ be able to explain why profit maximisation occurs where marginal revenue equals marginal cost

■ appreciate that firms may have a diverse range of objectives

■ understand why and how firms grow in size

■ appreciate the effect of technological change upon firms.

Culling Cullinan

Richard Burton probably knew nothing of the small South African town of Cullinan when he bought yet another chunky diamond for Elizabeth Taylor in 1969. But the rock, still known as the Taylor Burton, was found there, together with a quarter of the world's diamonds over 400 carats. The Cullinan mine has also produced what is still the largest rough gem in the world, the whopping 3,106-carat Cullinan Diamond, parts of which adorn England's Crown Jewels. Now the mine itself, like so many of the diamonds unearthed there, is about to change hands. On 22 November De Beers, the diamond giant that has owned the mine since 1930 said it was selling it to a consortium led by Petra Diamonds, one of South Africa's emerging diamond producers, for 1 billion rand ($147m) in cash.

De Beers is selling because the mine is no longer profitable, despite attempts to turn it around. But Petra reckons the mine still has another 20 years of production in it and plans to extract at least 1m carats a year. The unexploited 'Centenary Cut' deposit, which lies under the existing mine, could yield a lot more.

Petra is a relatively small outfit, listed on London's Alternative Investment Market that specialises in buying mines that bigger companies see as marginal. Its trick is to extract better returns by rationalising production and processing, and keeping operating costs and overheads down. It has already bought two of De Beers, South African mines, both of which are now profitable, and is finalising the 78.5m rand acquisition of the group's underground operation in Kimberley which stopped working in 2005.

It already operates four mines in South Africa and has promising exploration in Angola (a joint-venture with BHP Billiton), Sierra Leone and Botswana. Petra expects to produce over 1m carats by 2010; quite a jump from 180,474 carats in the year to June. The company has yet to make a profit, but expects to be making money by the middle of next year.

In the 1990s De Beers decided that it was no longer a good idea to try to monopolise the diamond market. It started focusing on higher returns rather than market share, and has been revamping its mine portfolio, selling off mines that are no longer profitable and investing in more enticing operations, such as its mine off the west coast of South Africa, its Voorspoed operation in the Free State province, and two new mines in Canada.

Adapted from The Economist, 12 January 2007

1	(a)	Explain the meaning of the term 'marginal' in the statement 'Petra specialises in buying mines that bigger companies see as marginal.'	*(5 marks)*
	(b)	With the aid of a diagram explain how Petra may be able to exploit new technology to benefit from a mine that De Beers sees as 'no longer profitable'.	*(10 marks)*
	(c)	According to the extract De Beers is 'focusing on higher returns rather than market share'. With the aid of the data evaluate the alternate objectives that De Beers could pursue.	*(25 marks)*
2	(a)	Examine three reasons that explain why firms seek to grow larger.	*(15 marks)*
	(b)	Evaluate the methods that firms might adopt in order to grow.	*(25 marks)*

3 Competitive markets and perfect competition

This chapter builds on the material encountered in Chapters 1 and 2 and starts to look at what are referred to as the forms of market structure. This is how different markets react according to the numbers of firms in the industry in which they operate. We can see this as a spectrum ranging from a large number of small firms in competition with each other; price takers who have to accept the market price, to an industry which is dominated by one firm which can influence the price as it has no competition.

Figure 3.1 *Not a perfect market – doctor and patient*

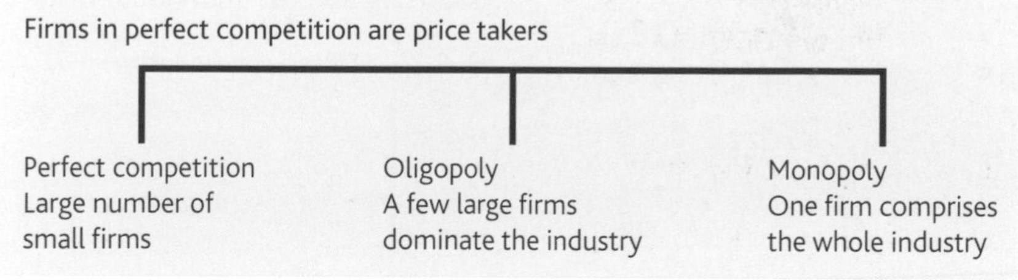

Firms in perfect competition are price takers

Perfect competition	Oligopoly	Monopoly
Large number of small firms	A few large firms dominate the industry	One firm comprises the whole industry

Figure 3.2 *The market spectrum*

Figure 3.2 shows the a spectrum ranging from very intense competition, where firms have no market power, to a situation where there is no competition as the firm is the only one in the market.

An introduction to perfectly competitive markets

Firms operating under conditions of competition will not only need to remain price competitive but will strive to improve the quality of their product or service to stay ahead of their competitors.

Perfect competition is an extreme form of competition and is based on the following assumptions.

- Large number of buyers and sellers – this is to ensure that the product is sold and the firm is a **price taker**.

Key terms

Price taker: a firm that has to accept the price ruling in the market.

Key terms

Homogeneous: all products are the same irrespective of who makes them.

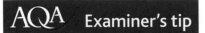

AQA **Examiner's tip**

You must know the assumptions as they are crucial to understanding the working of the theory.

■ No one firm or individual buyer is large enough to affect the market price.

■ A perfect market exists – therefore buyers and sellers have perfect knowledge of the product and prices.

■ **Homogeneous** products – all products are the same, which means that consumers have no preference over who they buy from and will purchase from the cheapest provider.

■ Freedom of entrance to and exit from the industry – any firms can enter the industry as there are no barriers to keep them out. Firms that do not make normal profits can leave the industry and use their factors of production elsewhere. This means that firms will make normal profits in the long run.

■ Readily available information – we assume that all firms have equal access to any technological improvements and that all firms have equal advantages. Thus firms are unlikely to engage in research and development (R&D) as the results will be immediately available to other firms.

■ Factors of production are perfectly mobile which means that they can undertake any types of work in any location.

While you may consider the assumptions of perfect competition to be unrealistic (and you would be right) they lead to certain efficient outcomes which economists find useful: the performance of the model is taken by economists as a benchmark for the efficient performance of markets in general and as a result the theory has a degree of importance which is greater than its practical application. Economists appreciate that competition is important to achieve efficiency and while perfect competition may not be possible, some degree of competition would be welcome.

Firms in perfect competition have no influence over the market; they can sell all they produce at the going price. Figure 3.3 shows both the industry and the individual firm.

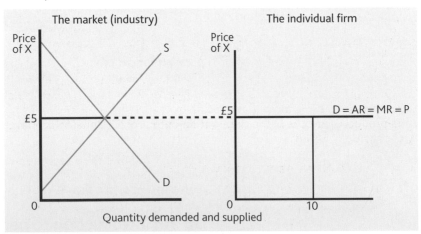

Figure 3.3 *The firm and the industry*

Firms in perfect competition are price takers

In Figure 3.3 the market price for product X reaches an equilibrium at £5, and this is the price that the individual firm has to accept – it has to 'take its price' from the market. If the firm tries to sell above the price of £5 it will not have many customers as consumers will go elsewhere. If it sells below £5 it will be deluged with customers but will not be maximising its returns.

The diagram of the firm shows that the demand curve for X is perfectly elastic as the firm can sell all that it produces at the going price. We will assume that the firm is producing 10 units of output.

- Total revenue = price × output (£5 × 10 units): firm's total revenue is £50.
- Average revenue = total revenue (£50) ÷ output (10) = price £5. The average revenue curve is the same curve as the demand curve.
- Marginal revenue = revenue obtained from the sale of the extra unit and, as all units sell at the same price, is £5. So the horizontal line at the price of £5 equals D = AR = MR = P.

The diagram of the industry shows that both the consumer and producer surpluses (see Figure 4.7 on page 43) are maximised so the industry is using its factors to produce what consumers want to buy – in economists' language it is **allocatively efficient**.

How many does the firm produce?

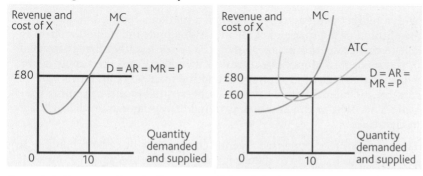

Figure 3.4 *How many does the firm produce?*

Figure 3.5 *Short-run supernormal profit*

In Chapter 2 we saw that firms would decide on their level of output by the relationship between marginal revenue and marginal cost and derived the maxim that 'any firm wanting to maximise profit will produce where marginal revenue equals marginal cost.'

Once we have the marginal revenue and the marginal cost curves we are in a position to determine the output of the individual firm.

In Figure 3.4 MR = MC at the output of 10 units, and in order to maximise profits the firm will produce 10 units. Once we have the output of the firm we can calculate that the total revenue = price × number of units produced. Price is £80 per unit at an output of 10 units, which gives total revenue of £800.

Short-run profits and the industry response

To work out the level of profits we need to be able to compute total costs. We can do this using the ATC, as ATC × Output = total cost. Figure 3.5 takes the previous diagram, Figure 3.4, and adds an ATC curve.

At the output of 10 units the ATC is £60 per unit produced. Thus total cost is ATC × output = £60 × 10 = £600. So the firm's total cost is £600. But the total revenue is £800: the firm is making £200 profit. Revenue, minus cost, equals profit, £200. But as we include normal profit in costs this £200 must represent supernormal or abnormal profit. If abnormal profit is being made then other firms will wish to enter the industry to maximise the opportunity cost of using their resources, and as there are no barriers to entry they will do so until all supernormal profits are competed away.

Link

To recap, look at Chapter 2 where we examined the individual firm's demand curve.

AQA Examiner's tip

You must be able to explain why D = AR = MR = P.

Key terms

Allocative efficiency: the optimum allocation of scarce resources that best accords with the consumers' pattern of demand.

Activities

Using the diagram (Figure 3.3) assume that more firms enter the industry.

1. What would happen to the price ruling in the market?
2. Explain why the individual firm has no option but to trade at that price.
3. Explain what will happen to the AR and MR and why.

AQA Examiner's tip

It is essential when drawing a diagram that you indicate where marginal revenue equals marginal cost because profit-maximising firms will produce at that point.

Note that at the profit-maximising output profit per unit is the difference between average revenue and average total cost.

Link

See Chapter 2, p20.

Activities

The market demand and supply curves for an industry in perfect competition give a market price of 60 and an output of 200 units. The supply increases such that the equilibrium price is now £40 where 300 units are demanded and supplied. The costs curves for the individual firm are as follows.

Table 3.1 *Cost table for firm*

Output	ATCEs	MCEs
0		
		20
1	60	
		40
2	40	
		60
3	50	
		80
4	60	

1 Using graph paper construct a diagram showing the industry position and, using the equilibrium prices and information from the table above, construct the diagram of the firm.

2 At a price of £60 what quantity would the firm have been producing?

3 What was its level of supernormal profits or losses?

4 Explain why a price of £40 is sufficient to keep the firm in the industry.

Market response

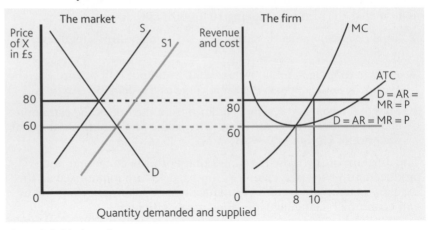

Figure 3.6 *Market adjustment*

With a market demand curve of D and a market supply curve of S the price ruling in the market is £80 and at this price the individual firm is able to make supernormal profits of £20 per unit. Other firms attracted by the supernormal profits will enter the industry and the supply curve will shift to the right, from S to A1 and the price will fall. Firms will continue to enter the industry until supernormal profits are competed away. The effect of this on the individual firm is shown on the right side in Figure 3.6.

The firm now faces a revised revenue curve as the price has changed. To maximise profits it has to reduce its output to 8 units as at 10 units MC would be greater than MR as MC is at £80 while MR has fallen to £60. Any unit produced beyond the output of eight units adds more to costs than revenue; the firm's output has fallen as, due to the entry of other firms, its market share has fallen.

Its total revenue is now £60 × 8 (price × output) and its total cost is £60 × 8 (ATC × output). Both total cost and revenue are the same and as normal profit is included in cost the firm is making normal profit and this implies no hardship whatsoever to the firm. This is the long-run equilibrium position for a firm in perfect competition where the average total cost and the average revenue are equal, which is at eight units in the Figure 3.6. This allows us to state another maxim: that normal profit is where average total cost equals average revenue.

■ Long-run equilibrium and efficiency

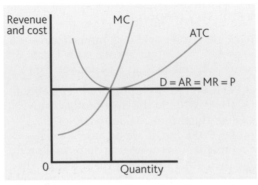

Figure 3.7 *Long-run equilibrium for a firm in perfect competition*

In Figure 3.7 the firm is in equilibrium as it is making normal profit as AR = ATC.

Notice that in equilibrium profit maximisation (MR=MC) corresponds to **optimum output**, where the ATC is at its lowest point. This is the point of productive efficiency where the firm is producing its products at the lowest possible cost using existing technology. Also at this position the MC of the last unit equals the price of the last unit and the firm is allocatively efficient as the price is equal to the lowest resource cost of supplying the product. Firms in perfect competition are likely to be **statically efficient**, that is, both allocatively and productively efficient at a point in time.

The assumptions of perfect competition seem to imply that while a firm will not grow large enough to exploit the economies of scale its activities will result in an efficient allocation of resources. However, a firm in perfect competition may, in the search to reduce costs, dispose of its waste in ways that create negative externalities and will not therefore be allocatively efficient.

Dynamic efficiency is efficiency over time and concerns the production of new products, new techniques and new processes, and for firms to undertake the investment in research and development they need to make supernormal profits. Firms in perfect competition are unlikely to embark on research and development as according to the assumptions all firms in the industry have perfect knowledge, and free entry means that supernormal profits are competed away. Without being able to protect their investment and earn supernormal profits, it is unlikely that firms in perfect competition would invest in the research and development required to achieve dynamic efficiencies.

Key terms

Optimum output: the (optimum) combination of fixed and variable factors that minimises ATC.

Static efficiency: efficiency at a point in time – includes allocative and productive efficiency.

Dynamic efficiency: efficiency over time – new products, techniques and processes which increaases economic growth.

 Examiner's tip

Examiners often ask questions about efficiency – ensure you know what efficiencies apply to perfect competition.

Case study

An example of perfect competition?

The Internet economy: Towards a better future

Can you remember life before the Internet? Though quite a new technology, already a world without the Web has become as unthinkable for many of us as a world without telephones. But what of the future? Can the benefits of this extraordinary technology be multiplied, and how can the thornier challenges be met? How times have changed since the OECD convened its first-ever ministerial conference on e-commerce in Ottawa, Canada, in 1998. Google was a month old, and was still operating in a garage with just three employees. Amazon and eBay were fledgling ventures, but have since gone on to become successful mainstream companies. And in the last few years, new services, such as iTunes, Skype and YouTube, have become part of the daily vocabulary of millions of people around the world. Underneath, the network's infrastructure has also fundamentally transformed in the last decade. Dial-up Internet access has given way to always-on broadband technology.

Moreover, users are accessing the Internet via all manner of wireless devices, from laptops to mobile phones. Along the way, communications became the fastest-growing part of household expenditure since 1993, even faster than health and education.

Millions of people now use the Internet for everything from doing homework to buying books, or playing or downloading games, music and movies. Levels of user participation and publication on the Internet have also surged, from blogs, podcasts and interactive wikis that anyone can modify, through to services for sharing photos and video clips, such as Flickr and Daily Motion. Social networking sites such as Bebo, Facebook and MySpace represent another rapidly developing frontier of communication.

*Adapted from **Susanne Huttner**, Director, OECD Science, Technology and Industry Directorate*

Firms making losses

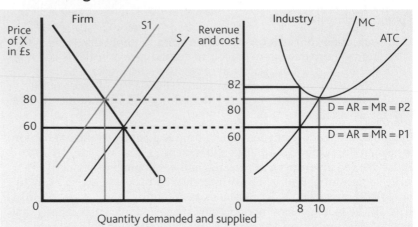

Figure 3.8 *Market adjustment for firms making losses*

At a market price of £60 the firm in Figure 3.8 is making losses as at an output of eight units; the ATC is £82 whereas the AR is only £60 and a loss is being made of £22 per unit. The firm is producing at the profit-maximising/loss-minimising output as MC = MR, which means that it is making the smallest loss possible, but as total costs exceed total revenue losses are made. In the diagram showing the industry the equilibrium price is £60 as a result of the interaction of demand and supply. If firms are making losses, some of them will be leaving the industry and the industry supply curve will move to the left from S to S1 and this will lead to a higher price of £80. At this point the firm is able to make normal profit as the ATC and the AR are equal at an output of 10 units. The firm's market share has increased as other firms have left the industry.

Entering and leaving the industry

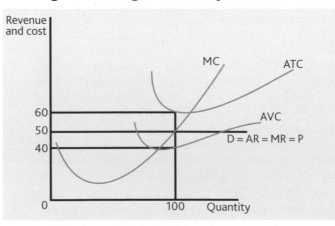

Figure 3.9 *Entering and leaving the industry*

In Figure 3.9, the firm is producing at the point where MR = MC and so is maximising its profits or minimising its losses.

At the output of 100 units the firm's total revenue (price £50 × output 100) is £5,000. But at this output its total cost (ATC × output) is £6,000 and the firm is making losses of £1,000 per week! The firm is faced with the decision as to what to do; it is not using its resources efficiently and will gradually shift them.

The question is how fast will it leave the industry? Whether it closes down slowly or leaves immediately depends on the relationship between the price and the average variable cost. While it is possible for a firm in the short run to continue in production without covering all its fixed costs this is not a situation that can continue in the long run as the firm must cover all of its costs.

In the diagram, the AVC is £40 per unit, giving a total variable cost of £4,000 (AVC × output £40 × 100 units). The firm's total cost is £6,000 (£60 × 100 units); total cost (£6,000) − total variable cost (£4,000) = total fixed cost (£2,000).

The firm faces fixed costs of £2,000 and these must be paid whether the firm produces or not. At present running the firm only results in a loss of £1,000, so running the firm is paying £1,000 towards the fixed costs; shutting immediately would mean that all fixed costs would have to be paid out of the owner's pocket. So if the price is above the AVC it pays the firm to continue production to offset some part of its fixed costs and close down slowly. If price falls below the AVC there is no point in carrying on and the firm will shut down immediately.

The short-run supply curve for a firm in perfect competition

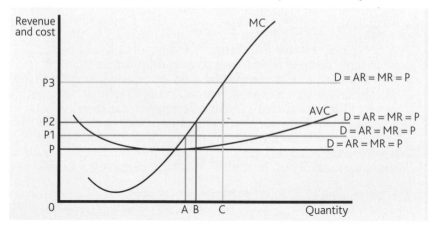

Figure 3.10 *The short-run supply curve for a firm in perfect competition*

In perfect competition the firm will leave the industry immediately if price falls below AVC as it cannot afford to pay for its labour and raw materials, let alone its fixed costs. Thus in Figure 3.10, below the price of 0P it is not cost effective for the firm to supply any of its products. Conversely, some firms expecting price rises in the future will enter the industry as price rises above variable cost. At price P1 the firm will supply 0A.

Above the level of AVC the firm equates MR and MC. As the MR is also the demand curve the firm equates MC and demand. If price increases to 0P2 the firm will increase its output until MR and MC are equal and supply 0B. In perfect competition the MC curve above the AVC is the firm's supply curve. Further increase in price leads to further extension of the supply curve, for example, if price increases to 0P3 the supply extends to 0C.

Activities

The price ruling in a perfectly competitive market is £40. The individual firm's costs curves are shown between the output of 6 and 12 units. Plot the situation of the firm on graph paper. The marginal cost can be plotted on the outputs as shown.

Table 3.2

Output	MC	ATC	AVC
	20		
6		65	38
	25		
7		59	34
	30		
8		54	30
	40		
9		52	32
	50		
10		50	35
	60		
11		52	40
	70		
12		55	43

1 Explain what level of output the firm will produce and why.

2 What is the firm's level of losses at this output?

3 You have been called in to advise the managing director as to whether the firm should close immediately. Write a brief to explain the costs/benefits of the firm's options.

Entering an industry

British Telecom (BT) – one of the largest telecommunication operators in Europe – is expected to become the first foreign company to enter China's telecom sector after the nation joined the World Trade Organization (WTO). BT is scheduled Friday afternoon to announce its cooperation with Chinese privately owned telecom service provider 21 ViaNet (China) Inc. Sources from both companies said the cooperation will expand both companies' business coverage and is mutually beneficial. According to the agreement, 21 ViaNet will become the service arm for BT Ignite – the broadband service branch of BT - on the Chinese mainland; while 21 ViaNet will adopt technology from BT Ignite to jointly develop new services.

Humphrey Penney, director of BT Ignite Global Solutions, said BT is looking for potential opportunities in China, adding: 'In the midst of the sluggish telecom market around the globe, we see the growth all across the board, ranging from the Internet, information technology and telecom sectors to traditional enterprises only here in China. China is the last land on earth for a new round of prosperity.'

BT's involvement in China's telecom market will benefit both sides, industry experts commented. For BT, suffering from the pressure of heavy debts, China may become its future revenue pool. For 21 ViaNet, BT's reputation and customer base may help it move into the international market. China vowed to gradually open its telecom market after accession to the WTO. Value-added services in Beijing, including e-mail, on-line data searching, call centre, Internet access and Internet content services – are widely regarded by industry insiders as the first fields that foreigners may step into. Zhang Xinzhu, a telecom expert said, with China's outstanding performance in the telecom industry, more foreign telecom carriers may follow BT's lead. Foreign telecom carriers could also test the water in the value-added business, and then develop into the basic telecom and other industries, he said.

Adapted from 'BT Becomes First Foreign Firm Entering China's Telecom Market',
People's Daily, http://english.peopledaily.com.cn

Key terms

Structural performance and conduct model: individual performance depends ultimately on the industry structure where the variables in the model are structure, conduct and performance.

The structural performance and conduct model

Economists can analyse how an industry is likely to operate using the structure, performance and conduct model. The industry structure (which is assumed to determine the conduct of the industry) includes such variables as the number and size of buyers and sellers, degree of product differentiation and the level of barriers to entry.

Conduct refers to the activities of the industry's buyers and sellers. Sellers' activities include use of their productive capacity, pricing policies and research and development, while buyers' activity concerns whether any buyers are in a position of power.

Performance is measured in terms of welfare maximisation where resources are employed where they achieve the highest value output for the economy. The structure of perfect competition should lead in the long run to the optimal allocation of resources in the economy where welfare will be maximised. This outcome means that other market forms can be subjected to this analytical model and their outcomes judged relative to the outcome under perfect competition.

Action may be required by governments to ensure that other market forms achieve maximum welfare, in terms of competition policy to ensure that groups of firms are unable to 'rig the market'. Both the European Commission and the UK have a competition policy that is aimed at ensuring that consumers are not exploited by restrictive or monopolistic practices.

AQA Examiner's tip

Practise the diagrams – it is essential that you can construct and explain these diagrams.

At the end of this chapter you should:

- realise that perfect markets do not exist but that some degree of perfection is possible
- understand the structure/conduct/performance relationship
- appreciate that profit-maximising/loss-minimising firms equate marginal costs and marginal revenue
- realise that normal profits are included in costs
- understand the benefits of competition to the consumer
- understand what is meant by efficiency
- be able to use diagrammatic analysis to explain situations that arise in perfect competition.

Extract A – Models and reality

Agriculture is often said to resemble the economist's model of perfect competition as the theoretical structure of the market resembles the conditions under which agriculture operates. While it is unlikely that a model can totally reproduce reality the assumptions of perfect competition seem to be borne out by the farming industry.

Extract B – Cheap no more

In early September the world price of wheat rose to over $400 a tonne, the highest ever recorded. In May it had been around $200. Though in real terms its price is far below the heights it scaled in 1974, it is still twice the average of the past 25 years. Earlier this year the price of maize (corn) exceeded $175 a tonne, again a world record. It has fallen from its peak, as has that of wheat, but at $150 a tonne is still 50 per cent above the average for 2006.

As the price of one crop shoots up, farmers plant it to take advantage, switching land from other uses. So a rise in wheat prices has knock-on effects on other crops. Rice prices have hit record highs this year, although their rise has been slower.

Normally, sky-high food prices reflect scarcity caused by crop failure. Stocks are run down as everyone lives off last year's stores. This year harvests have been poor in some places, notably Australia, where the drought-hit wheat crop failed for the second year running and farmers have been leaving the industry.

Yet what is most remarkable about the present bout of 'agflation' is that record prices are being achieved at a time not of scarcity but of abundance. Two things are affecting the world's demand for cereals. One is increasing wealth in China and India. This is stoking demand for meat in those countries, in turn boosting the demand for cereals to feed to animals.

Not surprisingly, farmers are switching, too: they now feed about 200–250 million more tonnes of grain to their animals than they did 20 years ago. Because this change in diet has been slow and incremental, it cannot explain the dramatic price movements of the past year. The second change can: the rampant demand for ethanol as fuel for American cars. In 2000 around 15mn tonnes of America's maize crop was turned into ethanol; this year the quantity is likely to be around 851mn tonnes. America is easily the world's largest maize exporter – and it now uses more of its maize crop for ethanol than it sells abroad.

It is risky to predict long-run trends in farming – technology in particular always turns out unexpectedly – but most forecasters conclude from these conflicting currents that prices will stay high for as much as a decade. However in the long run the operation of a perfectly competitive market will result in the efficient allocation of resources and is totally dependent upon the free entrance and exit of firms in response to profit making or loss making circumstances.

If food prices are to stay more or less where they are today, it would be a radical departure from a past in which shoppers and farmers got used to a gentle decline in food prices year in, year out. It would put an end to the era of cheap food. And its effects would be felt everywhere, but especially in countries where food matters most: poor ones.

Adapted from 'Cheap no more', The Economist, 6 December 2007

1 (a) Using the information in extract A outline the assumptions under which perfect competition operates. *(5 marks)*

   (b) Extract B refers to the Australian farmers leaving the industry. With the aid of a diagram(s) explain how under what circumstances a firm that cannot cover its costs will decide whether to continue production or cease production. *(10 marks)*

(c)   Extract B says 'However in the long run the operation of a
       perfectly competitive market will result in the efficient allocation
       of resources and is totally dependent upon the free entrance
       and exit of firms in response to profit making or loss making
       circumstances.' Analyse and evaluate this statement.   *(25 marks)*

4 Concentrated markets: theory of monopoly

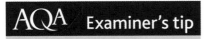

AQA Examiner's tip

Make sure you know the assumptions of monopoly.

Key terms

Barriers to entry: obstacles that stop new firms entering a market.

In this chapter we will look at the opposite end of the spectrum to perfect competition and begin our study of market concentration: a situation where the majority of the market share is in the hands of one (monopoly), two (duopoly), or a few (oligopoly) firms. In this chapter we will consider the situation where the total market is made up of one firm and no other firms are able to enter the industry. Given this structure you may well expect that the conduct and performance will be different from firms that are in perfect competition.

Monopoly

The assumptions of monopoly are as follows:

- The firm is the industry – the whole output of the industry is in the hands of a single firm.

- There are **barriers to entry** – no other firm is able to enter the industry.

As the firm is the industry it faces a downward sloping demand curve with a marginal revenue curve that slopes down beneath it. If you are unsure of why this is so look back at page 18 where it is explained in detail. The revenue curves for monopoly are reproduced in Figure 4.1.

Constructing the diagram

Figure 4.1 represents the first stage of constructing the monopoly diagram. In order to decide the monopolist's level of output the next stage is to add a marginal cost curve. In Figure 4.2 the MC cuts the MR curve at an output of 20 units, so this is the point of profit maximisation. The price is found from the AR curve and in this case is £50. The total revenue of the monopolist is £1,000 price × output (£50 × 20).

In order to find the level of profit we need to add the ATC curve to Figure 4.2 and this is shown below in Figure 4.3.

In Figure 4.3 the marginal cost curve cuts the ATC at its lowest point. The profit maximising output for the monopolists is where marginal revenue equals marginal cost at an output of 20 units. At the profit maximising output the ATC is £30 per unit, giving a total cost of £600. (ATC = £30 × output 20.) The monopolist is making supernormal profit of £20 per unit (AR – ATC: £50 – £30), or a total profit of £400 (total revenue – total cost).

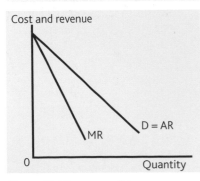

Figure 4.1 *The monopolist revenue curves*

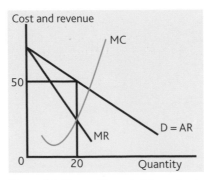

Figure 4.2 *The profit maximising output*

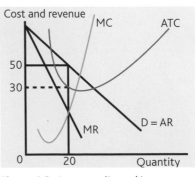

Figure 4.3 *A monopolist making supernormal profits*

Notice that at the profit maximising output the monopolist is not productively efficient as it is not producing at the lowest level of the ATC. It will not be spurred on to reduce its costs by the threat of other firms entering the industry, and may not be over-concerned about wastage or reducing costs to the minimum. For example, it may be **X-inefficient** in terms of providing its sales force with cars far more luxurious than are actually required, or wasting resources that under a more competitive environment would be used effectively.

Under a situation of perfect competition, if supernormal profits were made, other firms would move into the industry until the level of profits returned to normal. But with monopoly there are barriers to entry that prevent other firms from entering the industry and as a result the supernormal profits can be maintained.

Sources of monopoly power

A source of monopoly power is barriers to entry that a monopolist can use to keep other firms out, and maintain abnormal profits in the long run. Some firms operate in industries where a vast amount of investment is required in capital equipment to achieve the minimum efficient scale and, as a result, the number of new entrants is likely to be low. Other firms not in such a fortunate position may be able to create other barriers to entry:

- **Patent laws** that allow the designer of a product the sole right to the exploitation of the invention for a number of years. This can be seen in terms of patents by pharmaceutical companies and Dyson's vacuum cleaner. **Copyright** is virtually the same but applies to music, publications and intellectual property, rather than products.

- Where the government has **nationalised** an industry and granted it a charter which prohibits competition by law.

- Where the **incumbent** firm has exploited the economies of scale and can produce at a lower cost than any would-be new entrant. Such a firm could reduce its prices, **limit pricing** and threaten potential entrants with a price war that might bankrupt any possible competitor.

- Where the incumbent can create fixed costs that will make it extremely expensive for new entrants, especially if these costs are **sunk** and unlikely to be recoverable if firms leave the industry. An example of this would be advertising on a massive scale that makes it too costly for any new entrant to enter the industry.

- In an industry where some firms may be **legal monopolies** rather than pure monopolies, firms may endeavour to **differentiate their products** from those of their closest competitors, for example, soap powder manufacturers indulge in heavy advertising expenditure and produce a multiplicity of brands.

- In an industry where a firm may have control of an essential raw material, for example, local water companies, or where a firm has obtained most of the prime retail outlets making it difficult for new entrants to purchase suitable sites.

 Examiner's tip

- Questions on monopoly are usually based on a pure monopoly where the firm is the sole supplier of a particular good or service.

- It is essential that you can construct and explain the monopoly diagram.

- Appreciate how the assumptions of monopoly determine the structure.

Monopoly and efficiency

Figure 4.9, monopoly and competition, shows a perfectly competitive industry where price is 0PC and output is 0QC. Both the consumer and producer surplus are maximised so the industry is allocatively efficient. The consumer surplus is indicated by the triangle FEG.

Assume that the industry is taken over and monopolised by one firm. We can adapt the diagram to this situation by making the industry supply curve, the monopolist's marginal cost curve and adding a marginal revenue curve. The monopolist will equate MR and MC to maximise profits, output will fall to 0QM and the price will increase to 0PM. The consumer is now presented with a smaller quantity available at a higher price and the consumer surplus has fallen to EHI.

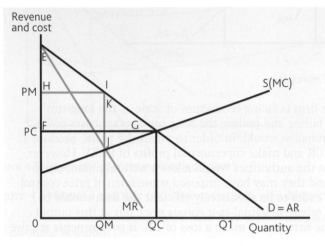

Figure 4.9 *Monopoly, competition and static efficiency*

We have seen in Figure 4.3 that the monopolist is not productively efficient in that it does not produce at the lowest point of the ATC. Neither is the monopolist allocatively efficient as, in monopoly, the consumers pay a price that is above the opportunity cost of producing the last unit of output. In Figure 4.9 the profit-maximising output is 0QM. The marginal cost of producing the last unit is QMJ, but the price at which it sells is QMI. Consumers put a much higher value on the last unit than the cost of producing it.

The triangle KJG shows the gain in both consumer and producer surplus that could be achieved by increasing output to 0QC. This area is called **dead-weight loss** and is due to the allocative inefficiency of monopoly. To be allocatively efficient the monopolist needs to produce up to the output 0QC where MC equals price. Between QM and QC the demand curve, reflecting the benefit consumers derive from these units, is above the MC curve, which shows the cost of producing these units – production of them would increase consumer welfare. The monopolist will not produce units between QM and QC because every unit produced beyond QM adds more to costs than revenue as MR is falling while MC is rising and this would reduce monopoly profit.

As monopolists do not produce at the point of either productive or allocative efficiency they cannot be said to be economically efficient.

While the diagrams above show that the monopolist is neither allocatively or productively efficient it must be remembered that these are static efficiencies and that monopolists may be dynamically efficient. They may be using the monopoly profits to fund research and development, which may lead to the development of new products, new processes and new techniques that increase consumer welfare.

Monopoly and dynamic efficiency

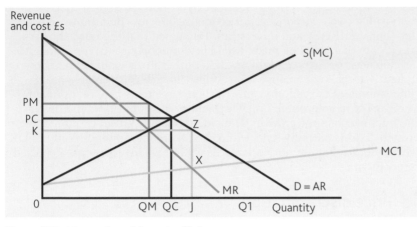

Figure 4.10 *Monopoly and dynamic efficiency*

Figure 4.10 reproduces the previous diagram, showing the situation under both perfect competition and monopoly. However in this diagram the monopoly is able to achieve economies of scale and the marginal cost curve moves downwards to MC1, output increases to 0J, in excess of the competitive output, 0QC at a price of 0K, which is lower than the competitive price, 0PC. While the monopolist is still not allocatively efficient, as the price of the last unit JZ is greater than the cost of the last unit JX, exploitation of the economies of scale could benefit the consumer more than a perfectly competitive situation.

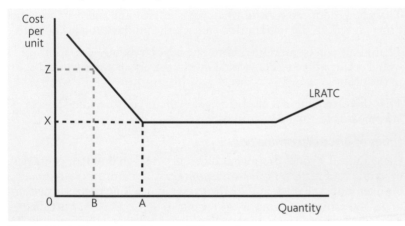

Figure 4.11 *Achieving the minimum efficient scale*

The minimum efficient scale

In some industries the minimum efficient scale (MES) does not occur until an extremely high level of output is reached. In Figure 4.11 the firm only reaches an output large enough to achieve the MES at 0A where its unit cost is at its lowest at 0X. A firm that produces less than this, for example, 0B, is unlikely to be able to compete as its unit cost will be higher at 0Z.

Under a situation of competition, especially where the market is fairly small as in the UK, prices are likely to be higher to cover costs than if there was only one firm that achieved the MES. Consumers could actually benefit as a result of the monopoly, and due to its lower costs it is likely to be competitive with foreign firms. In the context of the UK a number of firms competing may mean that no single firm has an output large enough to achieve the MES – in which case a single firm monopoly may be preferable.

Figure 4.12 *Joseph Schumpeter*

■ Key terms

Price discrimination: where an identical good/service is sold to different customers at different prices for reasons not associated with costs.

**Admission Price
£13.50
With Student ID
£7.25**

Figure 4.13 *A form of price discrimination*

Innovation

Joseph Schumpeter, an Austro–American economist, argued that monopolists were responsible for economic progress due to research and development (R&D) and innovation. He argued that the huge short-run profits that could be made would lead monopolists to innovate and develop new products, and if they didn't other firms would enter the industry, as 'gales of creative destruction', to grab the available profits. As innovation assists economic growth then a greater degree of monopoly or oligopoly in an economy may accelerate this innovation and increase the rates of economic growth. Reducing monopoly power could reduce growth. This is partially reflected in the control of monopolies in the UK where monopolies are not declared illegal but where every case is judged on its merits.

■ Price discrimination

Both monopolists and oligopolists may be in a position to **price discriminate** – be able to vary prices according to the customer. Price discrimination occurs when a producer sells an identical product to different buyers at different prices for reasons not associated with costs.

Firms who sell a product at one price realise that their profit could be increased if they could appropriate more of the consumer surplus, and this can be done if the producer can indulge in price discrimination

Conditions necessary for price discrimination

For firms to engage successfully in price discrimination certain conditions need to be met.

- That the vendor can control whatever is offered and there are no other firms present in the market that can sell the product at a lower price.

- That resale can be prevented from one buyer to another or arbitrage would occur, where traders would buy in the cheaper market and sell in the dearer.

- That there are different elasticities of demand, in that some buyers are prepared to pay more than others.

Methods of price discrimination

- Geographical – goods are sold at different prices in different countries, or in different regions of the same country. Car companies are noted for increasing the price in the UK market and selling them cheaper in mainland Europe.

- Time – for example, train companies charge high prices in the mornings, at peak time, when passengers need to use the trains to get to work by a specific time, and lower prices during the day at off-peak times when passengers could use alternative means of travel. In the case of passengers, price elasticity of demand changes with time.

- Age of customer – adult, pensioner, child are all charged different prices for tickets to travel on trains, entry tickets to the theatre and so on.

Dynamic pricing with monopoly

A topic which has received much recent attention is dynamic price discrimination. There are many aspects to this phenomenon. A publisher sets a high price for a new (hardback) book, and then subsequently the price is reduced. Or a retailer might use information it has obtained from its previous dealings with a customer to offer that customer a special deal. This latter form of discrimination, sometimes termed 'behaviour-based' price discrimination, could be highly complex. If a supermarket has sufficient information, it could offer those customers who have purchased, say, nappies, a voucher offering discounts to a particular brand of baby food. If a customer regularly spends £80 per shopping trip, the supermarket might send the customer a discount voucher if he spends more than £100 next time. Or if the consumer appears to have started shopping elsewhere recently, the supermarket will send a generous discount voucher to attempt to regain that consumer.

Adapted from Recent Developments in the Economics of Price Discrimination
Mark Armstrong, *February 2006*

Types of price discrimination

First degree price discrimination, sometimes known as perfect price discrimination, is a situation where each unit is sold for the maximum price.

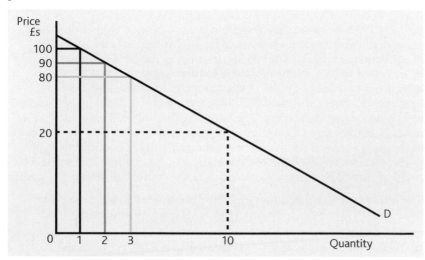

Figure 4.14 *First degree price discrimination*

First degree price discrimination: when the discriminating firm can charge a separate price to each individual customer.

Figure 4.14 shows first degree price discrimination where if 10 units are sold the price has to fall to £20, but if the monopolist is able to discriminate between customers then 1 unit can be sold for £100, the second unit for £90 and the third unit for £80 and so on. The benefit is the increase in profit, plus the fact that when the firm increases sales it does not reduce the price of all products sold. First degree price discrimination would rely on separation of markets and the seller reaching individual bargains with consumers. It also requires that the supplier can put an estimate on what the consumer would be prepared to pay for the good, and price accordingly. In doing so the supplier is trying to obtain as much of the consumers' surplus as possible.

Second degree price discrimination occurs where consumers are charged
different prices for different blocks of consumption. Less of the consumer
surplus is lost so less consumer information is required. In Figure 4.15
the first 100 units are sold at a price of 0P and the next 300 units are sold
at a price of 0P−. Without discrimination, if 400 units were sold the price
of all units would fall to P−, but with price discrimination total revenue is
larger, as shown by the shaded area in Figure 4.15.

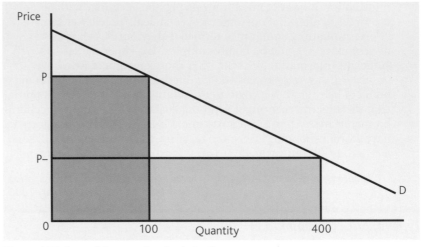

Figure 4.15 *Second degree price discrimination*

Third degree price discrimination is where the same product or service
is sold at different prices to different consumers in different markets.
Figure 4.15 shows a situation where if the goods were sold at the same
price in all markets then they would be sold at the price 0P, as shown
in the combined market. But by separating the markets the price can
be increased to 0P+ in the domestic market where demand is more
inelastic, and reduced to 0P− in the foreign market where demand is
more elastic. Firms will produce where marginal revenue equals marginal
cost in each separate market. The resulting level of profit is greater as a
result of market separation than if all were sold at one price; the addition
of the areas between the average revenue and average cost curves − (profit
as revenue exceeds costs) in the domestic and foreign market exceed what
could be earned charging a single price in the combined market.

The long-run average and marginal cost is assumed to be constant in all
markets.

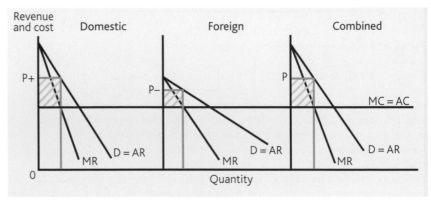

Figure 4.16 *Third degree price discrimination*

Consequences of price discrimination

Advantages for the price discriminator:

■ Increased profits redistribute income from consumers to producers.

■ Price discrimination is profitable and will provide a higher level of total revenue to the firm than the best single price.

■ Output will be larger with price discrimination than under single price monopoly. With single price monopoly, increases in output lead to a fall in MR, but the discriminator can sell more without lowering the price.

Effect on consumers:

■ Loss of welfare – consumers' surplus totally disappears under first degree price discrimination.

■ Inequitable – some consumers have to pay more than others, for example, users of peak time public transport.

■ If profits are reinvested, consumers might derive long-run benefits in terms of increased efficiency and lower costs and prices.

■ Lower prices might mean that poorer consumers may be able to afford the product, for example, cheap tickets for senior citizens.

After completing this chapter you should:

■ be able to recognise the conditions under which monopoly is likely to occur

■ be able to explain how the structure of monopoly may lead to particular outcomes

■ be able to construct and explain the monopoly diagram

■ feel comfortable with the concept of efficiency in relation to the monopolist

■ be able to explain circumstances under which price discrimination is possible and its likely outcomes for firms and consumers.

Activities

1. Explain why firms might want to employ price discrimination.

2. Analyse the conditions under which price discrimination is likely to occur.

3. Evaluate the use of price discrimination by a train operating company.

Extract A

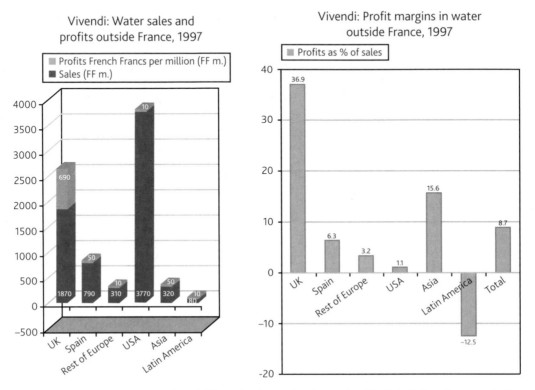

Vivendi: Water sales and profits outside France, 1997

■ Profits French Francs per million (FF m.)
■ Sales (FF m.)

Vivendi: Profit margins in water outside France, 1997

■ Profits as % of sales

From Public services international research unit by David Hall and Emanuele Lobina

Extract B

Why do the companies need to make profits?

Water and sewerage companies implement large scale investment programmes to maintain their assets and in order to meet their statutory environmental and quality obligations. By 2010 the companies in England and Wales will have invested almost £70bn since privatisation in 1989.

Price limits are set to allow companies to collect from customers, in the bills they pay, all operating costs in the year in which they are incurred. Operating costs cover the ongoing costs of running the company. At the price review in 2004 we assumed the industry would invest £17bn to maintain and enhance its assets in 2005–2010. Not all of this capital investment expenditure is collected from customers in the year in which the company spends the money. Therefore companies must fund a large proportion of this investment from the competitive financial markets, either through borrowing (debt) or shareholders (equity).

Just as mortgage providers for homeowners expect a return on the capital they lend, water companies must provide a reasonable return to capital providers. They must therefore make a profit to reward their investors.

Although the water and sewerage companies are largely monopoly service providers they must compete for capital with other companies. If they do not offer comparable returns to other companies after taking into account relative risks, they will be unable to secure the capital they need to finance their investment programmes.

The cost of capital is not intended to guarantee shareholders' returns. A poorly managed water company might earn a lower return because it underperforms our assumptions, for example on efficiency savings. On the other hand, outperformance of our efficiency assumptions will increase returns. This is important for the preservation of incentives.

From OFWAT Water charges and company profits: position paper

1   (a)   Using the data in extract A comment on Vivendi's level of profits. *(5 marks)*

       (b)   Extract B states that water and sewerage companies are largely monopoly service providers. With the help of a diagram explain how a firm's customers might be affected by its monopoly status. *(10 marks)*

       (c)   'Outperformance of our efficiency assumptions will increase returns.' In extract B the passage refers to the term 'efficiency'. Using both pieces of data and your own knowledge evaluate whether efficiency is likely to occur under the conditions of monopolistic water supply. *(25 marks)*

2   Explain why economists regard monopoly as an undesirable form of market structure. *(15 marks)*

Concentrated markets: the theory of oligopoly

In this chapter you will:

- learn about interdependence and reactive behaviour of oligopolies in a competitive market

- realise that there is no single theory of oligopoly

- appreciate the use of game theory as an analytical tool

- understand why collusive markets occur

- see that oligopolists may use a range of both pricing and non-price techniques to increase their market share

- learn about why and how oligopolists create barriers to entry.

Key terms

Oligopoly: where a few large firms have the majority of the market share.

Concentration ratio: the proportion of the market share held by the dominant firms.

Figure 5.1 *Sainsbury's owns 16% market share*

This is the second chapter concerning concentrated markets. Following the discussion of monopolies in Chapter 4, this chapter examines the theory of **oligopoly.** A large number of the goods and services purchased are produced and often marketed under oligopolistic conditions. The structure of the market is where the majority of the market is concentrated in the hands of a few large firms and this can be seen in such diverse industries as car production, food processing, banking, insurance, consumer electronics, to name but a few.

The structure of an oligopolistic market with the dominance of a few large firms leads to a range of possible behaviours. Unlike the theory of perfect competition and monopoly, which have been outlined in previous chapters, economists have no single definitive theory of oligopoly and how it is likely to act. There is no one theory that explains oligopoly as there is no simple set of rules for equilibrium, and the way firms operate in oligopoly depends upon the particular market circumstances. This has led to a number of different theories which seek to explain how oligopolists are likely to react in different situations.

Structure of the market

Before considering possible theories, the structure of the market requires further consideration. Although oligopolistic industries are dominated by large firms who have the majority of the market share, such as the big supermarkets, there might also be quite a large number of smaller firms operating in the same market. In the case of supermarkets consider the hundreds of little corner shops and stores which also operate in the market but have virtually no effect on the conduct or performance of the larger firms. Economists measure the market strength of the larger firms in terms of a **concentration ratio** which expresses the percentage of the market held by the large firms. A concentration ratio of say, 5:80 means that the largest five firms possess 80 per cent of the market share while the remaining 20 per cent is taken up by smaller firms. While concentration ratios can be expressed in terms of how many firms there are in the industry, three- and five-firm ratios are often used. The degree of market concentration is revealed by the figures so a ratio of 5:60 is less concentrated than a ratio of 5:80. A market with a concentration ratio of 3:80 would be even more concentrated.

Activities

Table 5.1 *Supermarkets' % of market share*

Tesco	31
Asda	17
Sainsbury's	16
Morrisons	12
Somerfield	4
Waitrose	4

1. Calculate the five- and three-firm concentration ratio in the supermarket industry.

2. Explain how Tesco may be seen as different from the rest of the firms in the industry.

3. What proportion of the market share is left to other firms?

4. How might the other firms in the industry be affected by the actions of the dominant five firms?

Barriers to entry

Another feature of oligopoly is the desire to keep other firms out so entry barriers may emerge that may be based on economies of scale. These barriers may be even stronger if the minimum efficient scale is large, for example, the car industry. In the absence of such barriers existing, oligopolists may decide to create them by using the following techniques:

- Limit and **predatory pricing** – the firm that has the lowest costs can use a technique that is known as limit pricing; it can lower its prices to a level where other firms are unable to compete, and drive them out of the industry.

- Advertising – large firms can spread the fixed costs of advertising over thousands of units which reduces the unit costs of advertising. New entrants to the market have to match the level of advertising expenditure but, without the volume of output, their unit cost of advertising will be higher. This may explain why there are only two firms in the UK detergent industry.

- Multiplicity of brands – if consumers switch brands frequently, an existing firm can capture a larger share of the market by running a large number of brands. By aiming at every area of the market it is likely to pick up more customers who engage in brand switching. This is true of both the soap powder manufacturers, cigarette manufacturers and car companies.

- **Integration** – as oligopolists grow in size they can integrate, both horizontally and vertically, forward and backward, to control the supply of resources and sources of distribution. This enables them to pursue a technique known as predatory pricing where they use their size and economies of scale benefits to drive down price and force smaller competitors out of business.

- Non-price competition – techniques to persuade customers to buy without changing the price and risk starting off a price war. This might include loyalty cards, buy one get one free (BOGOF) or the marketing mix that firms employ.

- Branding – manufacturers stress that their brands have unique characteristics, for example, Kellogg's cornflakes and Ferrari cars. A brand image is created through advertising and this should make demand more inelastic.

- Research and Development – by increasing their expenditure on research and development, firms can come up with products that give them an edge over their competitors so they can increase the price above that of their competitors.

Competitive oligopoly

In this situation, firms pursue an independent strategy and compete with each other but the firms are **interdependent** as action by one firm is likely to provoke a reaction by a competitor firm. Consider a situation where one firm, of a four-firm oligopoly, decides to increase its price. If its competitor firms leave their prices untouched the firm that raises its price will lose market share to the other firms. On the other hand, if it reduces its price, competitors are likely to reduce theirs or lower them further, possibly provoking a **price war** where all firms will lose revenue. Under these conditions firms will want to be able to anticipate how their competitors are likely to react to changes in their strategy when deciding their own price and output. Oligopoly is therefore characterised by **reactive behaviour** on the part of the firms in the market and by interdependence amongst the firms' pricing and output decisions.

Link

See Chapter 2, p25–6 for more on integration.

Key terms

Predatory pricing: setting a price that may bankrupt a competitor firm in order to try to take it over.

Integration: combining with other firms.

Interdependent: where actions by one firm will have an effect on the sales and revenue of other large firms in the market.

Price war: where firms competitively lower prices to increase their market share.

■ Key terms

Reactive behaviour: the action taken
by firms in response to a change in
behaviour of a competitor.

Kinked demand curve: a theoretical
approach that endeavours to
analyse the reasons for price
stability in oligopoly.

Brand loyalty: a measure indicating
the degree to which consumers
will purchase a firm's product
rather than a competing firm's
product.

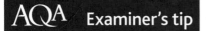

■ Key terms

Reactive behaviour: the action taken
by firms in response to a change in
behaviour of a competitor.

Kinked demand curve: a theoretical
approach that endeavours to
analyse the reasons for price
stability in oligopoly.

Brand loyalty: a measure indicating
the degree to which consumers
will purchase a firm's product
rather than a competing firm's
product.

AQA Examiner's tip

Make it quite clear to the examiner
that the kinked demand curve is
only one of a number of theoretical
possibilities.

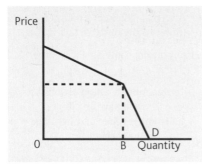

Figure 5.2 *The kinked demand curve*

AQA Examiner's tip

Figure 5.3 is for explanation only;
Figure 5.2 would be used in an
exam.

The kinked demand curve

The first approach that an oligopoly may adopt is to assume that
following a particular course of action, like that suggested above, will
provoke a response from other firms. On the basis of the example given
above, a firm that changes its prices may be punished by the reaction
of its competitors and its optimum strategy would be to promote price
stability. This is the basis of the theory of the **kinked demand curve**,
which seeks to explain, using the language of economics, why in oligopoly
there is a lack of price competition among firms and why prices tend to
remain stable.

Figure 5.2 shows an oligopolist selling an output of 0B at a price of 0A –
the point at which the demand curve is kinked.

The theory suggests that if the firm increases its price above 0A, its
competitors will leave their prices where they are and the firm will suffer
a drop in its market share (the size of the fall will depend on the degree of
brand loyalty the firm has built up). This is shown in the diagram by the
demand curve becoming elastic above the price 0A, so an increase in price
will lead to a fall in total revenue.

Below the price 0A the demand curve is assumed to become inelastic,
meaning that if the firm lowers its price, total revenue will fall. The logic
behind this is that if one firm lowers its price all other firms will follow,
or lower their prices even further, possibly leading to a price war. So below
the price 0A the demand curve is shown as inelastic, for if firms lower
their price the resulting price war means that their total revenue will fall.

Under the circumstances suggested above, firms competing on the basis of
price would lead to outcomes that were likely to promote losses!

The two parts of the kinked demand curve have different marginal
revenue curves and this is shown in Figure 5.3.

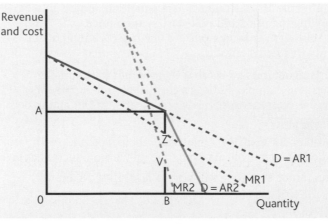

Figure 5.3 *The discontinuous marginal revenue curve*

The elastic section of the demand curve has been extended with the
dotted lines, labelled D=AR1 and the corresponding marginal revenue
curve is MR1. The inelastic part of the curve has been extended in the
same way, D=AR2 and the corresponding marginal revenue curve is
MR2. This leads to a discontinuity between the points Z and V and if the
MC curve fluctuates within this discontinuity there is no reason for the
firm to change its output.

Marginal costs and oligopoly

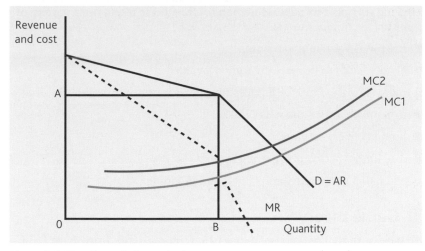

Figure 5.4 *The oligopolist's marginal cost curves*

Figure 5.4 shows the **discontinuous marginal revenue curve** indicated as a zigzag. As the marginal revenue curve is discontinuous the marginal cost curve can shift up and down, shown in the diagram as MC1, and MC2, without there being any effect on the level of output or the price. If marginal costs increased, the oligopolist would absorb the whole of the cost increase by taking a cut in profit. On the other hand, if marginal costs fall, the oligopolist's profit levels would increase. Techniques that can be employed to reduce marginal costs are likely to be employed by oligopolists.

While the model provides a plausible explanation of how price stability may occur there are a number of problems with the theory:

■ There is no explanation of how the original price was arrived at so it does not explain price determination.

■ The theory only deals with price competition and ignores non-price competition, which is an extremely important feature of oligopoly in the real world.

■ The theory fails to account for what can be considered to be limited price competition; the employment by oligopolists of the practice of giving discounts or interest free credit.

■ The model assumes a particular reaction by competing firms, and there is no guarantee that they will always react in the same way.

■ Under some circumstances a firm may decide that it could benefit by competing on price, reckoning that it is the strongest firm in the market and that it will be able to force its rivals out.

Non-price competition

Given the possible problems with competing on the basis of price, oligopolists may decide to compete using non-price competition. This is a marketing strategy that is employed to distinguish the firm's product or service from that of its competitors. Non-price competition is likely to increase expenditure for the firm in areas like advertising and sales promotions where it will try to promote its product above that of its competitors. This can be seen in terms of airlines, which offer larger seats, better in-flight entertainment or a more varied menu. Even though such measures are likely to increase the firm's costs it enables the firm to avoid changing prices and provoking a price war. However, the variety of

Key terms

Discontinuous marginal revenue curve: region over which a change in marginal costs will not lead to a change in the firm's price and output levels.

AQA **Examiner's tip**

You may need to discuss non-price competition in essays about oligopoly.

possible oligopolistic responses means that a firm may decide to employ non-price competition to promote its products at the same time as reducing its prices to increase demand. UK supermarkets use a variety of non-price techniques to increase their sales:

- in-store advertising/marketing
- loyalty cards to increase customer loyalty
- increasing the range of services on offer, for example, cashback
- in-store chemists and post offices
- home delivery services
- discounted petrol at hypermarkets
- extension of opening hours (24-hour shopping).

■ Game theory

We have seen that as a consequence of interdependence firms have to be able to predict what changes their rivals are likely to initiate and what strategies they need to have in place to respond. Also, if they decide to change strategy, they must work out how rivals will react and be ready to take further action as a result. This is the basis of **Game theory**, which explores the reactions of one player to changes in strategy by another player. When game theory is applied to oligopoly, the players are the firms, their game is played in the market, their strategies are their price or output decisions, and the payoff is their profits.

If we assume that competitive oligopoly is **a zero sum game** where any gain by one player is exactly offset by a loss by the other player, firms are likely to choose to leave their prices unchanged. They avoid risk; they are **risk averse.**

The Prisoners' Dilemma

Game theory supports **collusion** through an example which is known as 'the **Prisoners' Dilemma**'. This is where two prisoners, let's call them A and B, are accused of a joint crime, but kept apart in different prison cells and are unable to collude. They have been informed that if they both plead innocent they will receive a light sentence but if one protests innocence while the other owns up to being guilty, the one pleading innocence will receive a heavy sentence but the other will be let off. If they both plead guilty they get a medium sentence. If they could get together they could agree to plead innocent and get off with a light sentence, but in isolation they cannot trust each other, so each chooses to plead guilty and they both suffer.

A reasons as follows:

B will either plead guilty or innocent.

Assume B pleads innocent – then A gets a light sentence if A also pleads innocent but no sentence at all if A pleads guilty, so guilty is A's better plea.

If A assumes B pleads guilty – A gets a severe sentence if he pleads innocent and a medium sentence if he pleads guilty. So once again guilty is A's preferred plea.

B reasons in the same way, and, as a result, they both plead guilty and get a medium sentence, whereas if they had been able to communicate, they could both have agreed to plead innocent and get off with a light sentence.

■ **Key terms**

Game theory: an analysis of how games players react to changing circumstances and plan their response.

Zero sum game: where a gain by one player is matched by a loss by another player.

Risk averse: where one party does not take any action that might promote retaliatory activity by another party.

Collusion: where firms cooperate in their pricing and output policies.

Prisoners' Dilemma: where prisoners both choose the worst option.

The payoff matrix is shown in Figure 5.5.

		Prisoner A	
		Innocent	**Guilty**
Prisoner B	**Innocent**	A light sentence B light sentence	A no sentence B long sentence
	Guilty	A long sentence B no sentence	A medium sentence B medium sentence

Figure 5.5 *The Prisoners' Dilemma*

Competing or colluding

Firms in an oligopolistic market will consider how other firms will respond to their actions and what their own response might be to the actions of other firms. For example, firm A considers whether to raise or lower price or leave it unchanged. Before arriving at an answer, it will consider what the other firms will do in each of these cases; how will their actions affect the profitability of the decision it makes.

Using game theory we can illustrate the basic dilemma of oligopolistic firms – to cooperate or to compete. Figure 5.6 shows a two-firm oligopoly, or duopoly. If the firms cooperate then each firm can produce one-half of the total output and both earn profits of £40m.

In Figure 5.6, only two levels of production are considered. A's production is shown across the top, and B's production is shown down the left side. The top right square tells us that if B produces one-half, while A produces two-thirds, of the total output, A's profits will be £44m, while B's will be £30m.

		A's Output	
		One-half total output	**Two-thirds total output**
B's Output	**One-half total output**	B 40 A 40	B 30 A 44
	Two-thirds total output	B 44 A 30	B 34 A 34

Figure 5.6 *A pay-off matrix*

If A and B cooperate, each produces one-half of the total output and produces £40m as shown in the upper left box. But at that point each firm can raise its profits by producing two-thirds of the total output, provided that the other firm does not do the same.

Now assume that A and B make their decisions non-cooperatively. A reasons that, whether B produces either one-half or two-thirds of the total output, A's best output is two-thirds. B reasons similarly and in this case they reach the 'non-cooperative equilibrium', where each produces two-thirds of the total output. This is known as a **Nash equilibrium,** a non-cooperative equilibrium named after US mathematician John Nash, who developed the theory in the 1950s. A Nash equilibrium is one in which each firm's best strategy is to maintain its present behaviour, given the present behaviour of the other firms. Under this situation of competition they both make less revenue than if they had cooperated. The Nash equilibrium will be achieved if each firm chooses its optimal strategy by taking into account what the other firm may do.

> **Key terms**
>
> **Nash equilibrium:** where the optimum strategy is to maintain current behaviour.

Figure 5.7 *John Nash*

AQA Examiner's tip

Ensure that you are familiar with game theory; it is the technique used for analysing oligopoly.

Firm A's perspective:

- Producing half of the output assuming B does the same leads to a profit of £40m each.

- But by producing two-thirds of the total output it earns £44m.

- But if B produces two-thirds of the monopoly output and A only produces one-half, A only earns £30m, whereas if it produces two-thirds, earns £34m.

- The optimal strategy for A and B is to produce two-thirds of the output in each case.

Both of these examples of game theory suggest that firms in an oligopoly may be better off colluding than competing. In the examples above only two firms are shown but, if more firms are added, the range of possibilities becomes more complex, and in order to limit the possibility of choosing the wrong strategy, firms are likely to collude.

Collusive oligopoly

1 Formal collusion

This is a situation where oligopoly is defined by conduct as some form of agreement exists between the key firms in the industry about price and output policies. These collusive agreements have taken many forms, from **restrictive agreements** refusing to supply outlets which sold below the agreed price (for example, Volkswagen) to simply agreeing to all increase prices of selected products (for example, European pharmaceuticals and vitamin pills). The aim of all of these restrictive agreements is to increase the level of **joint profits** at the consumers' expense, in terms of price, quality or availability. The agreement is unlikely to be in writing as competition authorities in Western Europe levy huge fines on firms with restrictive agreements.

Collusion can be seen as a way of removing the uncertainty of competing when firms have a high degree of interdependence. Agreements may, for example, ban competition on the basis of price but may allow non-price competition to continue without restriction. Some agreements may divide the market on an area basis where one area is seen as the possession of a certain firm.

Under competitive oligopoly, firms are never certain how rivals will react, and they may decide to remove the uncertainty by colluding in order to maximise their joint profits and force up prices by restricting supply. They may also act to prevent other firms from entering the industry.

In order to operate successfully a **cartel** requires certain conditions:

- All major producers should be part of the cartel and be prepared to follow its rules.

- The market being supplied should be isolated from supplies by producers outside the cartel.

- High entry barriers to the industry either natural or created are necessary to stop other firms from entering the market.

- While firms in an oligopolistic industry will make more profits as a group if they cooperate, any one firm, may make more profits for itself if it defects while the others cooperate.

- The more homogeneous the product the greater the likelihood of success.

Key terms

Restrictive agreements: where firms collude to indulge in anti-competitive policy.

Joint profits: where firms agree to maximise shared rather than their individual profits.

Cartel: a group of firms working together, or colluding.

Most countries have a competition policy and competition commission to protect the consumer from market manipulation. The European Union has an active anti-cartel commission, as do the member countries, as they are aware that returns to a cartel can be substantial in terms of extremely high supernormal profits. Anti-competitive behaviour is considered to be a serious breach of the law resulting in fines which are extremely high, reaching 10 per cent of a firm's annual turnover.

Case Study

Antitrust: Commission imposes €38 million fine on E.ON for breach of a seal during an inspection

The European Commission has imposed a fine of €38 000 000 on E.ON Energie AG ('SON') for the breach of a Commission seal in E.ON's premises during an inspection. The seal had been affixed to secure documents collected in the course of an unannounced inspection in May 2006. When the Commission came back the next day, the seal was broken. The inspection formed part of the Commission's enforcement activities against allegations of anticompetitive practices on the German energy markets.

Competition Commissioner Neelie Kroes commented 'The Commission cannot and will not tolerate attempts by companies to undermine the Commission's fight against cartels and other anti-competitive practices by threatening the integrity and effectiveness of our investigations. Companies know very well that high fines are at stake in competition cases, and some may consider illegal measures to obstruct an inquiry and so avoid a fine. This decision sends a clear message to all companies that it does not pay off to obstruct the Commission's investigations.'

The seal had been affixed by Commission officials during an unannounced inspection carried out in May 2006. The inspection concerned the suspicion of anticompetitive practices on the German electricity market. It is the Commission's practice to seal rooms when carrying out surprise inspections in order to make sure that no documents can be removed by the company when the inspection team is absent (for example, at night).

IP/08/108 Brussels, 30 January 2008

Should collusion take place, the oligopolies are then in more of a monopolistic position in the market, the firms will equate MC and MR and make supernormal profits (shaded rectangle), as seen in Figure 5.8.

The cartel is likely to lead to certain outcomes for producers:

■ Increase in sales revenue and profit, that is, assuming the demand for the product is price inelastic, an increase in price will lead to an increase in sales revenue.

■ Increased likelihood that producers will compete by non-price methods in order to increase brand loyalty and their market share.

■ Increased profits might enable firms to finance increased investment leading to improved products, which could benefit consumers in the longer term.

For consumers the likely effects are:

■ An increase in price of the product – probably the major reason for the formation of the cartel.

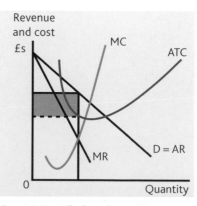

Figure 5.8 *Colluding oligopolists*

■ Increased costs for firms using the product in production of other goods. In the case of collusion by supermarkets over the price of milk the action would have led to a cost increase and a reduction in profits for firms that use milk as a raw material.

■ Reduction of the consumer surplus, which would occur as firms increased prices.

■ Increase in non-price competition, which may lead to some consumer benefit in terms of increased special offers or other techniques where associated products are bundled together and offered at a discount.

2 Informal collusion

Collusion may operate by one of the firms acting as a **price leader**; this firm signals changes in prices to the other firms in the cartel. When the firm raises its price all other firms in the cartel follow suit.

Price leadership may take various forms:

■ The price leader may be the dominant firm in the industry in terms of market share so when it changes its price all other firms follow.

■ A situation referred to as **barometric price leadership**, is where the role is taken by a smaller firm that is more sensitive to changes in market conditions than a larger firm.

■ Collusive price leadership and **parallel pricing** are where identical prices and price movements are maintained in the industry.

■ **Tacit collusion** may also occur where firms in the industry follow the industry norm, for example, cost plus pricing.

Activities

Table 5.2 *Major suppliers in the brewery and white goods market*

Company	Brand
Electrolux	Electrolux, Zanussi, Tricity Moffat
GEC	Hotpoint, Creda, Jackson, Cannon, English Electric
Hoover	Hoover
Whirlpool	Philips, Whirlpool
Lec Refrigeration	Lec
Merloni-Ariston Group	Ariston, Indesit
Birmid Qualcast	New World
Belling & Co	Belling
Servis	Servis
Candy	Candy, Domino

1 Why do some companies have a number of different brands?

2 With the aid of a diagram explain why GEC will have to consider the reactions of other firms to a change in their pricing and output policy.

3 Explain your reasons as to why you would see/not see this industry as a candidate for collusion.

■ Pricing techniques

In addition to the techniques that may be used by a cartel, other forms of pricing are common in oligopoly:

Transfer pricing

This is a technique where multinationals can alter costs and prices to benefit from different levels of tax in different countries. Consider a firm in the UK making component parts, for example, gear boxes for its cars and selling them to a subsidiary in a lower tax country making only a minimal profit on the sale. This would reduce their tax liability in the UK. The cars, after the components have been collected, can be assembled and sold in a low tax country where the resulting overall profit is taxed at a lower rate. Oligopolists, by overstating their costs in high tax countries and selling their products to subsidiaries at low prices and declaring their profits in low tax countries, can minimise their tax bill and maximise their profits.

Cost plus pricing

In most cases it will be difficult for large firms to decide the actual level of output where profit maximisation occurs so they may decide to use a different technique to determine price and output. One such is known as cost plus, mark up or average cost pricing. This occurs when the firm calculates the average cost of producing a given level of output and adds a 'mark up', say 50 per cent, and makes this the selling price.

This idea is given greater credence by the fact that real-world studies have concluded that average variable cost curves are likely to be saucer shaped rather than U shaped. So, over a wide range of output, large firms face the same LRAVC whether they increase or decrease output, as is shown in Figure 5.9.

The diagram suggests that firms may find it far easier to go for a cost plus pricing policy once it has achieved the minimum efficient scale 0A. Between A and B costs are fairly constant so a cost plus approach is relatively straightforward. A further point to be considered is that firms will be reluctant to change their prices too often as **menu costs**, the cost of changing lists and brochures, especially if the firm trades worldwide, are likely to be very high.

Competition Regulators would need to establish whether the mark up was decided individually by each firm or whether it was a result of collusion. Such distinctions can be extremely difficult to identify in practice.

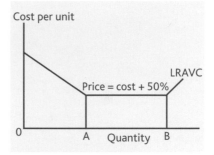

Figure 5.9 *Cost plus pricing*

Key terms

Menu costs: the time and money spent by businesses in changing their prices in line with inflation.

Link

Price discrimination is also a pricing technique and this can be found in Chapter 4, p47.

■ Case study

Transfer pricing

Bananas to UK via the Channel islands? It pays for tax reasons.

Think of Jersey and you think prosperous tax haven, or perhaps offshore financial centre as it prefers to be called. But exporter of bananas to the UK? Surely not. But a substantial volume of banana trade from the Caribbean has passed in the last 15 years through Channel Island-based offshore subsidiaries of Dole, Chiquita and Fresh Del Monte.

This routing of commodity trade and its associated activities through tax havens is typical of a growing trend among transnational corporations to shift their transactions between different countries to minimise their tax bills. The phenomenon, dubbed the flight of capital, is not illegal but is increasingly

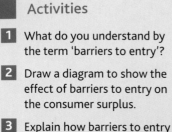

Activities

1 What do you understand by the term 'barriers to entry'?

2 Draw a diagram to show the effect of barriers to entry on the consumer surplus.

3 Explain how barriers to entry are likely to affect the efficient allocation of resources.

AQA Examiner's tip

Ensure you know the definitions used in the chapter.

depriving countries in which the profits were actually earned of the ability to raise money for development or for services.

Bananas are highly profitable – they are the largest single item by volume sold in British supermarkets and the third largest in value.

A *Guardian* investigation of the financial accounts of the three big banana companies has revealed that Dole, Chiquita and Fresh Del Monte had combined global sales of over $50bn (£24bn) in the last five years, and made $1.4bn of profits. They paid just $200m (or 14.3 per cent of profits) in taxes between them in that period. In some years the banana companies have paid an effective tax rate as low as 8 per cent, yet the standard rate of corporation tax in the US where they have their headquarters and file their accounts is 35 per cent.

*Adapted from The Guardian, **Ian Griffiths** and **Felicity Lawrence**, 6 November 2007*

After the completion of this chapter you should:

■ realise that the degree of concentration can be measured

■ appreciate that the kinked demand curve is only one possibility of oligopoly

■ understand the analysis underlying oligopolistic behaviour

■ understand that oligopoly can be defined by structure (few firms) or conduct (collusion)

■ appreciate the desire to create barriers to entry.

Extract A

Fingers pointed at credit rating agency monopoly

Credit rating agencies rank the value of debt as to its level of safety; they attempt to measure the likelihood of default. A credit rating measures credit worthiness – the ability to pay back a loan – and affects the interest rate applied to loans.

Charlie McCreevy, the European Union's internal market commissioner, last week launched a probe into the major agencies such as Standard & Poor's, Moody's and Fitch and their handling of the US sub-prime mortgage crisis with further regulation in mind.

But the dominance of the big three, who appear to be risk averse and who have become the gatekeepers to the new global financial system – is now raising questions in the market.

One senior executive at a major investment bank described the three-way monopoly of ratings as 'a bit like a protection racket'.

Rating agencies determine the likelihood that a company, fund or complex financial structure will go bust. Their ratings determine the rate of interest at which companies will be able to borrow money – and reflect the price investors will pay in the secondary markets.

The sub-prime crisis has shown, with hindsight, that many debt structures were given better ratings than they should have been. Now, some investors are questioning whether those flaws infuse the rest of the market. That has been a factor in the spreading of fear through the debt markets.

The Daily Telegraph dated 20 August 2007

Extract B

A beleaguered industry looks to reform itself

The agencies feel that criticism of their role in the (sub-prime mortgage) crisis was, in part, based on a misunderstanding: their ratings are based on risk of default, not market swings. Moody's said it was considering a new rating system for structured securities, using numbers, not letters, and a suffix that would indicate the expected level of volatility.

Some point to more profound concerns: because ratings are deeply embedded in financial regulation, the agencies have been handed an oligopoly; they suffer a conflict of interest, because they are paid by the issuers of the securities they rate, not by investors; and they are unaccountable because their ratings are deemed mere opinions and thus protected as free speech.

More competition should help, but it might just as easily lead to a race to the bottom, as agencies vie to offer the best terms to issuers.

Adapted from an article in The Economist 9 February 2008

Extract C

Who are the stakeholders?

Four credit rating agencies have NRSRO status (nationally recognized statistical rating organization) – Moody's, Standard & Poor's, the Fitch Group and Dominion Bond Rating Service. There are a host of smaller credit rating agencies typically focused on non-USA organizations or with specialist niches, for example, Capital Intelligence (international banks), and Japan Credit Rating Agency.

In such a competitive market investor credit rating agencies must be adding value for their customers, yet the financial community perceives that credit ratings are controlled by a duopoly – Moody's and Standard & Poor's – or at best a triumvirate – if Fitch is rated in the top group. 'There's too much concentration in too few hands,' said Dietrich Jahn, a German ministry official who focuses on banking [International Herald Tribune, 'Germans Call for Local Rating Agency', 4 March 2003].

Adapted from an article by Michael Mainelli, Z/Yen Limited

1   (a)   Using extract C explain what you understand by the terms 'duopoly' and 'concentration in too few hands'. *(5 marks)*

       (b)   Using extract A and with the aid of a diagram analyse why firms in an oligopoly **may** be seen as 'risk averse'. *(10 marks)*

       (c)   Using the data and your economic knowledge evaluate the view that (a) the ratings agencies are likely to collude (b) have the right characteristics to sustain such collusion and (c) the results will not benefit the consumer. *(25 marks)*

2   (a)   Explain how firms in oligopolistic markets are affected by interdependence and uncertainty. *(15 marks)*

       (b)   Discuss the factors which a firm operating in an oligopolistic market is likely to take into account when setting its prices. *(25 marks)*

6 Competition policy and contestable markets 💡 ✔️

Link

See *AQA Economics AS*, Chapter 8, p96 and Chapter 4, p44 in this book.

Link

The main theoretical arguments for and against monopoly have been covered at AS and also in Chapter 4 of this book.

Key terms

Incumbents: the existing firms in the industry.

Contestable market: where there is free entry and free exit of other firms.

Competition policy: methods that the UK government and EU authorities use in order to make markets more efficient.

Restrictive trade practices: methods used by firms to reduce competition in a market.

Competition Commission: a government organisation responsible for implementing policy in relation to monopolies.

The previous two chapters have looked at imperfect competition and it is relatively clear that barriers to entry allow existing firms to achieve supernormal profits by insulating the **incumbents** from the possibility of new entrants who would increase the levels of competition and reduce profits. In this chapter we consider the arguments for government versus private ownership, the regulation and deregulation of markets along with UK and EU competition policy. We then move to consider the arguments for markets being made more **contestable** as a technique to promote behaviour that would occur as a result of the possibility of increased competition.

Imperfect competition and competition policy

As outlined earlier, imperfect competition is broadly considered to imply productive and allocative inefficiency in the production of goods and services, though, in theory at least, this need not be so if monopolistic firms are encouraged to be dynamically efficient. As outlined below, the threat of market contestability and the implementation of UK and EU competition policy may do much to ensure firms with substantial market power act in the public's best interests.

Competition policy refers to the methods that the UK government and EU authorities use in order to make markets more efficient. Current competition policy has four main strands, covering:

- monopolies

- mergers

- **restrictive trade practices**

- the promotion of new competition.

Monopolies

Formerly known as the Monopolies and Mergers Commission, the role of the **Competition Commission** (CC) is to investigate monopolies and proposed mergers that might lead to a monopoly being created. This also involves investigating monopoly power in industries dominated by a few large firms, that is, oligopolies.

In the UK, the Competition Act 1998 outlaws the abuse of a **dominant market position**, defined as a market share of 40 per cent. The key objections are productive and allocative inefficiency, X-inefficiency and restricting output to generate supernormal profits. However, it is theoretically possible for a monopolist to benefit from economies of scale, which, if passed on to the consumer, can result in lower prices than under perfect competition. It is also possible that a firm with monopoly power is more innovative than a perfectly competitive firm.

In the UK two government agencies are responsible for implementing policy concerning monopolies, namely the **Office of Fair Trading** (OFT) and the Competition Commission. In turn, these agencies are responsible to the **Department of Trade and Industry** (DTI). The OFT uses a number of indicators relating to market structure, conduct and

Dominant market position: where a firm, or group of firms working together, have a market share of 40 per cent.

Office of Fair Trading: a government organisation responsible for implementing aspects of competition policy.

Department of Trade and Industry: the government department responsible for British industry.

Public interest: a term used broadly to cover the public's right not to be exploited by firms abusing monopoly power.

Nationalisation: state control of firms.

Privatisation: sales of government-owned assets to the private sector.

Deregulation: the process of removing government controls from markets.

performance to monitor the UK economy for evidence of monopoly abuse. Concentration ratios can be used to provide evidence of monopolies. Other indicators include:

■ evidence of price discrimination and price leadership

■ merger activity

■ ratios of advertising expenditure to sales

■ profit margins

■ the ratio of capital employed to sales turnover.

If the OFT discovers evidence of exploitation of a dominant market position it believes likely to be against the **public interest**, it refers the firm(s) to the Competition Commission for further investigation. The CC has legal powers to order firms to cease particular trading practices.

It is fair to say that relatively few firms and takeover bids are actually investigated. It seems that the threat of the possibility of CC investigation is a sufficient deterrent against the temptation of most large firms to exploit any monopoly power they might have. However, a number of firm approaches are available to the CC to deal with the problem of monopoly:

■ compulsory breaking up

■ price controls

■ taxes on 'excess' profits (sometimes known as windfall taxes)

■ **nationalisation**

■ **privatisation**

■ **deregulation**.

Much recent debate on the best way of dealing with and regulating monopoly has centred on the need to remove barriers to entry and make markets more 'contestable'. In contestable market theory, monopolies are defined by how easy or difficult it is for new firms to enter the market. High concentration of firms is not considered a problem, as long as an absence of barriers to entry and exit would potentially allow new firms to enter and hence contest the market. According to contestable market theory, it is not vital to have actual competition in a market, because the threat of entry by new firms is enough to ensure that existing firms in that market behave efficiently and do not exploit their position.

Mergers

For more on mergers, see Chapter 2, p25–6.

Merger policy falls under the 1998 Competition Act and also the 2002 Enterprise Act. The concern is that takeovers and mergers might create a new monopoly. A merger involves two or more firms joining voluntarily, whereas firms tend to be taken over involuntarily. The OFT surveys merger activity, with any that might be eligible for investigation on public interest grounds passed on to the Competition Commission, especially if it is anticipated that it will strengthen a dominant market position.

The European Commission has powers to prevent and control mergers in EU member countries. EU merger policy attempts to delegate policy as much as possible to national governments, though securing a dominant market position by buying out or otherwise acquiring competitors contravenes EU competition law.

Restrictive trade practices

Restrictive trade practices are those undertaken by firms to reduce competition in a market. Individual firms can use them to reinforce their dominance, whilst groups of firms working together as 'complex monopolies' or cartels, can use them to strengthen agreements and deter competitors.

Restrictive practices include:

- Decisions to charge discriminatory prices, for example, offering discounts if buyers also purchase other products, or for bulk orders.

- Resale price maintenance (RPM), where manufacturers fix the price that retailers eventually sell at, thus preventing any price competition in the market.

- Refusal to supply particular outlets or markets, especially retailers who do not participate in resale price maintenance agreements.

- 'Full-line forcing', where a supplier forces a firm that wishes to sell one of its products to actually stock its entire product range.

Public ownership versus privatisation

Nationalised industries

A nationalised industry or public corporation is one that is owned by the state. In the past, public ownership of essential utilities such as gas, electricity and water was judged by governments to be vital in order to ensure their production, for example, in times of war or crisis. Governments also came to provide a range of public and merit goods, such as national defence and education.

Nationalisation is supported for several reasons. First is that the very large economies of scale achievable in one enormous organisation may lead to lower costs than under private ownership. This is the essence of the **natural monopoly** argument. Nationalisation is also favoured for effective control of the economy. Government management of key strategic industries – the so-called 'commanding heights' – was seen as crucial in ensuring their provision, since market forces and the profit motive might lead to some products not being provided.

Key terms

Restrictive trade practices: methods used by firms to reduce competition in a market.

Natural monopoly: a firm that can theoretically gain continuous economies of scale and where it is thus uneconomic for more than one firm to supply the market.

Case study

The nationalisation of a UK commercial bank – Northern Rock

In February 2008 after a degree of procrastination in complete contrast with US Federal Reserve action over Bear Stearns, the Government announced that it was to take Northern Rock into public ownership – nationalisation.

It was abundantly clear that the Rock was in trouble when huge queues of customers formed outside it waiting to withdraw their money believing that the Rock was no longer safe. The Rock was a casualty of the sub-prime mortgage collapse in the US where loans were given to borrowers who at best were risky and at worse had no chance of repaying their borrowings. The loans were then repackaged with other debts and sold off to financial institutions worldwide.

The result was that when borrowers could not repay their mortgages, banks were not sure as to the size of their liabilities and the liabilities of other banking institutions. To maintain liquidity in

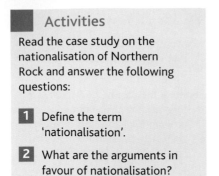

Activities

Read the case study on the nationalisation of Northern Rock and answer the following questions:

1 Define the term 'nationalisation'.

2 What are the arguments in favour of nationalisation?

3 Weigh up the arguments for private ownership of former nationalised industries.

Table 6.1 *Some key UK privatisations*

Company	Year
British Aerospace	1981
Cable & Wirelesss	1981
National Freight Corporation	1982
British Telecom	1984
British Gas	1986
British Airways	1987
British Airports Authority	1987
Rolls Royce	1987
British Steel	1988
British Leyland	1988
Water Boards	1989
Electricity distribution and generation	1990/91
British Coal	1994
British Rail	1995
British Nuclear Fuels	2000

the system banks borrow from each other on the 'wholesale market' and the crisis of confidence led to this market virtually collapsing. Banks would not lend to other banks in case they were unable to repay the loan.

The Rock raised most of the funds that it lent for mortgages from the wholesale market and had expanded at an increasing rate, reaping substantial financial benefits for its shareholders. Neither the Bank of England, the Financial Services Authority nor the Treasury appeared to appreciate the weaknesses of raising funds in this fashion and were caught off-guard when the run on the Rock started.

The Chancellor guaranteed depositors' funds but withdrawals still occurred and the authorities were afraid that the loss of confidence in the Rock might spread to other banks leading to a financial crisis. Under such circumstances the Government felt that it had to act.

Privatisation

Privatisation involves the transfer of assets or organisations from state ownership to the private sector. In the UK this has usually involved selling off previously nationalised industries and businesses. British Gas and British Telecom are examples of former public corporations that have been privatised.

Although the main privatisations have involved the sale of nationalised industries, privatisation takes a number of additional forms:

■ Deregulation, that is, the removal of restrictions on the provision of a good or service, for example, bus services.

■ Sale of local authority assets, for example, the sale of council houses to tenants under the 'right to buy' scheme.

■ Competitive tendering of services, introducing competition into the market for provision of public services, for example, local authority refuse collection.

■ Franchising and licensing, for example, regional rail services or ITV channels.

Advantages of privatisation

1 Promoting efficiency. This is the key advantage of privatisation from a free-market viewpoint. The profit motive creates incentives to cut costs, increasing dynamic efficiency and reducing the 'organisational slack' associated with X-inefficiency. If employees are also given shares in the company, or a share of profits, this may also lead to greater productivity. The 'stock market discipline' argument states that, through exposure to the threat of takeover and the discipline of the stock market, the privatisation of a state-owned monopoly should improve the business's efficiency and commercial performance.

2 Raises revenue for government. Selling former nationalised assets provides the government with a short-term source of revenue. In the mid-1980s, this was used to reduce government spending and the government's borrowing requirement, and also made income tax cuts possible.

3 Promoting competition. Privatisation arguably increases competition by breaking up monopolies. Many of the industries nationalised in the 1980s and 1990s had been legally protected from competition. However, natural monopolies are difficult to split into smaller companies without losing economies of scale and productive efficiency.

4 Reducing the size of the public sector. Free-market economists talk of 'rolling back the frontiers of the state' as a key step in improving economic efficiency.

5 Promoting popular capitalism. Encouraging an **enterprise culture** was an important justification for privatisation in the UK. It was argued, for example, that increased share ownership would turn the public against industrial action to protect their investments.

Disadvantages of privatisation

1 Worse allocation of resources under privately run monopolies. As outlined early in this book, profit-maximising monopolies will restrict output to a level that is neither productively nor allocatively efficient. A state-run organisation could produce at a level which equates the marginal cost of production with the value placed on the marginal unit by consumers. Thus a privatised monopoly could lead to a loss of economic welfare.

2 Externalities. Private firms may ignore the externalities of their activities, for example, pollution and scarred landscapes from coal extraction.

3 Closure of loss-making services. For example, railway branch lines, village stations and suburban bus routes.

4 Short-termism. There is a danger that under private ownership, investments that will only yield profits in the long term will not occur because commercial firms concentrate on the short-termism of delivering dividends to please shareholders and financial institutions.

Public-private partnerships and the private finance initiative

Public-private partnerships (PPPs) is the term used for a variety of partnerships between the private and public sectors to provide public services. They include competitive tendering and 'contracting out' of services such as street cleaning and refuse collection. PPPs have been important in the provision of health services, prisons, residential care homes and schools.

The **private finance initiative** (PFI), introduced by the Conservative government in 1993 and taken up by New Labour, is a common form of PPP. Under PFI, the government does not have to get fully involved in the planning, building and running of public investment projects. The government decides the service it requires and then seeks bids from the private sector for designing, building, financing and running the project. The advantages of PFI are that private sector partners may well have greater expertise in project management and that public sector services and infrastructure improvements can be provided without an increase in government borrowing.

Regulation and deregulation of markets

Regulation

Economic **regulation** involves setting rules and controls that restrict market freedom. External regulation involves an external agency, such as the OFT, Competition Commission, or European Commission setting and enforcing rules and controls. Self-regulation is where a group of firms regulate themselves, for example, through a professional association such as the British Medical Association. Governments can use regulation to correct various forms of market failure, for example, the over-production of negative externalities such as environmental pollution. The aim is to try to achieve the social optimum level of production and consumption.

■ **Link**

See Chapter 2, p25–6.

■ **Key terms**

Enterprise culture: a way of life that emphasises the importance of individuals who create their own businesses and create wealth.

Public-private partnerships (PPPs): partnerships between the private and public sectors to provide public services.

Private finance initiative (PFI): a form of public-private partnership in which private sector firms undertake the bulk of the work.

Regulation: setting rules and controls that restirct market freedom.

Link

See *AQA Economics AS*, Chapter 10 for more on market and government failure.

Regulation is also used to deter abuses of monopoly power. Rules and regulations are also imposed to promote health and safety at work, reduce discrimination and protect consumers' rights.

Case study

Utility regulators

In the UK, a number of specific regulatory bodies or 'watchdogs' have been set up by the government to oversee the activities of many of the companies that were privatised in the 1980s and 1990s. The main aim of the regulatory bodies is to subject the privatised companies to healthy doses of competitive discipline by making markets more contestable.

OFGEM: The Office of Gas and Electricity Markets is the regulatory body for electricity and gas supply in the UK.

OFWAT: The Office of Water Services regulates the privatised water and sewerage industry in the UK.

OFCOM: The Office of Communications regulates telecommunications and broadcast media.

ORR: The Office of Rail Regulation regulates the UK rail network.

Deregulation

Deregulation involves the removal of government controls on market activity. Significant deregulation has occurred in the UK in the last three decades. For example, access to BT's distribution infrastructure has been given to competitors in the telecommunications industry, and markets have been opened up for household energy supply and mail services. Deregulation is argued to promote competition and market contestability through the removal of artificial barriers to entry. It also reduces unnecessary costs imposed on economic agents by removing bureaucratic 'red tape'. The concept of **regulatory capture** is also an argument in favour of deregulation. This suggests that the agencies set up to regulate industries or firms can be 'captured' or influenced by the firms they are intended to oversee. The regulators then act in the industry's interest rather than that of the consumers they are set up to protect.

Traditional economic theory assumes that the market structure, the number of firms in a market, dictates the likely level of competition, so we have seen that perfect competition with a large number of firms leads to normal profits while monopoly and oligopoly with fewer firms and barriers to entry leads to supernormal profits.

In the 1980s an American economist W. J. Baumol developed the argument that the benefits of perfect competition might be achieved without all of the conditions being met. Baumol suggested that the benefits of perfect competition could be achieved as long as the market could be made contestable – as long as there was the potential for new firms to enter the industry.

Key terms

Regulatory capture: where agencies set up to regulate industries or firms can be 'captured' or influenced by the firms they are intended to oversee.

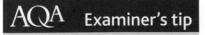 **Examiner's tip**

Do not confuse contestable market theory with the theory of perfect competition.

Contestable markets

The theory of contestable markets argues that the number of firms is not the most important factor; what matters is the absence of barriers to entry and the level of sunk costs. In order to fully understand both monopoly and oligopoly we must consider the effect of potential competition, from new entrants to the industry, on the behaviour of incumbent firms. An industry with a five-firm oligopoly with a concentration ratio of 5:75 would be analysed in a different way to our usual approach if the market was contestable.

Contestable markets are assumed to have free entry to new firms and free exit for both incumbents and new entrants. Free entry assumes that all firms, including both incumbents and new entrants, have access to the same technology and as a result have the same cost curves. New firms are not prohibited from entry by incumbents exploiting a huge minimum efficient scale or, for the new entrant, unachievable economies of scale.

However, any form of entry is usually costly to the entering firm as it may have to build a factory or engage in expenditure on advertising. These and other initial expenses are often called the sunk costs of entry. Free exit assumes that there are no sunk costs and that when it leaves the industry a firm can fully recover all of its previous investment expenditure including money spent on advertising and building up knowledge and **goodwill**.

Whether or not such a cost becomes a sunk cost depends on whether the costs can be recovered if the firm subsequently exits. For example, if the new entrant builds a factory that is product specific it may have little resale value and thus represents a sunk cost of entry. Alternatively, if it builds a factory that can have numerous uses and can be resold at a price close to its original value it is not a sunk cost of entry. Thus a market can be perfectly contestable even if the firm must pay some costs of entry, as long as these can be recovered when the firm exits. Contestability is likely to vary according to the industry under consideration but the lower the sunk costs of entry, the more contestable the market.

A contestable market allows **hit and run entry** where new firms can enter the industry and cream off some of the supernormal profits made by the incumbent firms. If the incumbent or incumbents are not behaving as if they were in a perfectly competitive industry at long-run equilibrium, producing an output where price equals marginal cost and at the minimum average costs, then a new entrant can step in, undercut them, and make a temporary profit before quitting again.

The bus industry at one stage could have been seen as an example of a contestable market. New operators can open up new routes or contest existing routes by reducing fares in order to take some of the incumbents' supernormal profit. If the route appears to be unprofitable, or the incumbent fights back with even lower prices, they can pull out. Bus firms do not have to spend huge sums of money to get into the industry, and as there is a ready market in second-hand buses, there are no large sunk costs or irrecoverable costs to concern the companies as buses can easily be sold on.

In Figure 6.1 the hatched rectangle indicates the monopoly profit that can be made in a particular industry. If the industry becomes contestable the incumbent, fearing new entrants will reduce the price from MP to CP, the normal profit level where average total cost equals average revenue. Output of the industry increases from 0A to 0B. Incumbents will also strive to be productively efficient in order to deter new entrants who could reduce costs even further.

The implications of Baumol's theory is that, given ease of entry to and exit from an industry, monopoly or oligopoly firms will behave as if they actually existed in perfect competition. They will only earn normal profits in the long run because if supernormal profits were made, new firms would be attracted into the industry increasing supply and driving down price. These are hit and run entrants. If losses are made, some firms will be forced to leave the industry causing supply to fall and price to rise back to a level consistent with the making of normal profits. They will be forced to operate with productive efficiency on the lowest point of the average cost curve where AC = MC, otherwise new firms could enter the industry producing at the most efficient output level, pricing their goods more competitively and forcing existing firms out.

Key terms

Goodwill: the value of a firm in excess of its asset value including reputation, brand name, trade contacts and general expertise.

Hit and run entry: where new firms enter the industry, cream off some of the supernormal profits of the incumbents and then exit.

AQA Examiner's tip

Figure 6.1 is a useful tool for illustrating the benefits of contestability.

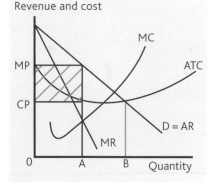

Figure 6.1 *The effects of contestability*

Activities

Using the passenger airline industry as an example:

1 Explain the difference between contestability and perfect competition.

2 Explain the meaning of the term 'sunk costs'.

3 Describe what is meant by 'hit and run entrants'.

The theory, however, postulates that actual entry to the industry is not required for the incumbents to act responsibly; the threat of entry can be sufficient. Potential entry can be as effective as actual entry as long as:

■ entry can be easily accomplished

■ existing firms take potential entry into account when making price and output decisions.

So, as long as there is a threat of competition, consumers will be protected from the worst abuses of monopoly/oligopoly power. At the same time, firms will be able to reach the MES and reap the benefits of large-scale production operating in accordance with the criteria for economic efficiency.

The assumptions of contestable market theory are:

■ Low barriers to entry, which means that there is both freedom of entry and exit into the marketplace.

■ No one firm has a significant share of the marketplace.

■ Firms compete so collusion does not occur.

■ Firms are short-run profit maximisers, producing where MC=MR.

■ Firms may produce a homogeneous or heterogeneous good.

■ There is perfect knowledge in the market.

Reality of contestable markets

However, the theory of contestable markets is controversial as there are many industries in which it will be difficult, if not impossible, to recover sunk costs, for example, vast sums spent on advertising are unrecoverable if the firm exits the industry. Furthermore, while firms may have access to the same technology the initial user expertise and elimination of glitches in the supply chain may take a new entrant some time to acquire or rectify, which will place it at a temporary disadvantage against incumbent firms.

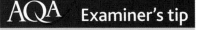

AQA Examiner's tip

Note that almost all markets have some barriers – it is the degree of contestability that is important.

Case study

Irish Outlook – If only we could harness hot air

The green paper has ruled out the nuclear option. If, however, other countries use nuclear power to generate electricity, we probably won't turn up our noses at importing it. The Irish solution to an Irish problem is alive and kicking.

We are still dependent on imported energy, despite our partial shift to an information economy. Our energy use is growing by 2 per cent to 3 per cent per year, more than twice the EU rate.

American companies located here demand the best. Good quality power without outages or surges is vital for many high-tech manufacturing companies such as Intel. Any emergent industrial relations problems in the ESB (Electricity Supply Board) would have to be settled at all costs. It is doubtful whether any public-sector workers have enjoyed so much bargaining power.

This strategic position means labour costs at generation plants in Ireland are 20 per cent to 30 per cent higher than in Europe. According to Deloitte, which compiled a report on the sector for the government, higher labour costs and generation plant inefficiencies cost Irish consumers €100m a year.

The green paper does not address the issue of wages, but prefers to highlight the mixture and price of fuels that are used in generation.

There is discussion on the subject of allowing freer entry into the energy markets and making them more contestable. But, reading between the lines, there is an implicit admission that not a lot can be done to make the sector more competitive.

Despite the recommendation of the Deloitte report, there is no question of splitting up or privatising the ESB or selling generation stations. From a global perspective we need expensive energy to force us to economise. But this does not mean production and distribution can be inefficient. If the policy is to use price to economise on energy then taxation is the route to follow — and not to facilitate excessive wages or other costs.

*Adapted from **Michael Casey**, Sunday Times, 8 October 2006*

In reality, entry barriers may be extremely difficult to remove and we can consider them on a number of levels:

a **Innocent entry barriers** are those that are part and parcel of the nature of the industry and have not been specially erected by the incumbents to hinder the entry of other firms. An example may be seen in terms of the economies of scale and the minimum efficient scale. If the minimum efficient scale is large an entrant may find it impossible to break in at a profit.

If such innocent barriers are large, incumbents may be able to virtually ignore the possibility of new entrant firms, and competition will then be restricted to the incumbents. Our analysis can then be in terms of game theory, as discussed in the previous chapter.

If, on the other hand, the industry is one where there are few innocent barriers to entry then existing firms will either:

■ accept competition and new entrants as part of their normal activity and be prepared to earn normal profits, or

■ try to invent barriers to keep other firms out so that supernormal profits can be earned.

b **Strategic entry barriers** – firms that create barriers are erecting strategic entry deterrents to stop other firms from entering the market. Such deterrents, as we have seen in Chapters 4 and 5, include such factors as hostile takeovers; product differentiation; predatory pricing; limit pricing; creation of brand loyalty; or expenditure on a massive advertising budget. Any new entrant will potentially have to match this in order to raise awareness of their product and gain a foothold in the market, and as it constitutes a large sunk cost it will prevent some firms entering.

In terms of empirical relevance, although contestable markets are a further development in terms of competitive market theory, in reality in most markets there are some barriers and in other markets there are huge barriers to entry.

In the case of the bus industry, takeovers and amalgamations have taken place and the original large number of small firms has coalesced into a six-firm oligopoly due to the takeovers, sell outs and mergers that have occurred. This has led to creation of entry barriers and the market has become less contestable. Apart from purchasing economies in terms of spare parts and petrol a new entrant must hire and train staff, and advertise extensively to inform customers of its services. New entrants also have to overcome the brand loyalty that incumbents have built up.

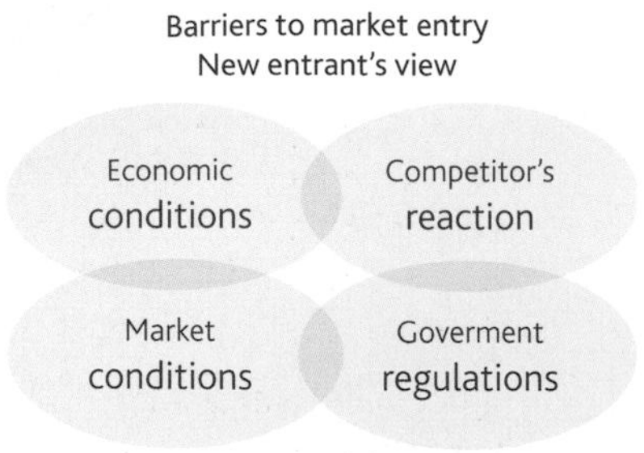

Barriers to market entry
New entrant's view

Economic conditions	Competitor's reaction
Market conditions	Goverment regulations

Figure 6.2 *Barriers to entry*

Entering a manufacturing industry usually requires a much larger investment in order to produce the required products. Current evidence suggests that a high degree of contestability is quite rare in purely domestic markets but the threat of new entrants may come less from domestic firms but from large foreign firms that may have lower set up costs.

Benefits of contestable markets

One important benefit is that it reduces likelihood of government failure – if contestable markets theory is correct in assuming that just the threat of competition can alter the behaviour of incumbents, it reinforces the link between barriers to entry and profit, while removing the association between barriers to entry and market concentration. The possibility that efficiency can be achieved in the absence of entry and exit barriers, but without actual competition indicates that as long as new firms can enter the market, just the threat of competition will control incumbents' actions. Governments, beyond removing entry and exit barriers, will not have to interfere in the market, for example, in terms of a windfall profits tax or trying to introduce new firms and this may reduce the likelihood of government failure.

Traditional monopoly/oligopoly theory concentrates on the number of firms currently in the industry. But contestable market theory, which concentrates on the possibility of contestability rather than the number of firms, may suggest a more useful analytical approach when trying to predict firms' pricing and output behaviour.

Criticisms of contestable market theory

■ Limited application – in practice, sunk costs may be extremely high. Once established in an industry the high sunk costs, like specialist machinery, would make a firm very reluctant to pull out. Takeovers and mergers may reduce long-run average costs and create unachievable economies of scale for new entrants.

■ The level of technical knowledge required to enter an industry may be high, and not freely available to firms considering entering the industry as information may be jealously guarded by the incumbents.

■ Incumbents protect themselves by taking out patents on products and do not make the results of their Research and Development (R&D) widely available, for example, pharmaceutical companies.

■ The theory ignores the possible aggressive actions of incumbents who may make it known to potential entrants that they will resist new entrants by limit pricing.

We can use game theory to analyse the effect on a contestable market; assume there are two players, A, the incumbent, and B, a potential entrant. The strategies for A are to set its price at the monopoly profit-maximizing level or at the competitive (normal profit) level. The strategies for B are to enter and set a price just below that of A or not to enter.

Figure 6.3 shows the payoffs for the two firms. If B does not enter, A earns a normal profit by setting a competitive price or earns maximum monopoly profit by setting the monopoly price. If B does enter and undercuts A's price, A incurs an economic loss regardless of whether it sets its price at the competitive or monopoly level. The reason is that B takes the market with the lower price, so A incurs a cost but has zero revenue. If A sets a competitive price, B earns a normal profit if it does not enter, but incurs an economic loss if it enters and undercuts A by setting a price that is less than average total cost. If A sets the monopoly price, B earns a positive economic profit by entering and a normal profit by not entering.

The Nash equilibrium for this game is a competitive price at which A earns a normal profit and B does not enter. If A raised the price to the monopoly level, B would enter and by undercutting A's price would take all the business, leaving A with an economic loss equal to total cost. A avoids this outcome by sticking with the competitive price and deterring B from entering.

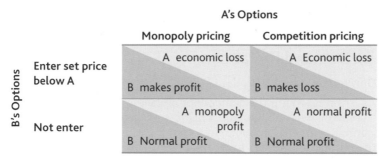

Figure 6.3 *A contestable market*

After completing this chapter you should:

- ■ demonstrate knowledge of the general features of UK and EU competition policy and evaluate the costs and benefits of such policies
- ■ understand the arguments relating to public ownership, privatisation, regulation and deregulation of markets
- ■ appreciate how contestability may change firm behaviour
- ■ understand the limitations of contestable market theory and that it is the degree of contestability that is important
- ■ appreciate that firms may have objectives other than profit maximisation
- ■ understand the possible conflict due to separation of ownership and control
- ■ Realise that making a sufficient level of profit is still a crucial activity for firms.

AQA↗ Examination-style questions

1   (a)   Explain the characteristics of a contestable market.   *(15 marks)*

    (b)   Evaluate the view that the increased contestability of markets will increase efficiency and will always be advantageous to consumers.

                                                                                         (25 marks)

2   (a)   Explain why economists usually regard monopoly as an undesirable form of market structure.   *(15 marks)*

    (b)   Evaluate policies a government might use to reduce the problems caused by monopoly.   *(25 marks)*

AQA, June 2005

7

The labour market: demand and supply

Key terms

Derived demand: occurs when the demand for a factor of production arises from the demand for the output it produces.

Theory of marginal productivity: key theory underpinning the demand for labour.

Marginal revenue product (MRP): the value of the physical addition to output arising from hiring one extra unit of a factor of production.

This chapter examines the factors influencing demand and supply of labour at different levels – economy-wide, by occupation and by individual firm. The key theoretical framework underpinning demand for labour, known as marginal productivity theory, is outlined. Also is the fact that there is a range of monetary and non-monetary factors influencing labour supply.

Demand for labour

Derived demand

As is the case with the demand for all factors of production, demand for labour is a **derived demand.** This means factors of production are not wanted as an end product, but rather for what they can produce. Thus the number of workers firms wish to employ depends mainly on the demand for the output produced. A rise in demand will usually lead to a firm employing more workers.

Aggregate demand for labour

The aggregate, or total, demand for labour depends principally on the level of economic activity. If the economy is growing and firms are confident that it will continue to grow in the future, employment levels will tend to increase. However, if national output falls or grows more slowly, firms will be less confident about levels of aggregate demand in the future and employment levels will fall.

The individual firm's demand for labour

In addition to the demand for the output produced, the number of workers that a firm seeks to employ is determined by a number of factors, including:

- **The price of labour**. A rise in wage rates which exceeds any rise in labour productivity will raise unit labour costs and will lead to a contraction in demand for labour.

- **Productivity**. As output per worker per hour increases, the more attractive labour becomes.

- The **price of other factors of production**. If capital becomes cheaper firms may seek to substitute some of their workers with machines, for example.

- **Supplementary labour costs**. For example, increasing employers' National Insurance contributions will lead to a fall in demand for labour.

Note that a change in any of the last three of these factors will lead to a change in the quantity of labour demanded at a given wage rate. Shifts in the demand curve for labour are examined below.

Marginal productivity theory

The **theory of marginal productivity** of labour states that demand for workers depends on their **marginal revenue product (MRP)**. Where the marginal cost of taking on an additional unit of labour equals its marginal revenue product, the equilibrium quantity of labour employed will be established.

In the short run, as a firm takes on more workers, output rises at first, because of increasing returns due to the benefits of division of labour, leading to an increase in marginal product. The **marginal product of labour** is the number of extra units of output a firm gains from employing an additional unit of labour. After a particular level of employment is reached, marginal product tends to fall due to the onset of diminishing marginal returns. The marginal revenue product of labour is the addition to a firm's revenue from employing an additional worker. It is calculated by multiplying the worker's marginal product (MP) by the marginal revenue (MR). The formula for marginal revenue product is thus:

$$MRP = MP \times MR.$$

With perfect competition in the product market, the firm becomes a price taker, implying the price of its output does not change if it sells more, so marginal revenue will be equal to price, and the firm can sell all its output at the ruling market price. If we also assume perfect competition in the labour market, firms can recruit workers at a constant wage rate. Table 7.1 shows how marginal revenue product is calculated and also demonstrates the profit-maximising condition.

Table 7.1 *Marginal revenue product*

No. of workers	Total product	Marginal product	Marginal revenue product	Marginal cost	Total revenue	Total cost	Profit
1	12	12	60	100	60	100	– 40
2	26	14	70	100	130	200	– 70
3	50	24	120	100	250	300	– 50
4	90	40	200	100	450	400	50
5	140	50	250	100	700	500	200
6	200	60	300	100	1,000	600	400
7	254	54	270	100	1,270	700	570
8	304	50	250	100	1,520	800	720
9	340	36	180	100	1,700	900	800
10	358	18	90	100	1,790	1,000	790
11	374	16	80	100	1,870	1,100	770
12	378	4	20	100	1,890	1,200	690

Table 7.1 assumes a constant market price for the product of £5 per unit and a constant wage rate of £100 per worker per week. It is clear that after the employment of the second worker and up to the employment of the ninth worker, each one adds more to revenue than to cost. After the employment of the ninth worker the situation is reversed and each additional employee adds more to costs than to revenue. Therefore profit is maximised when nine people are employed. You should be able to see that this level of employment is where the gap between total revenue and total cost is greatest, that is, £1,700 − £900 = £800.

The marginal revenue product of labour curve shows the quantity of labour demanded at each wage rate, as shown in Figure 7.1. The marginal revenue product curve of labour is thus the demand curve for labour. Figure 7.1 shows that a firm will demand labour at the point where MRP equals the marginal cost, that is, the wage rate. When the wage rate is W1, the firm will thus demand Q1 units of labour. If the wage rate rises, say to W2, the firm will continue to equate the wage with MRP, and thus demand Q2 units of labour.

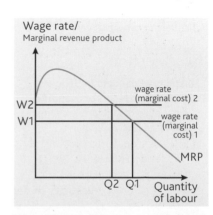

Figure 7.1 *Marginal revenue product and equilibrium quantity of labour employed*

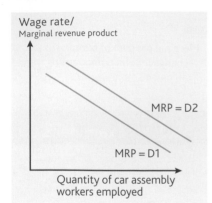

Figure 7.2 *An increase in marginal revenue product (MRP)*

Shifts in the demand curve for labour

The demand curve for labour will shift out to the right if the marginal revenue product of labour increases. This will come about if the marginal product of labour and/or the marginal revenue increases. So the demand for car assembly workers will increase if the productivity of car assembly workers rises, perhaps as a result of increased training and/or if the price of their output rises due to an increase in demand for cars. This increase in MRP is illustrated in Figure 7.2.

From Figure 7.1 you will see that MRP tends to rise at first, and then fall as diminishing returns set in. You will thus see it as possible that a firm may equate MRP with wage rate at two levels of employment. However, the firm will not be maximising profit at the lower employment level since if it expands employment further it can add workers that will generate MRP over and above the cost of employing them (it is fairly easy for you to see for yourself that this is true). To avoid ambiguity, it is therefore conventional to draw the demand curve for labour in the same way as demand curves are drawn at AS, that is, as downward-sloping.

Activity

Table 7.2 *Total product per week*

No. of workers employed	Total product per week	Total revenue	Marginal revenue product
1	8		
2	20		
3	34		
4	43		
5	50		
6	54		

The table above shows the total product per week for a small firm as the number of workers employed varies. The price of the product sold is £10 per unit.

a   Calculate total revenue at each level of employment.
b   Calculate marginal revenue product as the number of workers employed increases.
c   Explain how many workers per week the firm should employ if the weekly wage per worker were: (i) £40; (ii) £70; (iii) £90; (iv) £120.

Figure 7.3 *A team of accountants. Assessing an individual's MRP is likely to be difficult if they work in a team*

Key terms

Elasticity of demand for labour: the responsiveness of quantity demanded of labour to a change in the wage rate.

Measuring MRP can be difficult in reality. Work is often carried out in teams, which makes it hard to isolate the contribution to output made by an individual worker. In addition, it is difficult to measure the marginal product of a number of people who work in the tertiary sector. For example, how would you measure the contribution of each accountant working in a team carrying out an audit?

The elasticity of demand for labour

The elasticity of demand for labour is a measure of the responsiveness of the quantity demanded of labour to changes in the wage rate. The formula is:

$$\text{Elasticity of demand for labour} = \frac{\text{percentage change in quantity of labour demanded}}{\text{percentage change in wage rate}}$$

For example, if elasticity of demand for labour were 5 and wage rates increased by 10 per cent, then, all other things remaining equal, the demand for labour would fall by 50 per cent. If demand for labour fell by 10 per cent when wage rates rose by 100 per cent, then, all other things remaining equal, elasticity of demand would be 0.1, that is, inelastic.

There are a number of factors that determine the elasticity of demand for labour. These include:

Time period. In the long run, it is easier to substitute labour for other factors of production or vice versa. In the short run, firms may not have enough time to reorganise their operations and will thus have to employ the same number of workers even if wage rates increase. Workers will have contracts of employment and firms may have to make redundancy payments if they dismiss employees. Over time, the firm could buy labour-saving capital equipment and reorganise its working methods, reducing the amount of labour required. So elasticity of demand for labour will be higher in the long run.

Availability of substitutes. The easier it is to substitute other factors of production for labour, the more a rise in real wage rates will lead to a firm replacing labour with machines. For example, it might be relatively straightforward these days to replace production line workers with automated capital equipment. If there are plenty of good substitutes, then the elasticity of demand for labour will tend to be high.

Elasticity of demand for the product. As already explained, labour is a derived demand. So, if there is a collapse in demand for tin, then there will also be a collapse in the demand for tin miners. The elasticity of demand for labour in an industry mirrors the elasticity of demand for the product made in the industry. If the elasticity of demand for the product is low, a reduction in demand for it will have little effect on employment in the industry.

The proportion of labour cost to total cost. The larger the proportion of labour cost to total cost, the higher the elasticity of demand for labour. This is because an increase in the wage bill will have a significant impact on total costs. If a group of workers gains a 20 per cent pay rise but these workers accounted for 70 per cent of the costs of the firm, then a 20 per cent pay rise would have a dramatic effect on the supply curve and lead to a large decrease in quantity of the product demanded. This would subsequently lead to a large fall in employment.

Figure 7.4 *A car assembly line. The longer the time period, the easier it is to substitute labour for other factors of production*

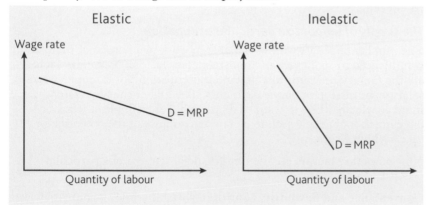

Figure 7.5 *Elastic and inelastic demand curves for labour*

The supply of labour

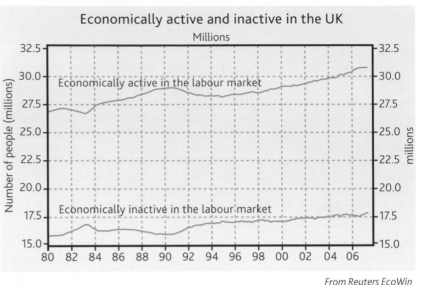

Figure 7.6 *Economically active and inactive in the UK*

■ Key terms

Economically inactive: the percentage of the population who are either not in work nor seeking it.

Participation rate/activity rate: the percentage of the population of working age currently in work or actively seeking work.

Monetary factors: the financial rewards to a particular occupation, for example, wage, commission, bonus.

Non-monetary factors: the non-financial rewards to a particular occupation, for example, holidays, leisure time and convenience.

In 2008, the population of the UK was just under 61.5 million, though not all of the population were available for work. The labour supply consists of all those who are economically active. The economically active are those who are either currently in work or are actively seeking work. Those not actually in work, but actively seeking it, are defined as being unemployed. The labour supply is also known as the labour force or working population.

Those sections of the population that are **economically inactive** are not part of the labour supply, since they are neither in work nor seeking it. The inactive include those not of working age (currently 16 to 65 for men and 16 to 60 for women). Other inactive sections of the population include students in full-time education, housewives, those who have retired early, prisoners and the severely disabled.

The **participation rate**, or **activity rate**, is usually calculated as the percentage of the population of working age that is economically active. The UK has one of the highest participation rates in the world, at around 75 per cent.

The supply of labour to a particular occupation

The number of people willing and able to work in a particular occupation is influenced by monetary and non-monetary factors. **Monetary factors** are the financial rewards to a particular occupation, for example, wage/salary, commission or bonus payments. The higher the wage rate, the more people are likely to want to do the job. For example, a relatively large number of people seek to be lawyers because of the potential for earning high wages.

Non-monetary factors are the non-financial rewards of a particular occupation, for example:

Convenience and flexibility. Long or unsociable working hours may deter potential workers, whereas if people have the flexibility to choose the hours they work, more may be attracted to a given occupation. For example, many financial advisers are able, to an extent, to choose when they work. In some occupations it is also becoming increasingly possible to work from home.

Status. People may be attracted to high status occupations, such as barristers.

Promotion prospects. Some people may be prepared to work for relatively low wages early in their careers, for example in the media, hoping for eventual promotion to high-paid jobs.

Job security. People will be attracted to more secure jobs. The teaching profession has high levels of job security which encourages some people to enter the profession even though pay is not especially high.

Working conditions. *Ceteris paribus*, more workers will be attracted to jobs with pleasant working conditions. For example, we might expect that the supply of refuse collectors would be low as it is not a pleasant job. This factor is offset by the low level of qualifications required.

Holidays/leisure time. Workers may be attracted to the long paid holidays in some occupations. Some people may be encouraged to become teachers or civil servants because of the relatively long holidays on offer.

Perks and fringe benefits. Workers will be attracted to firms that offer company cars, expense accounts, free private heath care and non-contributory pension schemes. Travel agents tend to receive cheap holidays for their families, for example.

Job satisfaction. A combination of the factors listed above, along with other, intangible features, such as relationships with colleagues, or a sense of making a difference in people's lives, can lead to job satisfaction and a greater supply of labour to an occupation. For example, the teaching and nursing professions may not have especially high monetary rewards but are often said to yield high job satisfaction. Stressful jobs where there is little sense of recognition may lead to job dissatisfaction and a reduced supply of labour.

One key concept, which dates back to Adam Smith, is that of **net advantage**. Smith postulated that the overall reward, taking into account monetary and non-monetary factors, should be equal across the various industries in which a particular occupation (for example, engineer) could be practised. As highlighted in Figure 7.8 those occupations with satisfying non-monetary features may have a higher supply at a given wage (S advantage), meaning that potential employees would be prepared to work for a relatively low wage rate (W1). Those occupations with less satisfying non-monetary characteristics may have a lower supply at a given wage (S disadvantage), and the monetary rewards must thus be higher to compensate (W2).

Case study

City teachers to get more cash incentives

The Education Secretary Alan Johnson has argued that additional cash incentives, or 'golden hellos' should be given to teachers who opt to teach in some of England's most deprived inner-city schools. The government's teacher training agency has been asked to investigate methods of attracting high quality teachers to areas of economic deprivation in a bid to raise academic performance there. Mr Johnson also wishes to address the gender imbalance of teachers in primary schools by attracting more men to the sector, along with more trainees from ethnic minority groups, increasing the government's target for recruiting teachers from ethnic minority backgrounds from 10.5 per cent to 12 per cent.

Mr Johnson said: 'Ensuring that schools serving areas of high disadvantage have good quality teachers will be critical if we are to make progress on narrowing the social class achievement gap. I want the agency to look creatively at how best it can use the

AQA **Examiner's tip**

It is worth making a list of the key terms and facts relating to the UK labour supply.

Figure 7.7 *Performance prospects in the media mean that workers are prepared to accept low initial wages*

■ **Key terms**

Net advantage: the overall rewards to a particular occupation, taking into account both monetary and non-monetary factors.

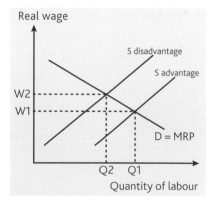

Figure 7.8 *The concept of net advantage explains the supply of labour to a particular occupation*

resources and levers at its disposal to make progress in this area. This might include (but not be limited to) consideration of more targeted use of incentives such as golden hellos.'

New maths and science teachers are currently offered cash incentives of £5,000 in response to a national shortage. Schools and local authorities have also been given the option of offering additional financial incentives for recruitment and retention of school leaders. Government cash is also to be used for language teachers in primary schools and science and maths teachers in secondary schools.

The head of the Government's teacher training agency said: 'The Government has shifted its focus from increasing the quantity of teachers in England, to ensuring the whole school workforce has the skills and tools to deliver a curriculum that is relevant to pupils now and in the future. The Government aims to attract the right numbers of teachers and train them to high standards.'

■ **Activity**

Read the case study 'City teachers to get more cash incentives'.

Use the concept of net advantage to compare the monetary and non-monetary factors prospective teachers may take into account when considering joining the profession.

■ **Key terms**

Unemployment: the number of people of working age who do not currently have a job but are actively seeking work at existing wage rates.

Elasticity of supply of labour: the responsiveness of quantity of labour supplied to a change in wage rate.

The supply of labour to a particular firm

In addition to the factors influencing the supply of labour to a particular occupation, some additional factors influence the supply of labour to particular firms:

Availability of training. If a particular firm offers a higher quantity and quality of training than others, it is likely to attract more workers.

Location. Firms based in cities will have a greater amount of labour to choose from. Good transport links for commuters are also important.

Level of unemployment. When the level of **unemployment** is low, there may be 'skills shortages' making it difficult for firms to fill vacancies.

Opportunities for overtime work. The availability of overtime hours paid at higher rates may attract people who wish to increase their incomes.

The industry labour supply curve

A change in the wage level in an industry causes a movement along its labour supply curve.

An industry's labour supply curve is generally upward sloping, left to right, as shown in Figure 7.9. An increase in real wage, for example W1 to W2, causes an extension of supply, for example, Q1 to Q2, even though the labour supply curves of individuals already in the industry may be backward-bending, as explained below. This is because a higher wage is likely to attract new workers into the industry.

The elasticity of supply of labour

The **elasticity of supply of labour** measures the responsiveness of the quantity of labour supplied to a change in the real wage rate, and will vary from industry to industry. The formula for elasticity of supply of labour is:

$$\text{Elasticity of supply of labour} = \frac{\text{percentage change in quantity of labour supplied}}{\text{percentage change in wage rate}}$$

The elasticity of labour supply depends upon:

The skills and qualifications required in the job. Jobs that require specific skills and higher-level qualifications will find it more difficult to attract workers when the real wage rises, since there will be few workers possessing the relevant skills. Elasticity of labour supply thus tends to be lower for skilled jobs than for unskilled jobs.

The length of the training period. Jobs with long training periods will have low elasticities of labour supply, because workers may be put off by the length of the training period, even if a higher real wage is offered. Even if some workers are attracted into such an occupation by a higher wage rate, it may take several years to complete the required training, for example, in the case of doctors, architects and lawyers.

Sense of vocation. For teachers and nurses, for example, the reward for the work is not wholly financial and thus supply may not change much in response to a change in wage. Jobs which have a vocational element will thus tend to be inelastic in terms of labour supply.

Time period. In the long run, supply of labour will tend to be more elastic. This may be because certain occupations require a notice period to be given before leaving one job for another, as well as the training period required for some jobs.

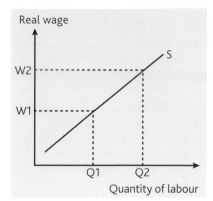

Figure 7.9 *The industry labour supply curve*

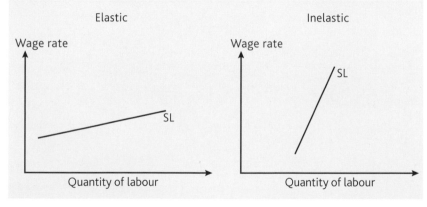

Figure 7.10 *Elastic and inelastic supply curves for labour*

The individual supply of labour

For most people, a choice is made between spending time at work or leisure. For each hour an individual works, he or she gives up an hour of leisure. The benefit that would be enjoyed from an hour of leisure is therefore the opportunity cost of supplying an hour of labour.

A possible shape for the individual's labour supply curve is shown in Figure 7.11. The **backward-bending supply curve for labour** suggests that at high wage levels an increase in the wage will actually lead to a reduction in the hours of labour supplied. This is because an individual worker will need to work fewer hours in order to earn his or her target level of income, that is, that level of income which secures the standard of living they aspire to, or that at least gains them an acceptable standard of living.

AQA Examiner's tip

The shape and slope of the individual supply curve for labour has important implications for fiscal and supply-side policies. Supply-side economists argue that higher rates of taxation lead to reduced incentives to work.

Key terms

Backward-bending supply curve for labour: the individual labour supply curve is thought to be this shape because it is assumed workers will prefer to work fewer hours as their income increases above a certain level.

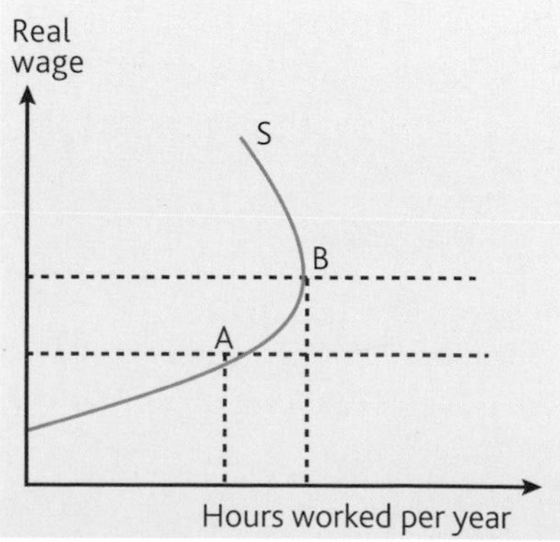

Figure 7.11 *The backward-bending labour supply curve*

Income effect (of a wage increase): depending upon an individual's target level of income, he or she can work fewer hours for the same overall pay.

Substitution effect (of a wage increase): individuals will tend to choose to work more hours, as the opportunity cost of leisure increases.

The effect of a change in wage on an individual's labour supply can be analysed in terms of **income and substitution effects**. If wages rise, leisure becomes relatively more expensive, that is, it has a higher opportunity cost. An individual will thus tend to substitute extra hours of work, replacing hours of leisure. Whilst the substitution effect always works in this way, the income effect is more controversial. If an individual's wage rises, the increase in income may encourage extra work, or alternatively the individual might opt for more leisure time while maintaining a sufficient level of income. Beyond point A in Figure 7.11, the negative income effect begins to offset the positive substitution effect. Beyond point B, the overall effect is negative because the negative income effect becomes strong enough to outweigh the positive substitution effect.

After completing this chapter you should be able to:

■ understand that the demand for a factor of production such as labour is derived from the demand for the product and that it will be influenced by the productivity of the factor

■ understand that the supply of labour to a particular occupation is influenced by monetary and non-monetary considerations. Non-monetary considerations include job satisfaction and dissatisfaction and the economic welfare derived from leisure time.

Extract A

Army offers bursaries to boost recruitment

The British Army is to introduce a bursary scheme for thousands of school leavers in an effort to boost recruitment and raise the calibre of graduates. The scheme will offer £1,000 to those who sign up but first study courses in areas useful to the armed forces such as IT and engineering. Recruits will receive a further £1,000 when they have completed their training.

The army further education bursary scheme is aimed at raising the standards of recruits; a Ministry of Defence survey in 2004 found that 41 per cent of recruits had a reading age of 11. The move is one of several initiatives intended to address a shortage of manpower in some army trades and regiments.

The commander of the army recruiting group denied there was a recruitment crisis but acknowledged there was a problem retaining good people already serving. The army came under attack this week from the National Union of Teachers which accused it of targeting school pupils, based on 'misleading propaganda'.

Audrey Gillan, The Guardian, 29 March 2008

Extract B

'The army has changed my life'

Private Robert Baldwin, 21, The Royal Regiment of Scotland

I left school without getting many qualifications. The army has changed my life completely. It has opened my eyes to cultures and things I would never have seen. If I had not got into the army I would have a real dead end job.

Sergeant Major Billy McLaren, 40, The Royal Regiment of Scotland

The army appealed to me because I was into sport and I fancied the travel because I had never even left Glasgow. I've had amazing experiences having been to Northern Ireland and Iraq and represented the army internationally for skiing and football.

Audrey Gillan, The Guardian, 29 March 2008

1   (a)   Outline **two** possible factors influencing the elasticity of demand for soldiers.   *(5 marks)*

    (b)   With the aid of a diagram, explain what might happen to the supply of labour to the army as a result of the bursary scheme outlined in Extract **A**.   *(10 marks)*

    (c)   Discuss whether monetary or non-monetary factors are most important in determining the supply of labour to the armed forces.   *(25 marks)*

2   (a)   Outline the marginal revenue productivity (MRP) theory of demand for labour.   *(15 marks)*

    (b)   Discuss the factors that are likely to determine the extent to which an increase in the wage rate offered to (i) barristers and (ii) waiters will lead to an increase in their supply.   *(25 marks)*

AQA Examiner's tip   No need to demonstrate evaluation in Question 2, part (a), just a sound theoretical understanding, ideally with a diagram. Question 2, part (b) will require more thought about a logical structure and the key concepts to include. High-quality answers here are likely to include accurate diagrams and possibly a real-world understanding of the nature of these two contrasting occupations. Thorough evaluation is crucial for higher-level marks in part (b).

8 | The labour market: wage determination

In this chapter you will learn:

- that wages are largely determined by the interaction of demand and supply, but these are not the only factors

- the difference between economic rent and transfer earnings

- how trade unions can influence the wages of their members, depending on the relative market power of employers

- that discrimination involves employers under or overvaluing the marginal revenue productivity of certain groups of workers.

AQA Examiner's tip

It may make understanding of this topic more straightforward to realise that the market for labour can be analysed like any other market, that is, with supply and demand.

Link

See Chapter 7 for more on demand and supply.

Key terms

Economic rent: the payment received by a factor of production over and above that which is needed to keep it in its present occupation.

Transfer earnings: the minimum payment needed to keep a factor of production in its present use.

In modern society we seem to be preoccupied with how much we earn in comparison to others. Many news reports pour scorn on the 'excessive' earnings of sports players and 'fat cat' company bosses. This chapter puts the theories of demand and supply of labour covered in Chapter 7 together to outline how wages are determined in the labour market, explaining how and why different groups earn different amounts. However, as shall be explored in this chapter, traditional theories of demand and supply are not the only reasons why some individuals earn more than others.

▌ Wage determination

Pay in a particular labour market, for example the market for City executives or teachers, is influenced by a number of factors. Along with demand and supply, these include the influence of trade unions and professional organisations, government intervention and esteem.

Demand and supply

Unsurprisingly, since the price of labour is determined in the labour market, the forces of demand and supply play a key role in determining relative wages. The wage paid to a particular occupation will rise following a rise in demand for their services or a decrease in their supply. For example, the wages of website designers have risen as increasing Internet use has increased demand for their services. This is shown in Figure 8.1.

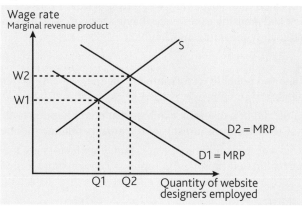

Figure 8.1 *An increase in marginal revenue product (MRP)*

In Figure 8.1 an increase in demand for website designers results in a rightward shift of the demand curve (D1 = MRP to D2 = MRP) and a subsequent increase in their wage rate (W1 to W2).

▌ Economic rent and transfer earnings

Demand for, and supply of, labour are also important determinants of **economic rent** and **transfer earnings**.

Transfer earnings are what a factor of production can earn in its next best alternative use, that is, the opportunity cost of a factor performing its current role. In the labour market, then, they are the equivalent to the minimum which has to be paid to keep a worker in his or her current job.

Economic rent is the surplus payment over and above transfer earnings and is thus total earnings minus transfer earnings. For example, a top football player may earn £5,000 per week. If the next best paid job he is willing and able to do is an estate agent earning £800 per week, his economic rent is £4,200 and his transfer earnings are £800.

In Figure 8.2 the total earnings received by the workers is 0WAQ. Of this, WAB is economic rent and 0BAQ is transfer earnings. This shows that economic rent is the area above the supply curve and below the wage rate. The amount of economic rent earned by individual workers will differ. The first worker taken on would have been prepared to work for much less than the wage rate actually paid, so a relatively high proportion of his or her earnings will be economic rent. Conversely, the last worker employed would have been prepared to work only for the going wage rate and so earns no economic rent.

The proportion of earnings made up of economic rent depends on the elasticity of supply. Economic rent will be a large proportion of earnings when supply is inelastic. For example, many Premiership footballers, Hollywood movie stars and hedge-fund managers are thought to earn substantial economic rents. Supply will be inelastic since most footballers enjoy playing the game and would continue to do so even if their wage was reduced, as most would earn much less in their next best paid jobs. Top sports players also tend to be highly paid. High demand for their skills is derived from high attendance figures at fixtures and valuable TV rights, along with merchandise sales, whereas the supply of top athletes and players is limited. Figure 8.3 shows the market for Premiership football players, with the equilibrium wage rate at the high level of W1.

Trade unions

In reality, there are few examples of highly competitive labour markets. A **trade union** seeks to further the interests of its members through a process of 'collective bargaining' with employers. The effect of introducing a trade union on the labour market is analysed in Figure 8.4. A trade union will act as a monopoly seller of labour to bid up the wage of its members from W1 to W2. This effectively creates a new supply curve, W2aS, since no workers will be prepared to work for any wage less than W2. However, employment will fall from Q1 to Q2. Thus, while some workers are able to benefit from higher wages, others may lose their jobs. The wage increase that trade unions are able to secure for their members is known as the **trade union mark-up**.

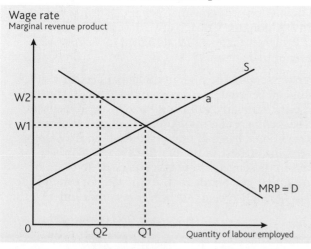

Figure 8.4 *The effect of a trade union on the labour market*

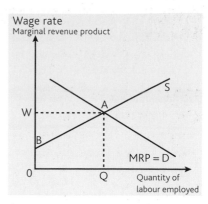

Figure 8.2 *Economic rent and transfer earnings*

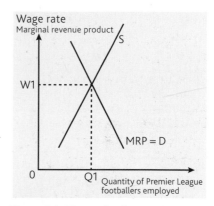

Figure 8.3 *The market for Premier League football players*

Key terms

Trade union: an organisation of workers who join together to further their own interests.

Trade union mark-up: the addition to wages secured by members of a trade union, compared to what they would earn if there were no union.

AQA **Examiner's tip**

Note that the analysis presented in Figure 8.4 can also be used to explain the effects of imposing a national minimum wage above the free-market equilibrium.

It could be argued that a trade union's attempts to raise wages will inevitably be at the expense of jobs, and that if unions wish to reduce unemployment, they should accept wage cuts. This need not be the case, however. By increasing the productivity of their membership through working with new capital equipment and new working methods, and by improving their skills and possibly motivation, a union can ensure that the MRP curve of labour shifts rightward. This creates the possibility for both increased wages and increased employment.

Case study

Trade union membership trends

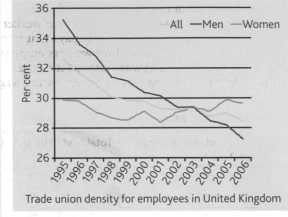

Trade union density for employees in United Kingdom

ONS Labour Market Trends

Figure 8.5 *Declining trade union density, 1995–2006*

Since Mrs Thatcher came to power in 1979, trade unions have seen a large decline in membership. Total membership has declined from 13 million in 1979 to just over 6 million in 2006. Union density (the percentage of employees who are members of a trade union) was 39 per cent in 1989, compared to 28 per cent in 2006. The number of working days lost through industrial action peaked at over 29 million in 1979, remaining at a high level through the early 1980s. In contrast, during the 1990s, an average of 0.6 million were lost through industrial disputes.

Part of the explanation for the reduction in union membership lies in the decline of manufacturing industry. It was in manufacturing that powerful unions existed; now many manufacturing jobs have disappeared. In addition, the Conservative government passed several Acts of Parliament after 1979, designed to progressively reduce the power of trade unions.

Union membership tends to be high in the public sector, with a density of around 60 per cent, compared to less than 20 per cent in the private sector. Similarly, full-time workers are 50 per cent more likely to be members of a trade union than part-time workers. Reflecting the traditional bases of manufacturing industry, union membership remains highest in the North East and Northern Ireland. Workers in these regions are twice as likely to be union members than those in the South East. In the US, for example, less than 10 per cent of employees are members of a trade union.

ONS Labour Market Trends

Employers with labour market power

Firms who employ a high percentage of workers in a particular labour market can influence the wage rate. In a labour market a **monopsonist** employer is a firm which is the only buyer of labour. Remember that a monopoly is a single seller. An example is the government, as the main employer of soldiers for national defence. Monopsonists are price makers, that is, they dictate the wage rate. In order to employ more workers they have to increase the wage rate. This means that the marginal cost of labour will exceed the average cost of labour (equivalent to the wage rate).

Monopsony in a market without trade unions

Table 8.1 shows how the average cost of labour (ACL) exceeds the marginal cost of labour (MCL). For example, to attract a fourth worker costs the employer an extra £50 since he or she not only pays that worker £32 but also pays an extra £6 to each of the first three workers employed. Because the monopsonist will face increasing wage rates as it increases employment, it will thus prefer to restrict employment, depressing wages below the free-market level.

Table 8.1 *Cost of labour per hour under monopsony*

No. of workers	Average cost of labour (wage rate) per hour (£)	Total cost of labour per hour (£)	Marginal cost of labour per hour (£)
1	20	20	20
2	22	44	24
3	26	78	34
4	32	128	50
5	40	200	72
6	50	300	100

Figure 8.6 shows that the number of workers employed will be Q1 (where MRP = MCL1) and the wage rate will be W1 (derived from the ACL curve). For the purposes of comparison, the competitive market outcome is also shown (Wc, Qc).

Monopsony in a market with trade unions

In a monopsony labour market, a union can theoretically raise both the wage rate and the level of employment, without a rightward shift of the MRP curve. Figure 8.6 highlights this. If the labour market is not influenced by trade unions, the equilibrium wage rate is W1, and the level of employment is Q1. Again for the purposes of comparison, the competitive market outcome (Wc, Qc) is shown.

A trade union has the same effect on the labour supply curve in perfect competition or monopsony. When the union sets the wage rate at W2, as shown in Figure 8.7, the kinked line W2AB is the labour supply curve and the average cost of labour curve (ACL). The marginal cost of labour (MCL) curve is the line W2ACE which has a double kink. As long as the monopsonist employs a labour force smaller than, or equal to Q2, the marginal cost of taking on an extra worker equals both the average cost and the wage W2, as set by the trade union. Beyond Q2 and point A, the monopsonist has to offer a higher wage in order to attract additional workers. Since the firm now has to pay all workers the higher wage, the marginal cost curve lies above the average cost curve. This is indicated by the upward sloping line CE.

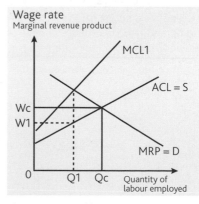

Figure 8.6 *Equilibrium in a monopsony labour market*

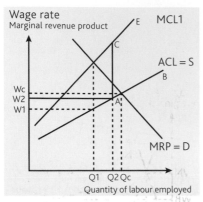

Figure 8.7 *Introducing a trade union into a monopsony labour market*

Key terms

Wage differentials: differences in wages arising between individuals, occupations, industries, firms and regions.

This gives rise to a vertical discontinuity between the horizontal section of the marginal cost curve (for levels of employment at or below Q2 and point A) and the upward-sloping section of the curve (CE). With the introduction of a trade union setting the wage rate at W2, employment is at Q2, compared to Q1 with no trade union. Thus, under monopsony conditions, the trade union has actually managed to increase both the wage rate and the quantity of labour employed. You can see from Figure 8.7 that the closer the union's target wage is to the competitive equilibrium (Wc), the higher the level of employment will be.

■ Wage differentials

Wage differentials exist when labour markets are not perfectly competitive. They are the differences in wages that can occur between different groups of workers. Wage differentials can also have a regional dimension.

Demand and supply

Economic theory would predict that wages will be high when demand is high and inelastic and supply is low and inelastic. Conversely, wages will be relatively low where supply is high compared to demand and when both demand and supply are elastic. For example, surgeons are paid considerably more than cleaners. The supply of surgeons is low compared to demand, due to the lengthy training and the high qualifications needed to gain access to the training. Supply will also be inelastic as a result. An increase in the wage rate will not lead to an influx of many new surgeons in the short run. Demand will also be inelastic due to the vital role that surgeons have, with no substitute. Conversely, the supply of cleaners is high and elastic. No qualifications are required for the job, along with little training. The large number of people capable of doing the job will mean that an increase in the wage rate will lead to a large extension of supply. The marginal revenue productivity of cleaners is also low, meaning demand is low. Figure 8.9 contrasts the market for surgeons and cleaners.

Relative bargaining strength

Surgeons working in the UK tend to be members of the British Medical Association (BMA), which is a prominent professional organisation with significant bargaining power. If the BMA was to take industrial action it would have major consequences. There is little scope for replacing specialist medical workers with other factors. In contrast, cleaners have low bargaining power. Few are members of a trade union and they are much easier to be replaced by unemployed workers, or possibly capital equipment.

Government policy

The introduction of the national minimum wage will have had a positive impact on the pay of cleaners. Similarly, public spending on health care

Figure 8.8 *Members of the National Union of Teachers march in protest against proposed pay cuts in 1979*

has increased, with an ageing population increasing the demand for surgeons. This will increase the MRP of surgeons.

Esteem

Some occupations are held in high public esteem, such as vets, surgeons and barristers. This is because they are perceived as providing an important service, and being composed of people who are well qualified and have particular skills and talents. This will help to boost their perceived MRP, and could be seen as a form of positive discrimination (see below). In contrast, jobs such as cleaning, though important, are not held in particularly high regard and are perceived as easy for anyone to do.

Wage differentials between particular groups

Skilled and unskilled workers. Skilled workers receive higher wages than unskilled workers primarily because the demand for skilled workers is higher and they are fewer in supply. The marginal revenue productivity of skilled labour is higher because their skills generate high output per worker. It is also more difficult to substitute skilled labour with capital equipment or unemployed workers.

Male and female workers. Men still receive higher pay than women, despite equal pay legislation. This is partly explained by the fact that more women work part-time than men. Even if hourly rates of pay are compared, however, men still earn more than women. The main reasons seem to be on the demand-side. The average marginal revenue productivity of women is less than that of men. In the past the qualifications of men were greater than that of women, since social convention was that more men went to university. A greater percentage of women work in low-paid occupations. Also, a smaller percentage of women are members of trade unions or professional organisations, giving them less bargaining power. Some women also miss out on promotion because they leave work to have and raise children. Negative discrimination also exists, with some employers undervaluing the marginal revenue productivity of female workers.

Part-time and full-time workers. Part-time workers tend to receive a lower hourly wage than full-time workers. The supply of people willing and able to work part time is relatively high compared to demand. It is also more convenient for people raising children, or studying. Part-time workers are also less likely to receive training than full-time workers, so their productivity will be lower. Also, a smaller proportion of part-time workers are members of trade unions or professional organisations. In addition, a higher percentage of part-time workers are women.

Ethnic origin. Workers from ethnic minority groups on average receive lower wages than white employees. Pakistani workers, for example, receive relatively low pay. One reason for this is that a high proportion work in the catering industry, which is relatively low paid. Also, the qualifications of Pakistanis, especially females, are typically lower than the rest of the population. Discrimination is another factor.

Activity

Using an appropriate diagram, highlight and explain the reasons for the likely wage differential between skilled and unskilled workers.

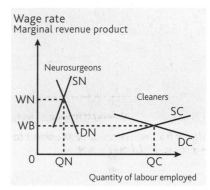

Figure 8.9 *The market for neurosurgeons and cleaners*

Case study

Mr Average of football nets £1m

The average annual salary of a footballer in England's top flight has broken through the £1m ceiling for the first time. Players in the Premier League are now earning 15 times more than the 'golden generation' who lifted the World Cup in 1966, even when inflation is factored in. In 1966, First Division players were paid an average

Activity

Read the case study and discuss in a group whether the pay of top footballers is justified, with reference to economic theory.

Figure 8.10 *What factors might influence the earnings of a premiership footballer compared to a nurse?*

of £100 a week by their clubs. Today, that figure, when performance related bonuses are taken into account, stands at an eye-watering £21,000 a week, according to Deloitte, the accountants. Those at the pinnacle of the game, such as the England captain, reportedly make more than six times that amount. The rate of increase means that footballers now earn almost as much in a week as the average person is paid in a year. The England women's football team have criticised the Football Association for paying them just £40 per day as they competed for five weeks at the World Cup in China.

Occupation	Weekly wage in 1966 (£)	Weekly wage in 2007 (£)	% increase after inflation
Top footballer	100	21,154	1,459
GP*	71	2,115	120
Teacher	27	661	80
MP	63	1,167	37
National average	18	452	85

* Excludes allowances and expenses

Roger Waite, Sunday Times, 18 November 2007

■ Discrimination in the labour market

Discrimination is a cause of **labour market failure**, and occurs when a group of workers or potential workers are treated differently to other workers in the same job in terms of pay, employment, promotion, training opportunities and working conditions. Discrimination can be negative or positive.

Negative discrimination

Negative discrimination occurs when workers of similar ability are treated less favourably than others, and are paid lower wages because of race, gender, age or disability. Prejudice leads employers to believe that the marginal revenue producttivity of these groups is lower than it really is. Figure 8.11 shows the effects of negative discrimination against women.

Whilst discrimination predominantly affects the demand curve for labour, there may be impacts on the supply side. For example, workers who are refused employment with discriminating firms will look for employment with firms who do not discriminate. The effect of this will be to increase the supply of labour to firms who do not practise discrimination; leading to lower wages for groups discriminated against. Negative discrimination can also occur on the part of consumers and fellow workers. If consumers boycott shops with workers from ethnic minorities, or other workers are racist, an employer may feel forced into not employing non-white workers.

The costs of negative discrimination

As shown in Figure 8.11, negative discrimination will lead to lower pay for the groups who experience negative discrimination. Such groups are likely to experience greater difficulty in finding work, and may thus resort to taking less demanding jobs than they are qualified to do. They may also not be considered for promotion, and subsequently not apply for more senior roles. Firms themselves may have less workers to choose from if they discriminate, which will increase their production costs and hence damage their international competitiveness. These higher costs are likely to be passed on to consumers.

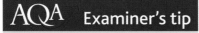

AQA Examiner's tip

Exam questions may be set on the impact of gender, ethnic, age and disability discrimination on wages and levels of employment.

■ Key terms

Discrimination: where groups of workers are treated differently to other workers in the same job regarding pay and employment.

Labour market failure: where the free market fails to achieve an efficient allocation of resources in the labour market.

Negative discrimination: when a group of workers is treated less favourably than others.

There may be economy-wide effects if government spending on welfare benefits has to be increased to support the incomes of groups discriminated against. Opportunity costs also arise if time and money is spent introducing and monitoring legislation to end discrimination and tackling social tension.

Positive discrimination

Firms may, however, discriminate in favour of certain groups. This is known as **positive discrimination**. In this case, employers perceive the marginal revenue productivity of a particular group of workers to be higher than it actually is. This results in the demand curve being further to the right than it should be, and thus some groups will earn higher wages than others of similar ability. The government may also discriminate positively in order to offset negative discrimination. In the US, this is referred to as 'affirmative action'. In this vein, the Conservative Party recently launched the Equal Pay and Flexible Working Bill, for which it hopes to secure cross-party support, mainly in a bid to address what it sees as pay discrimination against women.

After completing this chapter you should be able to:

■ understand the economists' model of wage determination in perfectly competitive labour markets and be able to assess the role of market forces in determining relative wage rates

■ understand how various factors, such as monopsony power, trade unions and imperfect information contribute to labour market imperfection, and appreciate how, in a monopsony labour market, the employer can use market power to reduce both the relative wage rate and the level of employment below those that would exist in a perfectly competitive market

■ understand the various factors that affect the ability of trade unions to influence wages and levels of employment in different labour markets, and be able to analyse these with relevant diagrams

■ understand the conditions necessary for wage discrimination and be able to discuss the impact of gender, ethnic and other forms of discrimination on wages, levels and types of employment.

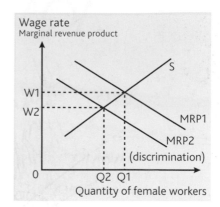

Figure 8.11 *Sex discrimination in the labour market*

■ **Key terms**

Positive discrimination: when a group of workers are treated more favourably than others.

Study Extracts A and B and answer all parts of the questions that follow.

Extract A

NHS consultants given 27 per cent pay increase

Too large a slice of the extra billions pumped into the NHS ended up in the pockets of hospital consultants, says a highly critical report by MPs. Consultants' pay rose by more than a quarter in three years while their working hours fell and there was no 'measurable improvement' in their productivity, the powerful Commons Public Accounts Committee has concluded.

Botched negotiations over a new contract, introduced in 2003, led to the higher-than-intended pay rise which was over 10 per cent more than the Department of Health expected. An average consultant's pay increased by 27 per cent over the first three years of the new contract, from £86,746 in 2003–4 to £109,974 in 2005–6, but productivity fell in the first year by 0.5 per cent. The report follows figures published earlier this month showing that average pay for GPs rose by 35 per cent during the same time to £110,004. Despite this, average working hours fell and most GPs dispensed with their out-of-hours responsibilities.

The consultants' contract, implemented in 2004, following two-and-a-half years of wrangling between the Government, NHS employers and the British Medical Association, was intended to reward those who gave most time to the NHS, halt the rise in private practice, increase productivity and create a more flexible workforce by giving managers greater control. But these benefits have mostly not been realised. The number of consultants rose by 13 per cent, while total consultant activity rose by just 9 per cent and the number of patients treated fell. The average weekly hours of work fell from 51.6 to 50.2.

Adapted from Jeremy Laurance, The Independent, 22 November 2007

Extract B

The medical pay gap

£000s

*Consultants and nurses are on a salary – GPs are not (they are self employed)

The Independent, 22 November 2007

1   (a)   Using **Extract A**, compare the relative earnings of consultants, GPs and nurses in the UK between 2003–04 and 2005–06.   *(5 marks)*

        (b)   With the aid of a diagram, outline how a trade union such as the British Medical Association can increase the earnings of its members.   *(10 marks)*

        (c)   Discuss whether factors affecting demand or those affecting supply of labour are most important in determining the relative earnings of doctors and nurses.   *(25 marks)*

2   (a)   Explain how the equilibrium wage rate in a labour market is determined **both** by the marginal productivity of labour **and** by influences upon supply of labour.   *(15 marks)*

        (b)   Do you agree that if a trade union persuades employers to increase wage rates in a labour market, employment must inevitably fall in that labour market? Justify your answer.   *(25 marks)*

AQA, June 2007

> **AQA**
> **Examiner's tip**
>
> Question 2, part (b) is technically quite a difficult question and will need a good, clear structure and well-explained diagrams. A detailed comparison of trade union intervention in perfect competition and monopsony labour markets should lead naturally to your conclusion.

9 The distribution of income and wealth

In this chapter you will learn:

■ that wealth is a stock of assets, while income is a flow of money

■ that both wealth and income are unequally distributed throughout UK households

■ that inequality of income and wealth can be shown diagrammatically using Lorenz curves

■ about the difference between absolute and relative poverty, and policies to address poverty

■ about the effects of the introduction of a national minimum wage.

Key terms

Wealth: a stock of valuable assets.

Marketable wealth: wealth that can be transferred to others.

Non-marketable wealth: wealth specific to a person, which cannot be transferred.

Distribution of wealth: how wealth is shared out between the population.

In a modern market economy, inequality of income and wealth may be regarded as inevitable. Should we be concerned, however, at news headlines telling us that a quarter of the UK population live in households with incomes below half the national average? This chapter outlines what is meant by income and wealth and what tends to determine who in society gets what. At the lower end of the distribution of income and wealth, the chapter also covers definitions and consequences of poverty, along with government policies to address them.

Wealth

Wealth is a stock of valuable assets. It can be divided into marketable wealth and non-marketable wealth. **Marketable wealth** is that which can be transferred between individuals, for example, property, whilst **non-marketable wealth** cannot be transferred between individuals, for example, life assurance, or non-marketable tenancy rights.

The **distribution of wealth** can be broken down among the population as a whole, between particular groups and the various types of wealth.

The distribution of wealth among the population

Wealth has tended to be more unequally distributed than income in the UK. Table 9.1 shows the distribution of marketable wealth among the UK population in 1986, 1996 and 2003.

Table 9.1 *Distribution of wealth in the UK*

Marketable wealth – % of wealth owned by:	1986	1996	2003
Most wealthy 1%	18	20	21
Most wealthy 5%	36	40	40
Most wealthy 10%	50	52	53
Most wealthy 25%	73	74	72
Most wealthy 50%	90	93	93
Total marketable wealth (£bn)	955	2,092	3,588

Office for National Statistics

You can see clearly from Table 9.1 that the UK's distribution of wealth has become more unequal between 1986 and 2003. You might be surprised to note that the wealthiest 1 per cent of the population own around a fifth of the nation's entire marketable wealth. You should also be able to see that the least wealthy half of the population own 10 per cent or less of the country's wealth.

Wealth distribution between different types of assets

Wealth can be held in many forms including life assurance, pension rights, property, shares, art, wines, bank deposits and cash. Non-marketable wealth made up of life assurance and pension fund holdings have traditionally accounted for over a third of all household wealth, and are more evenly distributed than marketable wealth including property, shares and bank deposit accounts.

The proportion of wealth held in property is liable to fluctuation over time resulting from changes in house prices. Increases in owner-occupation and house price rises in the 1980s increased the share of wealth held in property, whereas in 2008 a fall in property prices led to a decline in property as a proportion of marketable wealth.

Wealth distribution between different groups

Wealth tends to be skewed towards older age groups. Clearly, older people have had more time to build up savings and other forms of wealth than younger people. In addition, white adults are wealthier than those from ethnic minority groups, while men are wealthier than women.

Sources of wealth

There are four main sources of wealth:

Inheritance. This is the main route to wealth. Assets, including property, can be accumulated over generations, with each successive generation being wealthier than the preceding one. Wealth can therefore, to an extent, be self-perpetuating.

Saving. Wealth can be accumulated through saving, though this is easier for high income earners. Older people generally have more savings than younger ones because they have had longer to accumulate them.

Entrepreneurship. There is an increasing incidence of people being 'self-made' through taking a risk and successfully building up a business, with highly successful examples including Bill Gates, Richard Branson and James Dyson.

Chance. Numerous 'instant millionaires' are made each year through winning the jackpot payment on the national lottery or via premium bond holdings.

Wealth inequality

The causes of wealth inequality include:

Inheritance. In the UK large stocks of wealth including estates and titles (for example, dukedoms) are passed down from one generation of already wealthy families to the next. This tends to perpetuate holdings of wealth among already wealthy families.

Marriage. Wealthy people tend to marry other wealthy people, reinforcing the concentration of wealth among relatively few people.

Income inequality. High earners are better able to save and earn interest, as well as getting access to higher-interest savings accounts. Indeed, those who have a propensity to save a higher percentage of their income will build up more wealth than those who save a smaller percentage.

Chance. The fortunes of business start-ups may depend on chance unforeseen events, such as the closure of a competitor. Winning probability-based competitions such as the national lottery also depends on chance.

■ Income

Whilst **income** is unevenly distributed in the UK, it is nevertheless more equally distributed than wealth. We can analyse the **distribution of income** by factor of production (also known as the functional distribution of income), between households and between regions.

Link

Income differences have already been explored in Chapter 8.

Figure 9.1 *It could be you! (Though it is statistically unlikely…)*

Key terms

Income: a flow of money to a factor of production. An individual's income may include wages and state benefits.

Distribution of income: how income is shared out between the factors of production.

■ The functional distribution of income

Income is a flow of money generated and received over a period of time. We can analyse the distribution between labour, capital, land and entrepreneurs. We could also consider the distribution of income within a factor category, for example, wage differentials for labour. Household income includes income from wages, salaries, investment income, pensions and transfer payments such as welfare benefits. Figure 9.2 shows sources of household gross income in 2005/6.

Measuring the distribution of income

A method of measuring and illustrating the degree of inequality in the distribution of income and wealth is the **Lorenz curve**.

The horizontal axis measures the cumulative percentage of the population, whilst the vertical axis measures the cumulative percentage of income earned. A 45-degree line is included, which is the line of perfect equality, as it shows a situation in which, for example, the bottom 30 per cent of the population earned 30 per cent of the income and the bottom 90 per cent of the population earned 90 per cent of the income. The actual cumulative shares are then included on the diagram. In reality, this will generate a curve which starts at the origin and ends with 100 per cent of the population earning 100 per cent of income but which lies below the 45-degree line. The greater the degree of inequality, the further the curve will be below the 45-degree line. Figure 9.3 shows that income is more unevenly distributed in Country X than Country Y.

For example, in Country X the poorest 10 per cent of the population earn only 5 per cent of the income, whereas in Country Y they earn 8 per cent. The distribution of income is often measured in quantiles, or equal-sized divisions of the population. The population can be divided, for example, into fifths of the population, known as quintiles, or tenths, known as deciles.

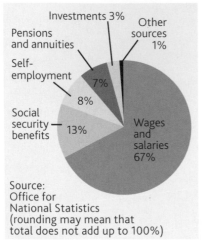

Source: Office for National Statistics (rounding may mean that total does not add up to 100%)

Figure 9.2 *Sources of UK household gross income, 2005/6**

■ Key terms

Lorenz curve: a diagrammatic representation of the distribution of income and wealth.

Gini coefficient: a statistical measure of the degree of inequality of income or wealth.

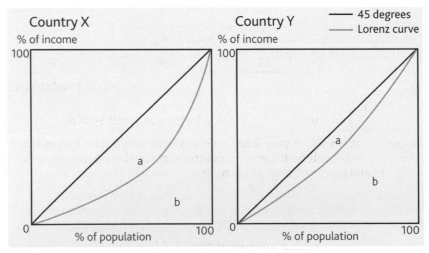

Figure 9.3 *Lorenz curves to show a comparison of income inequality*

A statistical measure of the degree of inequality shown on a Lorenz curve is known as the **Gini coefficient**. It is the ratio of the area between the 45-degree line and the Lorenz curve divided by the total area below the 45-degree line. In Figure 9.3, this is the ratio of (a ÷ a + b). Perfect equality would give a ratio of 0 and perfect inequality 1. The ratio will tend to lie between 0 and 1. The closer it is to 1, the more unequal the distribution of income. Table 9.2 below shows Gini coefficient data for the UK, 1980 to 2003, for gross income and disposable income. Gross income of households includes wages, salaries, pensions and investment income. Disposable income is gross income minus income tax and National Insurance contributions, but includes state benefits. Gini coefficients for both gross and disposable income show reduced inequality between 1990 and 2003, but the 2003 figures are considerably worse than in 1980.

Table 9.2 *Gini coefficient data for the UK, 1980 to 2003*

Year	Gross income	Disposable income
1980	0.34	0.28
1990	0.38	0.36
2003	0.37	0.33

■ The distribution of household income in the UK

The distribution of income between UK households has become more unequal in recent decades. One reason for this was the reduction in the top rates of income tax which, of course, benefited higher earners most. Large-scale privatisation also led to a rise in executive pay. For lower earners, the real value of benefits such as Jobseeker's Allowance fell. In addition, the percentage of single-parent families, who are often not in work or only in part-time jobs, more than doubled between 1975 and 2000. Table 9.3 shows the distribution of income in the UK, 1979–2005/6.

Table 9.3 *Distribution of household disposable income in the UK, 1979–2005/6 (% of total)*

Quintile group	1979	2002/3	2005/6
Bottom 20%	10	7	7
2nd 20%	14	12	12
3rd 20%	18	17	17
4th 20%	23	24	24
Top 20%	35	40	40

Office for National Statistics

The causes of income inequality between households

Impact of the State. A pure free-market system would not provide any welfare benefits, whilst income differentials, particularly between those who can and can't work are likely to be very significant. Government intervention to redistribute income should narrow such differentials.

Wealth inequality. Wealthier households will be able to earn more income such as dividends and interest from their asset holdings.

Household composition. Individual households will contain different numbers in employment.

Level of skills and qualifications. Individuals with skills or qualifications that are in high demand will tend to earn more. The lifetime earnings of graduates are often considerably higher than those of non-graduates.

Differences in earnings. Some workers earn more income than others. For example, full-time workers tend to earn more than those who work part time. Jobs with opportunities to work overtime will also boost earnings.

The geographical distribution of income

There is an uneven distribution of income between the regions of the UK. The average disposable income per head has tended to be considerably higher in London than in the North East of England and Northern Ireland. Table 9.4 highlights the regional distribution of income in the UK.

Table 9.4 *UK regional distribution of disposable income per head, 2005/6*

Region	Gross disposable income per head (£)
UK	13,279
London	15,885
South East	14,941
East	14,198
South West	13,258
Scotland	12,544
East Midlands	12,522
North West	12,186
West Midlands	12,133
Yorkshire and Humber	12,197
Wales	11,851
Northern Ireland	11,564
North East	11,356

Office for National Statistics

Income inequalities at a regional level are even more pronounced in Germany and Italy. For example, Germany still has considerable differences between what was formerly East Germany and West Germany. Similarly, the southern region of Italy is much less affluent than the industrialised north. Throughout Europe, there are significant differences in income per head, as Table 9.5 shows. Some economists identify a so-called 'core' of more developed economies in the north and west of Europe and a 'periphery' of less well-off countries of the former Eastern Bloc and in the more agriculturally dependent Mediterranean economies, including Portugal and Greece.

Table 9.5 *Differences in GDP per capita across EU27 in 1999 and 2006 (measured in purchasing power standards, EU27 index = 100)*

Country	1999	2006
EU27	100	100
Austria	133.1	127.7
Belgium	123.4	120.0
Bulgaria	27.0	35.4
Czech Republic	69.8	78.7
Cyprus	87.7	92.1
Denmark	131.3	126.0
Estonia	42.5	68.5
Finland	115.6	117.1
France	115.2	111.1

Country	1999	2006
Germany	122.6	114.3
Greece	83.1	97.4
Hungary	53.7	65.0
Ireland	126.7	145.7
Italy	118.0	103.5
Latvia	36.2	54.2
Lithuania	38.9	56.2
Luxemburg	238.2	279.6
Malta	81.3	77.0
Netherlands	131.7	130.8
Poland	48.7	52.5
Portugal	78.6	74.6
Romania	26.1	38.9
Slovakia	79.7	88.0
Slovenia	50.7	63.8
Spain	96.7	105.1
Sweden	125.8	124.8
United Kingdom	116.1	118.1

There are several reasons for differences in the geographical distribution of income, including differences in industrial structure, unemployment rates and the proportion of the population claiming benefits. Linked to the process of deindustrialisation and the move to an economy dominated by service-sector employment, the more developed nations in the EU, including the UK, tend to have lower relative levels of unemployment and lower dependency on state benefits. This is also reflected at a regional level within nations; for example, regions such as the north-east of England and Northern Ireland, historically more dependent on manufacturing and heavy industry, have suffered relatively high rates of unemployment and subsequent dependency on social security benefits. Often, the qualifications and skills of the labour force have not been appropriate for changes in industrial structure, leading to structural unemployment.

Differences in regional living costs may complicate matters slightly, for example, average house prices tend to be considerably cheaper outside London, though wages and salaries in some professions attempt to offset this with added 'London allowances'.

Government policies

The degree of government intervention to influence the distribution of income and wealth depends upon whether or not it feels the distribution that would arise if it were left to free-market forces would be inequitable.

Some economists do not favour substantial intervention, arguing that differences in income and wealth can act as signals, providing important incentives. However, Keynesians argue in favour of intervention since market forces may not ensure an equitable allocation of income and wealth, and that major differences can cause social division and the development of an 'underclass'.

Link

Structural unemployment is explained further in Chapter 13.

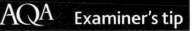

AQA Examiner's tip

The fact that the widest variations in income per head can often be within individual regions is an important point not realised by some students.

Methods of intervention

Governments can influence income and wealth distribution in society in a number of ways:

Taxation. Taxes can be categorised by their incidence as a proportion of income. While progressive taxes, such as income tax, take a higher percentage of the income or wealth of the rich to make the distribution more equal, regressive taxes, such as VAT, take a higher percentage of the income of the poor and thus make the distribution more unequal.

Monetary benefits. Monetary benefits are of two types – means tested and universal. Means-tested benefits, for example Working Families Tax Credit (WFTC), are available only to those who can prove their income is below a certain level. Universal benefits are available to everyone in a particular group regardless of income. Any family with young children receives child benefit, for example.

Direct provision of goods and services. These include the provision of, for example, health care, education and school meals, in order to give all citizens equality of opportunity. These are 'free at the point of consumption' funded through taxation.

Legislation and labour market policy. The introduction of a national minimum wage in 1999, anti-discrimination legislation and government subsidising of training serve to reduce income inequality. Also, measures to reduce unemployment may benefit low-income families.

Table 9.6 gives two measures of distribution in the UK. As outlined earlier, gross income of households includes wages, salaries, pensions and investment income. Disposable income is gross income minus income tax and National Insurance contributions, but includes state benefits.

Table 9.6 *Distribution of gross and disposable income in the UK, 2002/3*

	Gross income %	Disposable income %
Bottom 20%	7	8
2nd 20%	11	12
3rd 20%	16	17
4th 2t0%	23	23
Top 20%	43	40

Office for National Statistics

■ Activity

With reference to Table 9.6, explain whether or not intervention appears to have successfully redistributed income in the UK in 2002/3.

■ Key terms

Absolute poverty: when an individual or household's income is insufficient for them to afford basic shelter, food and clothing.

Relative poverty: when people are poor in comparison to others.

■ Poverty

In the last three decades the number of households with incomes below 40 per cent of the average level has grown to almost 10 million. At the time of writing, it is estimated that in the UK a third of children, almost 5 million, live in poverty, and that around half of those live in households where no adult is in paid employment. Economists discuss inequality in terms of **absolute poverty** and **relative poverty.**

Absolute poverty

Absolute poverty occurs when people's income is too low for them to afford basic necessities such as food, shelter, warmth and clothing. Even in developed countries such as the UK, there are some people who are undernourished or homeless. Absolute poverty is rare in the UK, and the largest problems of absolute poverty exist in less developed countries.

Relative poverty

Relative poverty exists when people are poor in comparison to others in society. By this definition, there will always be relative poverty in society. The relatively poor may be unable to afford a certain standard of living at a particular time. As a result, they will experience some form of social exclusion.

Relative poverty differs between countries and over time. Someone who is judged to be poor in the UK might be regarded as relatively rich in Somalia. Ten years ago in the UK, a DVD player might have been seen as a household luxury.

A rise in a country's income will result in a fall in absolute poverty. However, relative poverty may rise if those on high incomes benefit more than those on low incomes.

Measuring poverty

There is no official measure of poverty. However, the Joseph Rowntree Foundation, a charity set up for social research, has defined a household as being in poverty if its disposable income is less than 60 per cent of the UK median.

Table 9.7 *Proportion of people whose income is below percentages of median income*

Year	< 60% of median income	< 50% of median income
1961	12.8	7.4
1981	12.1	4.5
1991	20.1	11.7
2004	16.8	9.4

Office for National Statistics

The New Labour government from 1997 established a target of eradicating poverty within a generation. In this regard, it regularly carries out and publishes a **poverty audit**, which compares the government's performance against a set of targets.

The targets include:

- an increase in the proportion of working-age people with a qualification
- improving literacy and numeracy at age 11
- reducing the proportion of older people unable to afford to heat their homes properly
- reducing the number of households with low incomes
- reducing homelessness
- reducing the number of children in workless households.

Groups such as the elderly, the disabled, the sick, lone parents with children, the unemployed and those from ethnic minorities are more likely to suffer poverty than others.

Causes of poverty

The causes of poverty include the following:

Unemployment. Workless households are especially prone to poverty.

Low wages. Workers in unskilled, casual employment tend to earn relatively low wages, due to their resultant low marginal revenue productivity. Such workers may be disproportionately found in regions such as Northern Ireland and the North East.

Activity

In a group, discuss the things that you think are required to contribute to your basic standard of living. Do you imagine that these are the same things a citizen of a less developed country would include in their list?

Key terms

Poverty audit: assessment of the government's performance in eradicating poverty.

Figure 9.4 *Reducing homelessness is one of the government's poverty targets*

Sickness and disability. Dependency on sickness and disability benefits gives people relatively low incomes.

Old age. State benefits are still the major source of income for the elderly. However, this cause is becoming less important as more of the elderly build up occupational pensions and investment income.

The poverty trap. This reduces the incentive for those on low wages to earn extra income. If they do, they may be little better off, or even worse off because of the combined effects of paying income tax and having benefits withdrawn.

Imperfect information. Some people are simply unaware of their entitlements to benefits, or do not claim payments because of fear of social stigma.

Activity

Outline what you consider to be the economic costs and implications of poverty.

Case study

A vicious circle

People can get caught in a vicious cycle of poverty. Children from poor households tend to receive less education, and are less likely to enter into higher or further education. They are also likely to attend poorer performing schools. As a result children in poorer households tend to gain fewer qualifications. Statistics show that the poor tend to suffer worse physical and mental health and have a lower life expectancy, partly because they have poorer housing, less healthy diets and less access to quality health care. Because of their inability to afford consumer goods that most take for granted, such as cars, restaurant meals and holidays, the poor can also feel cut off from society, unable to live the type of life that the majority can experience, leading to low self-esteem and depression.

Government policy measures

Policies used by governments to address poverty will depend upon whether the intention is to tackle absolute or relative poverty. Absolute poverty may be addressed by introducing measures to raise the income of the very poorest groups in society, whereas tackling relative poverty implies using measures to reduce the gap between the rich and the poor. Measures to tackle poverty might thus include:

A national minimum wage. A national minimum wage is designed to increase the wages paid to low-income earners. See below for a detailed explanation.

Cutting the bottom rates of income taxes. Making income taxes less regressive will reduce the extent of the poverty trap and provide more incentive for people to work.

Tackling unemployment. Unemployment is a major cause of poverty.

Training and education. This should increase the productivity and potential productivity of the low paid and thereby improve their long term job prospects and earning potential.

Exploiting 'trickle-down' effects. Some supply-side economists argue that higher spending by the rich will stimulate the economy for the benefit of all, including the relatively poor. They argue that cutting corporation tax and income tax rates will create incentives for entrepreneurs to expand and thereby create employment for the poor. However, the idea of 'trickle-down' remains a controversial one, and it is unlikely that all groups experiencing poverty would benefit.

Increasing benefits. The direction of any incentive effects created by increasing welfare benefits remains controversial among economists. Free-market economists argue that it will lead to an increase in **voluntary unemployment** while Keynesians think increased government spending in this way can stimulate aggregate demand, creating jobs. However, the very poorest members of society dependent solely on sickness or disability benefits or the state pension may be unable to raise their standard of living in any other way.

Tax credits. Tax credits consist of benefits paid through the tax system as reductions in the amount of tax paid rather than receiving a cash benefit. The rationale behind tax credits is to create incentives to work whilst reducing child poverty. The working tax credit (WTC), introduced in 2003, replaced the Working Family Tax Credit (WFTC) available to those on low incomes and reduces the amount of tax they pay. The child tax credit (CTC), which streamlines all the various strands of income-related support for families with children into a single payment made to the main carer started in April 2001 and replaced the earlier married couple's tax allowance. Tax credits are one type of supply-side policy.

■ Minimum wage legislation

One way of addressing the problems associated with low pay is to impose a legal **national minimum wage**. Note that a minimum wage must be set above the market equilibrium wage rate if it is to have any impact.

Free-market economists argue that setting a minimum wage will distort the forces of supply and demand and have undesirable consequences, since firms' costs of production will rise, leading to higher unemployment. Figure 9.5 shows that setting a minimum wage of W2 above the free-market equilibrium wage rate W1 causes an increase in the quantity supplied of labour but also a reduction in the quantity of labour demanded. Thus, the minimum wage has caused an excess supply of workers equal to QS − QD. Those that keep their jobs may be better off, but compared to the free-market situation, equilibrium employment falls, from Q1 to QD, thus creating some additional unemployment. This could be seen as an example of government failure. You should be able to see that the extent of the unemployment created will depend upon the relative elasticities of supply and demand.

Some economists argue, however, that the introduction of a national minimum wage may not necessarily lead to higher unemployment. The low paid may have little bargaining power compared to their employers, especially if they are monopsonists. Setting a minimum wage could increase both the wage and employment level in such cases.

Furthermore, if a national minimum wage successfully increases average wages, this should, in turn, increase overall demand for goods and services which might well increase demand for labour. Those receiving higher wages may also feel a morale boost resulting in higher productivity. If employers also seek to gain higher returns from the now higher-paid workers by providing more training, productivity will increase further. Increases in productivity and demand for products will shift the marginal revenue productivity curve to the right, (D1 = MRP to D2 = MRP), as shown in Figure 9.6, eliminating any excess supply of labour at the national minimum wage W2.

Key terms

Voluntary unemployment: when a worker chooses not to accept a job at the going wage rate.

National minimum wage: a statutory minimum wage introduced to boost the earnings of the low paid.

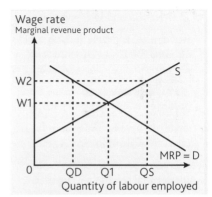

Figure 9.5 *The effect of introducing a minimum wage*

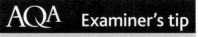

AQA Examiner's tip

Note that the analysis of a national minimum wage introduced above the free-market equilibrium is very similar to the analysis of the introduction of trade union.

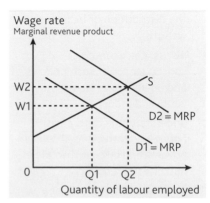

Figure 9.6 *The introduction of a national minimum wage may not create additional unemployment if MRP increases*

Read the 'Minimum wage set to rise by 21p' and answer the following:

1 Using a diagram, explain how a minimum wage works.

2 Evaluate the effectiveness of a national minimum wage in increasing the earnings of the low paid.

After completing this chapter you should be able to:

■ demonstrate knowledge of the distribution of household income and wealth in the UK

■ understand the various factors which influence the distribution of income and wealth and the possible costs and benefits of more equal and unequal distributions

■ demonstrate knowledge of the policies available to influence the distribution of income and wealth

■ discuss the economic consequences of such policies and be able to evaluate the various approaches

■ understand the difference between relative and absolute poverty and discuss the causes and effects of poverty

■ understand the effects of a national minimum wage upon labour markets.

■ Case study

Minimum wage set to rise by 21p

The minimum wage is set to rise from £5.52 to £5.73 this October, Gordon Brown said today. The Prime Minister began question time today by announcing the 21p increase in the pay of almost a million workers.

Brown told MPs in the Commons that the statutory rate will have risen by 60 per cent since it was first introduced in 1999. The hourly rate for 18 to 21-year-olds will increase from £4.60 to £4.77, while the statutory wage for 16 and 17-year-olds will go up from £3.40 to £3.53. Two-thirds of those who will benefit from the increase are women.

The Trades Union Congress (TUC) General Secretary, Brendan Barber, welcomed the announcement, although unions had wanted the Government to go further and announce an above-inflation increase for the eighth year in a row. 'The Low Pay Commission (LPC) was right to withstand pressure from business warning of economic trouble ahead. The truth is that employers will be able to absorb these sensible increases without too much difficulty,' Barber said. 'The LPC must continue to recommend the highest minimum wage increases that can be sustained as it provides very important protection for low paid workers.

'Bosses who fail to pay the minimum wage leave vulnerable workers in poverty and undercut the majority of employers who are happy to obey the law. Everybody stands to gain from making the minimum wage as robust as possible. We support the improvements to the enforcement regime that are currently going through parliament, and look forward to the introduction of tougher penalties for cheating employers and fair arrears for underpaid workers later in the year.'

Brown said at the start of Prime Minister's Questions (PMQs) that some people had warned that a National Minimum Wage would cost two million jobs, but three million jobs had been created. The business secretary, John Hutton, said: 'The National Minimum Wage remains one of the most important rights introduced by the Government in the last decade. Before it was introduced, some workers could expect to be paid as little as 35p an hour. Our legislation has ensured that can no longer happen. I am proud of the minimum wage. It makes a real difference to the lives of many of our lowest-paid workers and protects them from exploitation. It also creates a level playing field for business and boosts the economy.'

Paul Myners, chairman of the Low Pay Commission, said: 'This increase means that the minimum wage will have risen by 59 per cent since it was introduced in April 1999 – almost double the expected growth in prices over the same period. Despite many predictions to the contrary, job numbers in the industries most affected by the minimum wage have grown, and grown significantly, over the same period.'

The Government announced new measures to enforce the minimum wage, including a new method for dealing with arrears and an increase in the maximum penalty for non-payment to an unlimited fine. The minimum wage was £3.60 an hour when it was first introduced.

Deborah Summers, The Guardian, *5 March 2008*

Study Extracts **A, B, C** and **D**, and then answer **all** parts of the question which follows.

Extract A

Composition of the wealth of UK residents aged 50 to 65 by decile group, 2005

Percentage of total wealth

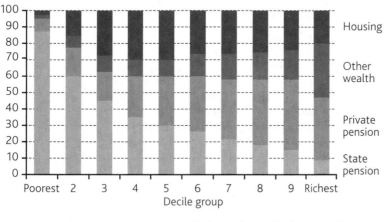

A New Pension Settlement for the Twenty-First Century,
The Second Report of the Pensions Commission, 2005

Extract B
Causes of wealth inequality

Two factors that promote wealth inequality:

People save as they age, which affects the distribution of wealth between young and old age-groups.

Home ownership is a very important determinant of overall wealth levels and inequalities.

Adapted from 'The long-term relationship between poverty
and debt', The Joseph Rowntree Foundation, November 2005

Extract C
Market failure and income and wealth inequality

Market failure can be caused by the existence of inequality. Wide differences in income and wealth between different groups within our economy lead to a wide gap in living standards between affluent households and those experiencing poverty. Society may come to the view that too much inequality is unacceptable or undesirable. The Government may decide to intervene to reduce inequality through changes to the tax and benefit system.

Economics of market failure, www.tutor2u.net,
accessed on 23 December 2005

Extract D

Young people face 'pensions time bomb'

Fewer than half of people under the age of 30 are in a pension scheme, a figure far lower than in the 1950s and 1960s. The Trades Union Congress (TUC) says that young people are failing to save, partly because employers have 'retreated' from contributing to a decent occupational pension, and partly because they face great pressure on their finances.

The TUC also says that the number of students leaving university with huge debts has increased, property prices are high and graduate jobs often pay low wages. Pensions scandals and mis-selling have made young people suspicious of pension companies.

TUC General Secretary, Brendan Barber, states: 'Young people have started a slow pension time bomb. Unless they take out pensions, a generation faces poverty in old age, dependent on the generosity of whatever government is in power. We used to think that slowly but surely we were all getting more prosperous. That's not likely to be true in retirement unless these trends change. The key change that needs to be made is to compel employers to make a proper contribution to pensions. All the evidence shows that employees understand occupational schemes and will join a work-based pension scheme, whereas they find making their own arrangements expensive and confusing. Young people, as much as today's pensioners, need to take a stand for a new pension agreement based on a good state pension topped up by decent occupational arrangements.'

The Press Association, published in The Guardian, 11 June 2004

1   (a)   Using Extract **A**, compare **two** ways in which the composition of
the wealth of UK residents aged 50 to 65 changes as their wealth increases.   *(5 marks)*

     (b)   'Society may come to the view that too much inequality is
unacceptable or undesirable' (Extract **C**, lines 3–4). Analyse
how the existence of inequality can cause economic problems,
such as market failure.   *(10 marks)*

     (c)   Using the data and your economic knowledge, evaluate the
view that the most effective way to reduce poverty is to increase
significantly the state pension.   *(25 marks)*

AQA, June 2007

2   'Workers in pleasant conditions, such as "soap celebrities", often receive
high pay, while those in disagreeable occupations, such as road sweepers,
are among the most lowly paid.'

     (a)   How does economic theory explain such differences in pay?   *(15 marks)*

     (b)   Assess the case for and against the government intervening to
raise the disposable income of workers on low pay.   *(25 marks)*

AQA, June 2005

At first glance, the case for government intervention appears very strong. However, might it always be justified when one considers opportunity costs, along with the costs and difficulties of implementation?

Link

Market failure is outlined in *AQA Economics AS*, p75.

Key terms

Market failure: where the free market fails to achieve an efficient allocation of resources.

Productive inefficiency: when firms are not producing at minimum possible average total cost.

Allocative inefficiency: when resources are not used to produce the goods and services wanted by consumers.

Fiscal policy: the use of government spending and taxation to meet economic objectives.

Government failure: when government intervention to correct market failure does not improve the allocation of resources or leads to a worsening of the situation.

Link

See *AQA Economics AS*, p111, for more on government failure.

This chapter extends the concepts of market failure and government failure introduced at AS and earlier in this book, and places emphasis on environmental aspects of market failure. While some aspects of government intervention, such as a national minimum wage, have been dealt with in previous chapters, here we cover methods such as regulation, taxation and extension of property rights. This chapter also covers the technique of cost-benefit analysis in depth.

Market failure and government failure

Market failure occurs when resources are inefficiently allocated, because of imperfections in the market mechanism, resulting in a loss of economic and social welfare. There are many possible cases of market failure, which include:

■ negative externalities

■ positive externalities

■ public goods

■ merit goods

■ demerit goods

■ imperfect competition

■ immobility of factors of production

■ equity issues, including poverty and inequality.

Market failure leads to productive and allocative inefficiency. **Productive inefficiency** occurs when firms are not producing output at minimum possible cost. This means that resources are being wasted which could have been used to satisfy wants and needs elsewhere. **Allocative inefficiency** occurs when resources are not used to produce the goods and services that consumers demand. The value society places on the last unit of output does not reflect the marginal cost of production.

Methods of government intervention that can be used to improve the workings of markets include:

■ government legislation and regulation

■ direct state provision of goods and services, including nationalisation

■ **fiscal policy** intervention, including indirect taxation and subsidies

■ improving the quality and availability of information.

Government intervention can sometimes fail to correct instances of market failure, and can even make existing problems worse. These are situations of **government failure**. The main types and causes of government failure include:

■ political self-interest

■ imperfect information

■ unintended consequences

■ regulatory capture.

■ Key terms

Negative externalities: negative spillover effects to third parties not involved with the consumption or production of the good. Social costs exceed private costs.

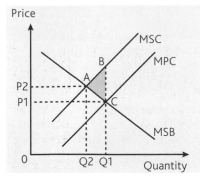

Figure 10.1 *Negative environmental externalities*

AQA **Examiner's tip**

Remember that marginal social cost = marginal private cost + marginal external cost and that marginal social benefit = marginal private benefit + marginal external benefit, or to use abbreviation, MSC = MPC + MEC and MSB = MPB + MEB.

Environmental market failure

One of the most important environmental market failures stems from **negative externalities** arising from production and/or consumption. Negative externalities occur when there is a divergence between private costs and social costs. For example, a chemical plant may operate with a private profit because its revenues exceed its private costs. However, it may be polluting the environment with waste materials, which it does not take account of. Thus the chemical plant creates a negative externality.

When there are negative environmental externalities, the free-market equilibrium price is less than the social equilibrium price (which includes both private and external costs), whilst the free-market equilibrium quantity will tend to be higher than the social equilibrium. In a free market, the organiser of a rock concert will have little direct incentive to limit noise pollution because it is external, and a profit-maximising firm will only take into account its own private costs. The market failure arising from negative externalities is shown in Figure 10.1.

Figure 10.1 shows that the marginal social cost of production is above the marginal private cost. Therefore there are external costs of production in this market, equal to the vertical distance between the two cost curves. The free-market equilibrium quantity demanded and supplied occurs where marginal private costs equal marginal benefits, that is, at Q1. However, the social equilibrium occurs where marginal social benefits equal the full costs of production, that is, where MSB crosses MSC, at Q2. Thus, if all costs to society were taken into account, the equilibrium quantity produced and consumed would fall to Q2, whilst price would rise to P2. Note that we are not saying that, using the chemical plant example, no chemicals should be produced, just that fewer should be produced if their production leads to environmental damage.

In a free market, there would be allocative inefficiency, because the socially optimal quantity is not being produced, and the price would not reflect the marginal cost to society. The extent of the welfare loss to society can be outlined in Figure 10.1, and is the difference between the cost to society of overproducing Q1 to Q2 and the value placed on this output by society (shown by the MSB curve). This difference is equal to the shaded triangle ABC.

Distributional effects

Environmental externalities can also create distributional problems. For example, in the case of global warming, the relatively poor citizens of developing countries are more likely to be significantly affected by flooding or drought and so on. They are less likely to have consumed the goods and services that are said to have contributed to global warming, whilst also being less likely to be able to afford to protect themselves or take insurance against localised flooding, for example. Thus we can say that there are inequities between those who contribute to global warming and those who suffer from it. Citizens of industrialised nations pay less for their goods and services than the social costs of their production.

An argument could therefore be made for imposing a tax on the output of industrialised nations, with the revenue used to compensate citizens of developing nations for their welfare loss.

■ Government intervention to correct environmental market failure

Economic measures to correct environmental market failure tend to be one of two types:

1 market-based measures, designed to modify the price mechanism using, for example, environmental taxes and subsidies

2 government regulation, sometimes referred to as 'command and control', designed to create incentives for firms to reduce harmful emissions, for example permits for factories to pollute up to a certain level.

Environmental taxation

An environmental tax is one placed on a good or service which is deemed to have a negative impact upon the environment. Environmental taxation is designed to 'internalise' any negative externality by increasing the private cost of production so that the producer and/or consumer is made to pay for some of the external costs. Environmental taxes thus seek to increase the firm's private marginal cost until it equals the social marginal cost curve, as can be seen in Figure 10.2.

Production levels should hopefully move towards the social optimum level, whilst revenues raised from environmental taxation could be used to fund spending on environmental clean-ups. Revenues could also be invested in developing new technologies that are designed to have low environmental impact, for example, 'clean' energy sources.

Examples of environmental taxes include fuel duty, air passenger duty, the landfill tax and the London Congestion Charge.

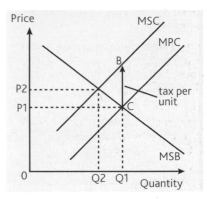

Figure 10.2 *Taxing negative externalities*

■ Case Study

Paying the price for environmental damage

Economists have argued that emissions of greenhouse gases such as CO_2 are best controlled by imposing a carbon tax.

In principle this seems simple – impose a tax on polluting firms according to the amount of emissions they release. Revenues raised from a carbon tax could be put to good use in developing low-carbon technologies and clean energy. This would create incentives for polluters, such as large power firms, to cut their emissions, whilst encouraging entrepreneurs to develop alternatives.

Revenues can easily be collected by the government using the existing tax system. However, some critics argue that a tax is too blunt an instrument, and will penalise certain sectors. A factory may be forced to reduce output in order to cut emissions, for example.

It is possible that a carbon tax would be politically difficult to pass, because of industry and pressure group resistance. However, those in favour say because it is universal it is not the same as distributing carbon credits.

Some critics believe, however, that polluting firms would attempt to pass on the increased cost to consumers rather than actually cutting emissions, though this would only work if consumers remained loyal despite rising prices, that is, if elasticity of demand was low. In addition, there is no guarantee that a government would spend tax revenues in the best way to encourage new low carbon technologies and cleaner energy sources.

Figure 10.3 *The Congestion Charge in Central London is an example of an environmental tax*

Problems with environmental taxation

There are a number of problems involved with using environmental taxation.

■ In practice it is very difficult to place an accurate monetary value on the environment and externalities, such as loss of habitat, resource depletion and consequences for human life. Thus there are clear problems in setting taxes so that marginal private costs are equal to marginal social costs.

■ Governments will also find it difficult to achieve a target reduction in total pollution, since they cannot be certain how consumers and firms will respond to increases in prices and costs. Price elasticities of demand and supply will not be known accurately and will vary over time.

■ If the demand for a product with an adverse environmental impact is inelastic, the imposition of an indirect tax may raise strong revenues, but only reduce equilibrium output slightly.

■ Imposing taxes on some demerit goods, such as cigarettes, may have a regressive effect in that they take a larger share of the incomes of low income consumers and thus may increase inequalities in the distribution of income.

■ Increasing environmental taxes in one country may reduce international competitiveness and encourage firms to shift production to countries with lower taxes. Perversely, this might serve to increase global pollution as firms take advantage of lighter environmental taxation elsewhere, for example in rapidly developing countries such as China and India.

Pollution regulation

Instead of using taxation, the government could regulate the level of output and pollution in a market. The government could set a quota it believes corresponds to the social optimum, or even impose a ban on certain pollution-generating activities. In the UK, the 1989 Environmental Protection Act set minimum environmental standards for a number of industries, including waste incineration and oil refining. Regulatory bodies such as Her Majesty's Inspectorate of Pollution monitor, that is, inspect, and fine firms that do not conform to the emissions standards that have been set. However, the monitoring system for environmental regulations can be expensive and difficult to enforce. In addition, regulation does not generate tax revenues that could be used to support environmental improvement schemes or compensate those who have been adversely affected by pollution.

Extending property rights

Externalities often occur because property rights are not fully allocated. A key problem relating to the environment is that commonly used resources such as the seas and the air around us are not privately owned and so no person or organisation takes responsibility if they are over-exploited. This is known as the **'tragedy of the commons'**.

Instead of using regulation and taxation, a government could create a market in property rights. 'Internalising' the externality in this way by, for example, setting up a tradeable pollution permit, could help limit the negative impacts of economic activity on the environment

Emissions trading has become a popular method of environmental protection in developed economies. A similar method of pollution control is carbon trading, which uses the signalling, rationing and incentive

Figure 10.4 *Can fly-tipping be solved with environmental taxation?*

functions of the price mechanism to influence the behaviour of producers and consumers.

With **pollution permits** the government sets a limit on the total level of pollution that is allowed and gives businesses the right to emit a given volume of pollution into the environment, designed to reflect the social equilibrium level of output. This will be where marginal social benefits equal marginal social costs, that is, at Q2 in Figure 10.5. Permits are then issued in an auction and polluting firms can bid for them as well as trade them with each other. Pollution permits should theoretically create an incentive for firms to reduce their emissions so that they are able to profit from the scheme. Evidence to date seems to favour pollution permits. For example, formerly high polluting firms have invested in new pollution control equipment, or 'cleaner' fuels. In addition, revenues raised from a pollution permit scheme can be used for other environmental schemes.

Case study

The Kyoto Protocol

The **Kyoto Protocol** was an international agreement signed by government representatives in 1997, designed to deal with some of the problems of climate change. Industrialised nations agreed to reduce emissions of greenhouse gases by over 5 per cent of 1990 levels by 2012. The Protocol allows carbon-trading between industrialised countries but worryingly, the US, which accounts for around a third of all carbon emissions, withdrew from the agreement in 2001. Rapidly developing countries such as China and India were also not bound by the Protocol, which seriously reduces the effectiveness of the agreement in reducing overall emissions.

Cost-benefit analysis (CBA)

Where major projects have important or controversial side effects, that is, where there are substantial spillover costs and benefits to third parties, **cost-benefit analysis (CBA)** is used as a means of decision-making. Cost-benefit analysis is thus a project appraisal technique that takes into account all costs and benefits of an economic decision. It is a technique that is used increasingly by governments in evaluating major investment projects.

The spillover costs and benefits upon third parties can be far-reaching and substantial. Cost-benefit analysis attempts to quantify the net cost or benefit to society of the various possible outcomes or sources of action, taking into account, as far as possible, their implications now and into the future.

The technique involves calculating **shadow prices** on costs and benefits where no market price is available, for example the loss of natural habitat or loss of agricultural land arising from a new house-building scheme in an attractive edge-of-city area.

The framework of cost-benefit analysis

There are four main stages to cost-benefit analysis.

- The first stage is to identify all of the relevant costs and benefits arising out of a particular project. These are divided into the private costs, private benefits, external costs and external benefits, as previously covered at AS. This is more difficult in reality than it seems. External costs and benefits are particularly hard to quantify, since investment projects may have wide-ranging consequences, affecting people beyond a specific location.

Activities

Suggest how property rights could be extended to deal with these environmental issues:

1 Burning of fossil fuels creating carbon emissions.

2 Pollution of waterways creating other externalities for users of waterways further downstream.

3 Logging of forests, for example, the Amazon rainforest.

4 Over-fishing of the oceans.

5 Fly-tipping of waste products on public land.

6 E-mail 'spamming' on the Internet.

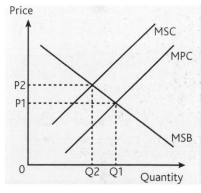

Figure 10.5 *Analysing pollution permits*

Key terms

Pollution permit: a right to emit a given volume of waste or pollution into the environment.

Kyoto Protocol: an agreement made at a global summit meeting in Kyoto, Japan, to cut world carbon emissions.

Cost-benefit analysis (CBA): an investment appraisal technique that takes into account all the private and external costs and benefits of an economic decision.

Shadow price: a price calculated to more accurately reflect the costs and benefits to society of a good, particularly where no market price has previously been calculated.

■ The second stage involves placing a monetary value on the various costs and benefits. This might be relatively straightforward where market prices are available, for example, on the jobs created or profits generated from building a toll bridge. For other variables, though, shadow prices must be calculated for costs and benefits where no market prices are available. For example, placing a value on time-savings as a result of widening a major motorway. Another example is how to put a monetary value on the cost of accidents, particularly where serious injuries or loss of life is involved.

■ The third stage involves the use statistical forecasting techniques, sometimes of a crude nature, to estimate costs and benefits over many years, where projects have long-lasting impacts. This applies particularly to projects where large-scale capital expenditure will be involved.

■ The final stage involves drawing together the data from the previous stages to compare social costs and social benefits. If the value of social benefits exceeds the value of social costs, then the project is worthwhile since it provides an overall net benefit to society.

Limitations of cost-benefit analysis

Whilst CBA provides a systematic approach to investment appraisal, in practice, the framework of cost-benefit analysis has a number of difficulties and limitations, for example, which costs and benefits to include, and how to put monetary values on them. Other problems include:

■ CBA may not fully reflect the distributional impacts of investment projects. In the case of a new shopping centre, external costs may be highly localised whilst external benefits, for example, job creation, are likely to be more widely spread.

■ Public sector projects are often controversial and may attract objection from pressure groups. The result of the cost-benefit analysis may be ignored for political reasons, with the eventual choice of project not being the one recommended by economists. While the CBA outcome may be ignored in favour of a sub-optimal project, the CBA process has at least obviated the important issues so that a decision can be taken on the basis of all the information available. In this case, CBA is an aid to decision-making and not a replacement for it.

■ In practice it is very difficult to accurately place a value on public goods, such as the environment, where there is no market established for the valuation of property rights. It will also be difficult to place a value on human life, though there are insurance markets which provide some information about how much people value their health and life.

AQA Examiner's tip

Whilst CBA allows governments to take a sophisticated view of the impact of major investment projects it does not mean that the technique is free from pitfalls.

Case study

Terminal 5 at Heathrow Airport

A new fifth terminal (T5) opened at the world's busiest international airport in 2008, heralded by an operational fiasco. In the run-up to the opening, the official cost-benefit analysis took five years and several million pounds to complete. Unsurprisingly, public debate over the opening of T5 has been fierce, with most arguments focusing on the likely negative environmental externalities, such as noise, increased pressure on local roads and reduced air quality. However, planning permission was granted and the cost-benefit analysis concluded that the new terminal project should go ahead.

Heathrow airport has around 90 airlines, which fly almost 70 million people a year to destinations around the globe. The airport provides thousands of jobs as well as crucial links between the UK and the world economy. It is central to the success of the economy of London and the south east. However, if Heathrow Airport was not allowed to grow, there were fears that the UK would lose out as international airlines and foreign firms relocated, for example, to mainland Europe. Whilst there were concerns about the environmental impact of T5, BAA, Heathrow's owners pointed out that it would be built on a disused brownfield site, and that any displaced flora and fauna would be carefully relocated. In addition, phasing out of older, noisier aircraft would keep any noise increases to a minimum.

After completing this chapter you should be able to:

▪ extend and develop the models of market failure introduced at AS

▪ discuss the causes of environmental market failure and the impact of environmental change on economic behaviour

▪ assess the consequences of the variety of government policies used to deal with environmental market failure

▪ understand the principles of cost-benefit analysis and evaluate the advantages and disadvantages of the approach.

Activities

Read the case study on Heathrow's Terminal 5, and answer the following questions:

1 Define the term 'cost-benefit analysis'.

2 Outline **two** external costs and **two** external benefits of the new terminal.

3 Discuss the usefulness of cost-benefit analysis in evaluating major investment projects such as Heathrow's fifth terminal.

Specimen Unit 3: The Global context
Study Extracts **A, B** and **C**, and then answer **all** parts of the question which follows.

Extract A
Global greenhouse gas emissions in 2000, by source
Table 1

Energy emissions	%	Non-energy emissions	%
Power	24	Land use	18
Transport	14	Agriculture	14
Buildings	8	Waste	3
Other energy related	5		

Energy emissions are mostly CO_2 (some non-CO_2 in industry and other energy related).
Non-energy emissions are CO_2 (land use) and non-CO_2 (agriculture and waste).

From official figures

Extract B

Climate change and global market failure

Greenhouse gases are, in economic terms, an externality. Economic activities that produce greenhouse gas emissions are bringing about climate change. Climate change imposes costs, both on the world today, and on future generations. However, the people responsible for greenhouse gas emissions do not themselves face the full consequences of their actions.

Climate change thus presents a unique challenge for economics; it is the greatest and widest-ranging market failure ever seen. If an appropriate price can be placed on carbon emissions, people will then be faced with the full social cost of their actions. This will cause individuals and businesses to switch away from goods and services associated with high carbon emissions, choosing instead low-carbon alternatives. Taxation and carbon trading can both be used to price carbon emissions. Pricing carbon emissions may then start to reduce the adverse economic effects of climate change.

The greenhouse gas emissions of most countries are small relative to the global total. A very large reduction in emissions is required to stabilise the concentration of greenhouse gases in the atmosphere. This means that the international management of common resources is needed to prevent countries free-riding. However, it will take many years before actions undertaken now to reduce climate change yield results. The long lead time means that costs are incurred in the short term, but the resulting benefits are long term.

Extract C

Climate change market could be worth billions to UK business

Introducing policies to reduce global warming could create a market valued at more than £25bn for UK businesses over the next ten years. Worldwide, the market created by concerted action to stop the rise in greenhouse gas emissions could be worth £750bn over the first five years alone. In the UK, the government will be mostly responsible for the climate change market growing so rapidly. Government action includes the extension of renewable energy schemes, the introduction of more environmentally friendly fuels and of measures to tackle the energy efficiency of the housing stock, and the tightening of building standards.

The introduction of new building regulations for industrial use and commercial use is expected to generate a market worth £950m by 2010. This will provide a big opportunity for smaller businesses. Other markets likely to grow include those for renewable electricity, biofuels for road transport and domestic energy efficiency. These markets are expected to grow by £800m, £500m and £400m respectively. There are many other ways in which private sector businesses are driving the climate change market.

1   (a)   Using Extract A, compare the contributions of energy emissions and non-energy emissions to total greenhouse gas emissions in 2000.   *(5 marks)*

       (b)   'Taxation and carbon trading can both be used to price carbon emissions' (Extract B). Explain how a government can use taxation and carbon trading to price carbon emissions.   *(10 marks)*

       (c)   Using the data and your economic knowledge, discuss whether government policies that aim to reduce the rate at which climate change is occurring benefit or harm UK firms.   *(25 marks)*

2   (a)   Explain how, by adversely affecting the environment, economic activity can lead to market failure.   *(15 marks)*

       (b)   Evaluate the view that government intervention can correct all the market failures caused by the effects of economic activity on the environment. *(25 marks)*

AQA, January 2005

AQA Examiner's tip   You may need to review your AS book on government failure to help you with Question 2, part (b). This is also a good example of a question where you can improve the quality of your answer with real-world examples.

The national and international economy

Introduction

Unit 4 builds on your AS knowledge of macroeconomic policies and objectives. Chapter 11 aims to broaden and deepen your understanding of what constitutes economic growth, along with the key determinants of growth. The phases and theories of economic cycles are presented, as are the potential costs of economic growth. The chapter then moves on to consider the usefulness of national income data as an indicator of living standards, and presents some modern alternative measures such as the Human Development Index. The challenge of 'sustainable' growth is also explained.

Chapter 12 begins with an explanation of how a consumer price index is constructed, and moves on to an in-depth explanation of the types and causes of inflation. To the demand-pull and cost-push causes introduced at AS is added a third cause – that of excessive growth of the money supply. This latter cause is presented in the context of the quantity theory of money. You will appreciate the various possible consequences of inflation, including reduced international competitiveness and redistribution of income. These are contrasted with the effects of deflation, and you will learn the difference between benign and malevolent forms of deflation.

In Chapter 13 we outline the differences between the key statistical measures of unemployment. The chapter then examines the types and causes of unemployment in considerable depth, contrasting between demand-side and supply-side causes. The various consequences of unemployment are assessed, and possible courses of action for governments to tackle them are presented. The concept of a 'natural rate' of unemployment is introduced, and the idea of a possible trade-off between unemployment and inflation is examined, in the context of the Phillips Curve model and its later expectations-augmented version.

Chapter 14 expands upon the aims of fiscal policy introduced at AS. However, the different types of taxes are explained, along with an examination of their effects, and their relative merits and demerits. The canons, or principles of a 'good' tax, which have their roots in Adam Smith's writings are illustrated. The significance of a government's budgetary stance is then outlined, with regard to the relative size of government spending and taxation, and subsequent impacts on aggregate demand. The chapter also outlines the limitations of fiscal policy as a demand-management tool and sets out the Labour government's fiscal rules, established to reinforce the credibility of fiscal policy. Since most supply-side policies are essentially fiscal in nature, the chapter moves on to recap the principles and effects of supply-side economics introduced at AS, whilst expanding upon some of the micro- and macroeconomic theories which underpin it.

Chapter 15 starts with a reflection upon what constitutes 'money' as we know it, and what the essential functions of money need to be. The difference between 'narrow' and 'broad' money definitions is then explained. The chapter then discusses the objectives and instruments of monetary policy, explaining in detail the modern monetary policy framework which has an operationally independent Bank of England at its heart. The theoretical framework of interest rate determination is simply outlined, as is the so-called 'transmission mechanism' of monetary policy. Monetary policy and, in particular, interest rates, are the key tool used today to influence aggregate demand in the UK economy.

Chapter 16 explains the process of globalisation, along with its implications and effects. At the heart of the process is the importance of international trade, and this along with key theories, such as David Ricardo's comparative and absolute advantage, are explained in detail. This develops the notions of specialisation and opportunity cost introduced at AS to the level of the individual country. However, whilst most economists are in no doubt about the benefits of unrestricted international trade, there are many examples of countries and trading blocs where methods of trade 'protection' are employed to protect domestic interests. The arguments for and against trade protection are thus outlined.

In Chapter 17 the key components of the balance of payments are outlined, though we continue to focus on the current account as the main indicator of a country's international competitiveness. We discuss the situations when a current account deficit might be considered to be a problem, along with possible solutions. The chapter also considers if a current account surplus is always desirable. As London has come to be regarded as the pre-eminent global financial centre, the chapter also reflects upon the economic importance of financial capital flows in and out of 'The City'.

Chapter 18 develops the international outlook of the previous two chapters and analyses the difference between the various types of exchange rate system. Using fairly straightforward demand and supply analysis, fixed, managed and freely floating exchange rate systems are analysed and evaluated. The euro represents the ultimate in a fixed exchange rate system and the chapter outlines the operation of a single currency along with its potential drawbacks.

Finally, Chapter 19 outlines some key background information about the European Union, including its major institutions such as the European Commission and European Central Bank, both of which will have some impact upon, and implication for, the UK economy. The main theoretical background of this chapter concentrates upon the nature of, and differences between, customs unions, free-trade areas, common markets and full economic union. The impact of the EU common external tariff will be analysed, along with the impacts of trade creation and trade diversion. The chapter could not be complete without a discussion of the effects of continued EU enlargement, both for the UK and accession countries.

11 Economic growth and the economic cycle

💡 ✅

Key terms

Recession: negative economic growth over two successive quarters.

Economic growth: an increase in the real output of the economy.

Long-term growth rate: the average rate of economic growth sustained over a period of time.

Real Gross Domestic Product (GDP) per capita: the total output of the economy in a year, divide by the size of the population, adjusted for inflation.

Material standard of living is much higher today than fifty or a hundred years ago, and this is a result of economic growth. By 2008, the UK economy had enjoyed over 60 quarters of unbroken economic growth since the last **recession** in 1992. What precisely is economic growth, what causes it, and is it always a completely beneficial phenomenon? Also, are national income statistics always a good indicator of the standard of living enjoyed by its citizens? Along with exploring these issues, this chapter also looks at the theory behind fluctuations in the economic cycle that seemed to be more pronounced a few decades ago.

The nature of economic growth

Economic growth may be defined as an increase in the real output of the whole economy. The **long-term growth rate** of the UK economy since the Second World War has been between 2.25 per cent to 2.5 per cent per year, a phenomenon usually linked to an increase in living standards.

The key statistic that is used to measure growth on an international basis is the change in **real Gross Domestic Product (GDP) per capita**. The UK's money (or nominal) GDP in 2007 was in excess of £1,000bn, which represents the value of all the income or expenditure or output generated in the UK economy in that year. Increases in money GDP then need to be adjusted for changes in (i) the general price level and (ii) the size of the population, in order to arrive at the change in real GDP per capita.

Activity

If money GDP in country A rises from £500bn to £600bn in a year and prices and population size both increase by 10 per cent, what is the change in real GDP per capita?

Although the level of real output may be increasing each year, that level will very probably be within the economy's full employment potential level of output. We therefore make a distinction between **actual GDP growth** and **potential GDP growth**. Figure 11.1 shows both potential and actual growth occurring. An outward shift of the Production possibility boundary (PPB) represents potential growth, whilst a move from point A to point B represents actual growth. It is possible for potential growth to occur without actual growth taking place. For example, the labour force of a nation may increase due to immigration, but if there is no demand for this factor, output will not rise.

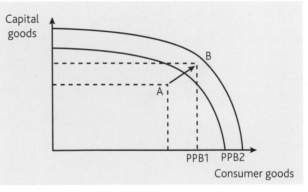

Figure 11.1 *Potential and actual growth*

The difference between the actual level of output and the full potential level is known as the **output gap**. This is where the economy is operating within its PPB. The gap represents the waste of resources arising from unemployment of scarce resources. In a recession, when actual GDP falls on a short-term basis, the output gap can be substantial.

When we consider a country's economic growth record we are looking at a long-term trend, that is, average GDP growth per year over a decade or more. This long-term average increase in GDP is often referred to as the **trend rate of economic growth**. This trend rate does not, however, tell us anything about the extent of any **economic cycle** fluctuations in GDP, which are the short-term increases and decreases in real GDP from year to year. These are highlighted in Figure 11.2.

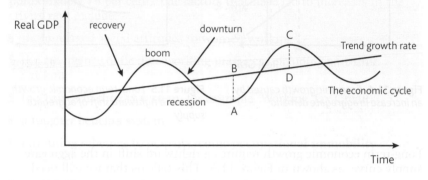

Figure 11.2 *The trend growth rate and the economic cycle*

We will consider the causes, difficulties and cures for economic cycle fluctuations later, but a government will clearly wish to maximise the long-term trend rate of economic growth, whilst minimising short-term fluctuations.

The UK's economic growth record

Figure 11.3 shows fluctuations in economic growth from 1990 to the present. You can identify the last period of recession from 1990 to 1992, when economic growth was negative.

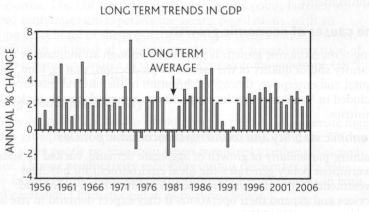

HSBC UK Economy explained

Figure 11.3 *The UK's growth record, 1956–2006*

Generating economic growth

If an economy is operating below its potential output, an increase in aggregate demand will cause a rise in equilibrium national output. Figure

Governments can have a key role in helping to generate high levels of top-quality, well-managed capital investment. Unsurprisingly, most of them are key elements of modern supply-side economics:

■ Lower taxation of business profits and business wealth

■ Tax relief for high spending on research and development

■ Promoting links between businesses and universities

■ Reforming trade union legislation, to make businesses easier to manage

■ Privatisation, opening up businesses to Stock Exchange discipline and sources of finance

■ Tougher competition policy

■ Encouraging foreign investment into the UK, bringing 'best practice' from our main international competitors

■ Encouraging macroeconomic stability (Gordon Brown's 'end to boom and bust').

Improved human capital – education and training

A world-class workforce has knowledge, skills and motivation. The first two of these require investment in education and training. An educated and skilled workforce will be more productive and thus help to generate economic growth, though investment in education and training is unlikely to yield immediate improvements in growth prospects.

In the UK there has been concern about the relatively poor educational standards of much of the school population. Reforms over many years in primary and secondary education, along with an expansion of numbers in tertiary education, have been intended to help, for example, the development of a National Curriculum, strategies for numeracy and literacy and the publication of school league tables. The government's target is to have 50 per cent of people under the age of 30 having passed through tertiary education by 2010. Education is likely to become increasingly important in the future as patterns of output and employment change increasingly rapidly. Strong future economic growth will need an increasingly 'flexible' labour force.

Enterprise

Generating strong motivation and a culture of enterprise is important, and will have a direct relationship with quality of management, along with a pro-business culture in society and appropriate tax reforms.

Advantages and disadvantages of economic growth

Economic growth can have both benefits and costs.

Advantages

The obvious benefit of economic growth is a rise in the material standard of living of households. Increasing real GDP per capita means that, on average, the population can enjoy more goods and services. Whilst developing countries are desperate to raise their output so that their people have enough food, housing and other necessities, most of the developed world also has an increasing range of luxury goods and services. Thus economic growth enables a country to reduce, if not eliminate, absolute poverty. In addition, economic growth raises tax revenue without having to raise tax rates, as national income increases, and some of this can be used to finance schemes to help the poor. Increased tax revenues can also be used to provide important public and

Figure 11.6 *Training and education are key foundations of economic growth*

merit goods, such as policing, education and health care as well as to correct negative spillover effects upon the environment.

Disadvantages

Economic growth can have costs, however. A fully employed economy, producing on its production possibility boundary, can only increase output by transferring resources from producing consumer goods and services to producing capital goods. In the short run, fewer consumer goods and services will be produced. However, in the long run, the extra capital goods will enable more consumer goods to be made. This is sometimes referred to as the choice between 'jam today, versus jam tomorrow'. Economic growth may be at the expense of negative externalities, such as environmental damage, if rapid industrial development is allowed without pollution controls. There are such fears about the rapid development of the Chinese and Indian economies. Economic growth may result in the depletion of non-renewable resources, such as oil.

Economic growth is also unlikely to benefit everyone equally. There may be some upheaval and stress as some people are forced to acquire new skills or change jobs, whilst the pace of work may also increase. While economic growth has the potential to reduce poverty, it may make some of the poor worse off. The gap between the rich and poor may increase, increasing the extent of relative poverty. In addition, having more goods and services does not guarantee happiness, instead creating a desire for even more goods and services and a feeling of discontent with one's lot. Some years ago most households were happy with one car, now many have two and some aspire to own more.

■ Uses of National income data

You may see references to three different terms for measuring the size of an economy:

- GDP = **Gross domestic product**
- GNP = **Gross national product**
- NI = **National income**

The measures are very similar for our purposes, and it doesn't really matter which is used provided there is consistency when making comparisons, though GDP is the more commonly used measure. If we add net property income from abroad (that is, interest, profits and dividends flowing into the country minus those flowing out) to GDP, we get to GNP. GNP minus depreciation of the nation's stock of capital equipment (a difficult to measure concept sometimes known as capital consumption) equals NI.

Difficulties in using GDP as a measure of living standards

GDP incompletely measures output

GDP statistics only measure the value of goods and services produced that are recorded as having been traded in markets. So they exclude the **non-monetised sector** of the economy including the unpaid labour of parents choosing to stay at home and the value of DIY. Even though these services add to the nation's output, because they are not traded in markets, their value is not included. They also omit the 'black' or informal economy, which is estimated at 10 per cent to 15 per cent of UK output. This is likely to be much higher in countries that have a greater tendency towards subsistence and where the framework for recording market activity is less developed.

AQA Examiner's tip

The Unit 4 specification requires candidates to be able to analyse and evaluate the various costs and benefits of economic growth. Use of a PPB and negative externality diagram will be useful tools here.

■ Activity

Write a list of all the potential negative externalities you can think of that may arise from economic growth.

■ Key terms

Gross domestic product (GDP): output produced by resources within the UK.

Gross national product (GNP): output produced by resources within the UK, plus net property income from abroad.

National income: output produced by resources within the UK, plus net property income from abroad, minus depreciation of the nation's capital equipment.

Non-monetised sector: valuable economic activity where no money changes hands.

AQA Examiner's tip

The limitations of national income statistics in measuring living standards over time and between different countries are important issues at A2. For the exam, try to remember at least three of the limitations outlined in this section.

GDP doesn't take account of quality improvements

If the quantity and price of computers, cars or clothes purchased stays the same, but their quality improves, for example, through technological progress, GDP figures will not pick up these improvements and therefore will tend to understate any welfare gains. Indeed, the prices of many computers have fallen in real terms whilst their capabilities have improved.

Distribution of income

It is possible for real GDP per capita to rise and yet for the distribution of income to become more unequal and for some families to have become poorer. Many believe that economic growth is maximised in societies which reward enterprise and success and penalise economic failure. This may not make for a healthy economic system and may promote the development of an 'underclass'. The USA is often criticised on this front. Whilst the USA is the world's largest economy in GDP terms, several sections of the population have not benefited equally from economic growth.

GDP ignores the amount and value of leisure

Leisure is crucial to people's welfare, and over recent decades most people have enjoyed longer holidays and a shorter working week. Even so, there has been comment recently about the UK eroding people's leisure time in pursuit of economic growth. A recent study showed the number of people working more than 48 hours a week had risen from 2.7 million to 4 million over the previous 15 years, and that British workers have the longest working week in Europe; 44 hours compared with the European average of around 42 hours. The stresses and strains of producing an ever-higher national output may lead to a loss of leisure time, and increased illness, leading to a loss of welfare.

Negative externalities

The pursuit of economic growth may deplete stocks of non-renewable resources or lead to increased levels of pollution and congestion. Indeed, the building of a road will add to GDP figures even if it goes through an area of outstanding natural beauty. Thus national income statistics will tend to overstate living standards.

GDP figures take no account of what is being produced

The USA spends a relatively high percentage of its GDP on defence and prisons. These may not contribute to happiness in the same way as consumer goods and services, though people may value national security and a low-crime environment highly.

Comparing national income between countries

International comparisons of national income per head will be unreliable if there are differences in the relative importance of non-monetised activity. This is compounded by differences in the depth of statistical data collection, particularly between developed and developing countries. There is also a lack of international agreement about how to classify and categorise items in national income accounts.

Accepting these difficulties, GNP per capita in different countries can be compared by converting GNP figures for each country into a common currency, with the US dollar typically used. The accuracy of such calculations suffer from the assumption that the exchange rates between local currencies and the dollar are correctly valued. However, the purchasing power of a currency may be difficult to compare internationally. Thus **purchasing power parity** (PPP) exchange rates are used. PPP exchange rates take into account how much a typical basket of goods in one country costs compared to another.

Figure 11.7 *The value of DIY is not measured in national income statistics*

■ Key terms

Purchasing power parity: exchange rates that take into account how much a typical basket of goods in one country costs compared to another country.

Alternatives to national income as a measure of economic welfare

Since there are a number of problems with using national income statistics to compare standards of living over time and between countries, other methods are becoming increasingly popular, which place less emphasis on GDP or GNP. Recent attempts to adjust conventional national income figures include the United Nations, **Human Development Index** (HDI), the **Human Poverty Index** (HPI), the **Measure of Domestic Progress** (MDP) and the **Misery Index**.

Human Development Index (HDI)

The Human Development Index (HDI) is calculated from the average of three indicators:

■ standard of living, measured by real GNP per capita, in US$ (PPP)

■ life expectancy at birth, in years

■ educational attainment, measured by a weighted average of adult literacy and enrolment ratio in schools and colleges.

The maximum value of the HDI is 1. The closer a country's HDI is to this, the greater its human development in terms of these three indicators. Table 11.1 shows the HDI of the top 10 and bottom 5 ranked nations. The UK was ranked sixteenth in 2007.

Table 11.1 *Human Development Index, 2007*

Country	Life expectancy index	Education index	GDP index	Human development index
Top 10				
1 Iceland	0.941	0.978	0.985	0.968
2 Norway	0.913	0.991	1.000	0.968
3 Australia	0.931	0.993	0.962	0.962
4 Canada	0.921	0.991	0.970	0.961
5 Ireland	0.890	0.993	0.994	0.959
6 Sweden	0.925	0.978	0.965	0.956
7 Switzerland	0.938	0.946	0.981	0.955
8 Japan	0.954	0.946	0.959	0.953
9 Netherlands	0.904	0.988	0.966	0.953
10 France	0.919	0.982	0.954	0.952
Bottom 5				
173 Mali	0.469	0.282	0.390	0.380
174 Niger	0.513	0.267	0.343	0.374
175 Guinea-Bissau	0.347	0.421	0.353	0.374
176 Burkina Faso	0.440	0.255	0.417	0.370
177 Sierra Leone	0.280	0.381	0.348	0.336

The Human Poverty Index (HPI)

The Human Poverty Index (HPI) is published annually by the United Nations and emphasises four dimensions of human life: longevity, knowledge, economic provision and social inclusion. The UK has not compared favourably with other developed nations, ranking only fifteenth in the 2004 version.

The Measure of Domestic Progress (MDP)

The Measure of Domestic Progress (MDP) is published by the New Economics Foundation as a reflection of how closely GDP actually mirrors the progress of the quality of life of British households. Taking account of some of the problems involved with using GDP as a measure of living standards, the MDP factors in the social and environmental costs of growth and benefits of unpaid work, such as household labour; both currently excluded from official GDP statistics. According to a recent report, UK GDP has increased 80 per cent in the last three decades, whilst MDP has been more erratic, and actually fell in the 1980s. The MDP argues that social costs have increased six-fold, along with spiralling costs of crime and the increasingly negative impact of family breakdown.

The Misery Index (MI)

Another indicator of economic welfare is pessimistically known as the Misery Index (MI), invented by the economist Robert Barro. The MI is arrived at fairly simply by adding the unemployment rate to the inflation rate, on the assumption that a combination of higher unemployment and higher inflation means a higher level of economic and social costs for a country. In recent UK history, according to this indicator, misery or unhappiness peaked in 1975, falling steadily thereafter.

Case study

Quality of life gets a higher profile

A radical move to extend the yardstick of progress from economic output alone to quality of life measures, such as education, pollution, and even the number of birds in the countryside, was yesterday unveiled by the government. A series of 13 new headline indicators (see below) intended to reflect everyday concerns will for the first time allow the Government's performance to be judged not only by growth rates but by the effect of policies on the environment and social welfare.

Launching the indicators yesterday, the Deputy Prime Minister, John Prescott, said, 'Sustainable development links the standard of living and the quality of life, not just in Britain, but right across the world.' Charles Secrett, Executive Director of Friends of the Earth, said, 'Often policy has been driven by the idea that more is always better…'

The 13 quality of life indicators:

Economic growth: Total output of the economy. Standard measure is gross domestic product (GDP). Since 1970 output has increased by 80 per cent in real terms.

Social investment: Measures investment in 'public assets' such as railways, buses, roads, hospitals, schools, water and sewerage. Accounts for 10 per cent of all capital spending and about 2 per cent of GDP.

Employment: Income enables individuals to improve living standards. Since 1994, the employment rate has increased slowly to 73 per cent of the population of working age.

Health: Average life expectancy is now around 74 years for men and 79 for women, but the time people can expect to live in good health is some years less.

Education and training: Based on qualifications at age 19.

Housing quality: Measures numbers of homes unfit to live in. In 1996, the private rented sector had the highest proportion of unfit stock – 15.1 per cent.

Climate change: Based on greenhouse gas emissions. UK emissions of the 'basket' of greenhouse gas fell by 5 per cent between 1990 and 1996.

Air pollution: In urban areas, the average number of days when pollution was recorded as moderate or worse fell from 62 days in 1993 to 40 in 1997.

Transport: Motor vehicle traffic in 1997 was more than 8 times the level in 1950, and car traffic was over 14 times higher.

Water quality: According to number of rivers of good or fair quality – currently 95 per cent of UK river network.

Wildlife: Based on population of wild birds – regarded as a good indicator of wildlife and the health of the wider environment. Populations of farmland and woodland birds have been in decline since the mid-1970s.

Land use: New homes built on previously developed land. In England, about 55 per cent of homes are built on brownfield sites, against a government target of 60 per cent by 2008.

Waste: An estimated 145 million tonnes of waste are produced in the UK each year, of which over 60 per cent are disposed of in landfill sites.

*Adapted from **Lucy Ward**, The Guardian, 24 November 1998*

Is economic growth sustainable?

Few people would argue in favour of zero economic growth. However, one current major issue, which lies at the heart of the Green Party's philosophy, is whether economic growth on a world scale is sustainable, that is, whether the pursuit of maximum growth today will impose costs on future generations that outweigh any benefits.

In 1987 the World Commission on Environment and Development defined sustainable development as that which meets 'the needs of the present generation without compromising the needs of future

AQA Examiner's tip

The Unit 4 specification states that candidates should be able to discuss issues relating to the sustainability of economic growth.

generations'. Put simply, economic growth today must not cause such destruction of the environment and depletion of raw material supplies that future generations will suffer substantial reductions in quality of life.

Some commentators argue that there are three main threats to **sustainability**:

Exhaustion of resources. In 1972 the Club of Rome's 'Limits to Growth' report argued that the world's mineral resources, including crude oil, are in finite supply and would be completely exhausted within 100 years. In 1992, the same authors warned that if the world's population reached 10bn, growth would become unsustainable and growth would become negative.

However, microeconomic theory would predict that as resources become increasingly scarce, with demand rising relative to supply, their market prices will rise. The market mechanism will help to deliver a solution via three effects:

1 Cause consumers to change their behaviour, for example, more fuel-efficient cars or homes

2 Increases in supply of, for example, oil as firms now find it profitable to exploit new, relatively expensive oil fields

3 Firms find it profitable to invest resources in substitute technologies, for example, solar power.

Governments can speed up the process via the use of indirect taxation.

Environmental damage. Economic growth seems inevitably to involve increasing industrial emissions, as well as huge piles of waste. However, as wealthy voters become increasingly interested in quality of life issues and governments introduce regulations, bans and tax incentives, businesses will look for products and processes that emphasise their eco-friendly credentials.

Global warming. Greenhouse gas emissions are linked to economic growth and are rising at an alarming rate. There is currently no realistic future prospect of fossil fuel burning not being the main engine of growth and the problem is going to get much worse as China and India industrialise rapidly.

The economic costs of global warming are very unclear, but may include (i) rising sea levels, leading to loss of agricultural land, population displacement and the cost of flood defences, (ii) structural adjustment problems for countries heavily involved in agriculture as climate changes and (iii) increasing storm damage.

There appear to be grounds for more pessimism on this issue as there seems little prospect of slowing the growth of CO_2 emissions in the near future, let alone reducing them. The Kyoto Protocol of 1997, later turned into an agreement by most industrialised nations, requires countries to make modest reductions in 1990 CO_2 levels by 2010. However, the USA refuses to ratify the Protocol, and accounts for 25 per cent of all greenhouse gas emissions. Also, rapidly industrialising countries such as China and India, with huge populations, are excluded from the Kyoto process.

The challenge of sustainability is seen as the main threat to future world economic growth. Whilst there are grounds for optimism on two of the above counts, global warming has raised questions for which we do not currently have satisfactory answers. Without conclusive scientific evidence it will be difficult to induce great urgency, though there is an increasing political weight behind global warming issues.

The economic cycle

Economic cycles, sometimes referred to as business cycles or trade cycles, describe the tendency for economic activity to fluctuate around its trend growth rate, moving from a high level of economic activity to negative growth and back again. There have been two recessions in the UK during the last 30 years. The first recession occurred between 1979 and 1981. The second recession occurred a decade later between 1990 and 1992. Both recessions raised unemployment considerably, but were followed by longer periods of recovery and boom throughout the rest of the 1980s and 1990s. However, less pronounced economic cycles (where the rate of annual growth simply decelerates in the downturn phase) can still be identified even if there is not a technical recession.

Figure 11.2 shows two complete economic cycles, together with a line showing the economy's trend, or long-run, growth rate. Actual growth, which is measured by the percentage change in real GDP over a 12-month period, varies in the different phases of the economic cycle. In the cycle's recovery phase, growth is positive, but, as Figure 11.2 shows, growth becomes negative if and when a recession occurs in the cycle.

Although, at the time of writing, there has not been a recession since 1992, the length of a cycle depends on the dates at which actual and trend growth rates converge. The choice of dates is important because the government's ability to meet its fiscal policy rules (explained in Chapter 14) depends on when the economic cycle starts and ends.

Phases of the economic cycle

Four phases of the economic cycle are identified, as illustrated in Figure 11.2.

Recovery. This can also be referred to as the upswing or upturn phase. During this phase, economic activity increases because there is optimism about prospects for the future. Consumer spending increases and firms are more keen to invest. Subsequently, employment rises, creating a further stimulus to spending and output. Some of the extra consumption and investment will be financed by increases in bank lending.

Boom. This is the peak of economic activity, where unemployment is low and economic growth is high as existing firms expand and new ones are created. However, after a point it is not possible for output to rise to meet the increasing levels of aggregate demand. As supply is not sufficient to meet aggregate demand, the economy overheats, resulting in inflation and **balance of payments** problems.

Downturn. Also referred to as a downswing. This is the phase when economic growth starts to fall below its trend rate. High inflation from the boom phase leads to reduced international price competitiveness causing some domestic firms to make output cutbacks whilst others go out of business. The government may also implement deflationary demand-side policies. The subsequent fall in economic growth along with rising unemployment is likely to reduce confidence about the future, causing households and firms to reduce their spending and investment plans.

Recession. A recession is a period of negative growth of real GDP over the course of at least six months. In this phase aggregate demand falls, whilst unemployment accelerates. The economy may even move into a depression or slump, which is a more prolonged period of falling output. Eventually, falling economic activity ceases and the economy moves into recovery. One reason for this is the constraint on demand. At some point households and firms have to raise their spending in order to replace

Link

See Chapter 10 on environmental market failure for more background information on these issues.

Key terms

Balance of payments: a record of the financial transactions over a period of time between a country and its trading partners.

such items as worn-out televisions, cars and capital equipment. Also, during a recession, net government spending is likely to rise. This may occur automatically as the lower level of economic activity will cause tax revenues to fall while government spending, especially on unemployment benefit, rises. It may also be the result of a deliberate government spending increase and/or cut in tax rates designed to boost aggregate demand.

Explanations of the economic cycle

Several demand and supply-side factors may cause or contribute to economic cycles.

Speculative 'bubbles'

Rapid economic growth can lead to a rapid rise and speculative 'bubble' in asset prices, as people seek to acquire assets whose value is increasing, for example, shares or houses. When people eventually realise that the prices of such assets have risen considerably above their real values, they will tend to sell them in an attempt to realise a profit before it is too late. This causes the speculative 'bubble' to burst, destroying consumer and business confidence. If households and firms stop spending, the economy may fall into recession.

Changes in inventories

As well as capital equipment, firms also invest in stocks of raw materials and stocks of finished goods ready to be sold, in order to ensure that there are no interruptions in production and to guard against fluctuations in demand. This type of investment is termed **inventory investment** or **stock-building**. Although inventory investment accounts for a very small percentage of GDP, fluctuations in inventories can be an important determinant of recessions. Changes in inventories can trigger and exacerbate economic cycles. Stocks of unsold finished goods build up when firms are too optimistic about demand for their products. The knock-on effect is that they are then forced to cut production by more than the original fall in demand. This 'de-stocking' can turn a slowdown into a recession.

Political cycles

In democracies such as the UK, the political party in power may attempt to engineer a boom in economic activity in the run-up to an election in order to secure votes. Once the election is over, the ruling party may then deflate aggregate demand to avoid **demand-pull inflation**. The pattern is repeated for the next general election.

Outside 'shocks'

These can be divided into 'demand shocks', affecting aggregate demand, and 'supply shocks', affecting aggregate supply. In some cases, an outside shock may bring both demand-side and supply-side shocks. For example, storm damage caused by hurricane activity in the Gulf of Mexico has led to reduced demand in southern US states, whilst also affecting the supply of crude oil, raising the price of oil and thus raising production costs across many economic sectors.

The multiplier/accelerator model

Keynesian economists have argued that economic cycles may be caused by the interaction of two processes known as the multiplier and the accelerator.

The **accelerator theory** of investment is that investment is determined by past changes in income. If national income is growing, this will tend

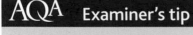

Examiner's tip

Ensure you are familiar with two or three causes of economic cycles.

■ Key terms

Inventory investment/stock-building: investment by firms in stocks of raw materials and stocks of finished goods ready to be sold.

Demand-pull inflation: inflation resulting from too much demand in the economy, relative to supply capacity.

Accelerator theory: the theory that the level of investment is related to past changes in national income.

to stimulate investment. This increase in investment will lead to an overall greater increase in national income via the **multiplier effect**. This leads to a further boost to investment, and the process repeats itself. However, if national income falls, this will tend to depress investment, and the **multiplier/accelerator model** will work in the opposite direction.

After completing this chapter you should be able to:

- analyse and evaluate the causes of changes in the various phases of the economic cycle, including demand-side and supply-side shocks
- analyse and evaluate the supply-side factors that are likely to determine the long-run trend rate of growth, such as investment, technology, education and training
- analyse and evaluate the various costs and benefits of economic growth
- discuss issues relating to the sustainability of economic growth
- evaluate the impact of growth on individuals, the economy and the environment
- discuss the use and limitations of national income data to draw conclusions on living standards
- interpret alternative measures of living standards, such as the Human Development Index.

Key terms

Multiplier effect: a change in one of the components of aggregate demand leads to a greater overall change in national income.

Multiplier/accelerator model: a model which describes how the interaction of the accelerator theory and multiplier effect lead to changes in national income.

The Global Context

Study Extracts **A, B** and **C**, and then answer **all** parts of the question which follows.

Extract A

Actual and forecast growth of GDP, UK 1997–2006 (annual % change)

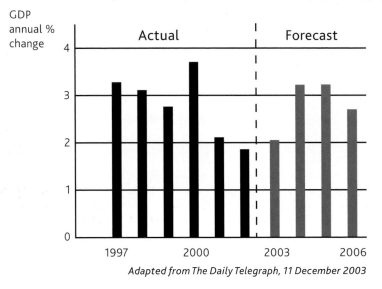

Adapted from The Daily Telegraph, 11 December 2003

Extract B

Causes and consequences of faster economic growth

There is a range of requirements for achieving faster economic growth. Saving needs to be stimulated in order to finance the investment needed for economic growth. Research and development (R&D) also need to be increased and high-technological industries targeted, perhaps with the help of government funding. Free international trade must be encouraged to allow exploitation of comparative advantage through specialisation. Improvements in the quality of education and training are also desirable. Finally, the economic climate needs to be favourable, both nationally and internationally, and appropriate demand-management policies will be crucial here.

The benefits of the faster growth thus achieved will be evident for all to see: increased consumption possibilities, including greater welfare and support for the disadvantaged; more expenditure on education, health, roads and housing; and improvements in other macroeconomic indicators. Such benefits must be central to the growth debate to help balance the views of those who believe that the costs, such as the rapid depletion of natural resources, environmental degradation, and a poorer quality of life, are much greater.

Extract C

British is best

While America, Japan and half the Eurozone have suffered recessions, the British economy has, uniquely, grown uninterrupted for every single quarter since 1997.

Growth in our biggest trading area, the Eurozone, is expected to be just 0.5 per cent in 2003. In the UK, real GDP growth is now expected to be 2.1 per cent. This is close to the government's estimate of the UK economy's trend rate of growth and means a minimal output gap. Clearly, stronger growth elsewhere would improve the UK's growth prospects and allow the fullest exploitation of its supply-side improvements.

Adapted from the Pre-Budget Report, HM Treasury, December 2003

1   (a)   Using Extract **A**, describe the actual and forecast growth performance of the UK economy for the period 1997 to 2006. *(5 marks)*

      (b)   Extract **B** (line 1) refers to the 'requirements for achieving faster economic growth'. Analyse **three** causes of a more rapid rate of economic growth in economies such as the UK and USA. *(10 marks)*

      (c)   Using the data and your economic knowledge, evaluate the economic consequences of a sustained, high rate of economic growth. *(25 marks)*

AQA, June 2005

2   (a)   Explain the main causes of economic growth. *(15 marks)*

      (b)   A recent EU survey reported that income per head was significantly lower in Greece and Portugal than in the Netherlands and Ireland. Evaluate the view that living standards in the Netherlands and Ireland must therefore be higher than those in Greece and Portugal. *(25 marks)*

AQA, June 2006

AQA Examiner's tip   Whilst Question 2, part (a) largely requires you to demonstrate a sound theoretical understanding of the various determinants of economic growth, Question 2, part (b) gives an excellent starting point for a technical and evaluative debate about the validity of national income statistics as a measure of economic welfare.

12 Inflation and deflation

In this chapter you will learn:

- that inflation is calculated using a weighted index of a 'basket' of goods and services

- that inflation has a range of demand-side and supply-side causes, which can come from both domestic and external sources

- that high inflation brings with it a range of largely negative consequences, especially if inflation is unanticipated

- that a falling price level may also have negative economic consequences.

Link

Look at Inflation in *AQA Economics AS*, p128.

Key terms

Deflation: a fall in the general price level.

Inflation: a sustained increase in the general price level.

Consumer price index (CPI): the headline measure of inflation, derived from movements in a weighted basket of consumer goods over a 12-month period.

Family Expenditure Survey: a representative monthly survey of UK household expenditure used to derive changes in the consumer price index (CPI).

Inflation was introduced at AS as a sustained increase in the general price level. It seems that, particularly since 1997, control of inflation has been made the key focus of macroeconomic management. In this chapter, we consider how an inflation index is calculated, and the causes and consequences of inflation in depth. We will also consider the issues surrounding **deflation**, or a fall in the general price level.

Inflation

Inflation is defined as a sustained increase in the general price level. The most common way of measuring this in the UK is to consider movements in the published **consumer price index (CPI)**. When the rate of inflation is published, what we mean is the percentage increase in the CPI over the previous 12 months, that is, we are measuring annual inflation. Our study of microeconomics tells us that prices in different markets are always changing relative to one another in response to supply and demand pressures, with some prices rising and others falling. With inflation we are describing a general movement upwards. The government's current target for CPI inflation is 2.0 per cent (+/− 1 per cent). This target range of 1 per cent to 3 per cent recognises that it is very difficult to accurately hit the central target of 2 per cent, and gives some room for manoeuvre. Figure 12.1 shows recent data for UK inflation using both consumer price index and retail price index (RPI) measures. Whilst the RPI takes into account the vast majority of items that consumers purchase, the CPI excludes a number of categories of expenditure, notably housing costs.

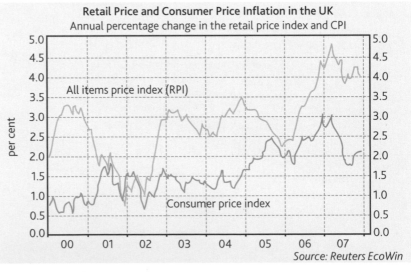

Figure 12.1 *UK Inflation*

The consumer price index (CPI)

The consumer price index (CPI) is a weighted price index used to measure the change in the prices of a typical 'basket' of goods and services. The categories of spending which make up this 'basket', along with their weights, are changed subtly each year using information from the **Family Expenditure Survey**. Changes in the weights attached to certain types of spending in the CPI reflect changes in the spending behaviour of UK households. In 2008, fruit smoothies, muffins and USB (Universal Serial Bus) drives were included for the first time in the CPI measure, whilst microwave ovens, 35mm camera film and CD singles have been removed. The consumer price index is used as the main official measure of inflation in the UK, reflecting the harmonised index of consumer prices (HICP) measure used in mainland Europe.

The shopping crunch

Research by the website Mysupermarket.co.uk suggested the price of an average shopping basket rose 11 per cent in the year to April 2008.

Table 12.1 *The average shopping basket*

Product	Price April 2007	Price April 2008	% Increase
Fusilli pasta 500g	£0.37	£0.67	87
Fresh chicken 1.5kg	£2.00	£3.54	77
British beef mince 500g	£1.00	£1.64	64
English butter 250g	£0.58	£0.94	62
Medium free-range eggs (12)	£1.75	£2.45	40
French baguette	£0.49	£0.65	33
Basmati rice 1kg	£0.90	£1.19	32
Mild cheddar 250g	£1.21	£1.52	26
Pure orange juice 1ltr	£0.72	£0.88	22
Semi-skimmed milk 3.4ltr	£1.68	£1.96	17

www.mysupermarket.co.uk, accessed on 15 April 2008

Calculating a weighted price index

The hypothetical example in Table 12.1 shows how to calculate a weighted price index.

Table 12.2 *Calculating a weighted price index*

Category	Price Index	Weighting (%)	Price × weight
Food	106	25	2650
Housing	112	25	2800
Clothing	98	15	1470
Transport	109	15	1635
Leisure	107	10	1070
Other items	103	10	1030
		100	10655

Government statisticians use the Family Expenditure Survey to discover what UK households spend their money on. This spending is divided into 14 categories and each category is 'weighted' according to its relative importance as a proportion of total spending. If, for example, 25 per cent of household spending is on food, this category will be given a weighting of 25/100 or 25 per cent. This weighting is then multiplied by the price index for a given year. To work out the price index for this year in the simplified example in Table 12.1, we firstly multiply all the price indices by their respective weights, which equals 10,655. We then divide this by the total of the weights, which we would usually expect to be 100. The price index for this year is thus 106.6 (to one decimal place). Use a calculator to check this for yourself.

Activities

Refer to Tables 12.1 and 12.2. Recalculate the price index if:

1 The index of food prices grew to 120.

2 Cheaper imports reduced the clothing price index to 95.

3 Increased car ownership increased the weighting of transport to 18 per cent, whilst the weighting of the 'other items' index fell by 4 per cent.

Activity

Discuss the view that, because the consumer price index (CPI) is not fully representative of the prices facing all households, it is therefore **not** a useful indicator.

Using index numbers

Economists make regular use of index numbers. These are straightforward to use as long as you are confident in calculating percentage changes. If we take the following (made up) index of house prices:

2005	100.0
2006	108.4
2007	120.0

2005 has been chosen as the starting point (also known as the base year), and this is given an index value of 100.0. By 2006 in this example, house prices had risen by 8.4 per cent compared with 2005, and so the index value for 2006 is 108.4. By 2007, house prices have risen by 20 per cent compared with 2005 and so the index value for 2007 is 120.0. It is easy to work out the relationship of every subsequent year with the base year, and the percentage change can easily be worked out without the aid of a calculator.

However, care is needed to calculate the percentage change between 2006 and 2007. The percentage change is not simply the numerical difference between 108.4 and 120.0. The percentage change calculation of $(120.0 - 108.4) \div 108.4 \times 100 = 10.7$ per cent must be worked out.

Limitations of the consumer price index as a measure of inflation

Although the CPI is the government's official indicator of consumer price inflation for the UK economy, there are some limitations in its usefulness.

- Different population groups experience different rates of inflation. Since the CPI is a reflection of the 'average' household's spending patterns, it will therefore not be representative of individual households, particularly 'non-typical' households. The weighting towards tobacco and motoring expenses will, for example, be irrelevant for non-smokers and those without a car.

- The CPI does not include house prices in its calculation, even though mortgage payments will represent a high proportion of the spending of younger house buyers. However, many older home owners may have paid off their mortgages.

- The CPI may over-estimate inflation. Price rises may hide improvements in the quality of goods and services. Prices of many cars and electrical goods have fallen in real terms over the last 30 years, whilst new innovations have made them significantly different to (and better than) early versions.

Causes of inflation

For any country, inflation can come from several sources. Some come direct from the domestic economy, for example, the pricing strategies of leading food retailers based on the strength of demand and competitive pressures. A rise in VAT would also be a cause of increased domestic inflation because it increases the firm's production costs and some of these costs are passed onto consumers in the form of higher prices.

Inflation can also come from external sources, for example an unexpected rise in the price of crude oil or other imported commodities, foodstuffs and beverages. Fluctuations can also affect inflation; for example a gradual depreciation in the value of the pound against the euro might cause higher import prices, which feeds through into the consumer price index.

The two traditional ways of categorising the causes (types) of inflation are (i) demand-pull and (ii) cost-push. At A2 level, a third factor, 'excessive' growth of the money supply, is also considered.

Cost-push inflation

Cost-push inflation occurs when businesses are faced with increasing production costs, and raise their prices in order to maintain profit margins. Sources of cost-push inflation may include:

■ **A rise in costs of imported raw materials**. Inflation in countries that export commodities or a fall in the exchange rate of the pound may increase the UK price of imported raw materials. There has been significant inflation in the price of commodities such as wheat and hard metals in recent years. Oil prices also accelerated through 2007 and 2008.

■ **Rising labour costs**, for example following aggressive pay bargaining by trade unions.

■ **Higher indirect taxes**, for example an increase in fuel duties or the rate of VAT. The ability of suppliers to pass the burden of these taxes onto consumers will depend on the price elasticity of demand and supply for their products.

■ **Wage-price spirals.** Rising expectations of inflation can themselves induce inflation. If workers expect prices to continue rising, they will be unwilling to accept pay rises less than their expected inflation rate in order to protect the purchasing power of their incomes. When workers are looking to negotiate higher wages, there is a danger of a **'wage-price spiral'** where firms will subsequently increase their prices in order to maintain profitability.

Cost-push inflation can be presented in terms of aggregate demand and aggregate supply analysis as shown in Figure 12.2. Rising costs of production shift the short-run aggregate supply curve leftwards from AS1 to AS2. The price level rises from P1 to P2, but equilibrium real GDP falls from Y1 to Y2.

Demand-pull inflation

Demand-pull inflation is most likely to occur when there is little spare capacity in the economy. An increase in aggregate demand will subsequently lead only to an increase in prices. Aggregate demand increases when one or more of its components increases, for example, increased consumption spending due to reduced income tax.

Demand-pull inflation can be presented in aggregate demand and aggregate supply terms, as shown in Figure 12.3. An increase in aggregate demand from AD1 to AD2 increases the equilibrium level of real GDP from Y1 to Y2, but also leads to price inflation, rising from P1 to P2. It is worth noting that an increase in investment, ceteris paribus, will increase aggregate demand in the short run, but will serve to increase aggregate supply in the long run.

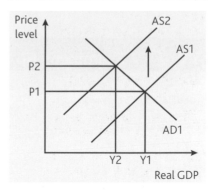

Figure 12.2 *Cost-push inflation*

■ Key terms

Cost-push inflation: inflation caused by economy-wide increases in production costs.

Indirect taxes: taxes levied on spending on goods and services.

Wage-price spiral: the process whereby increases in costs, such as wages, lead to increases in prices, which in turn leads to firms' costs increasing, and so on.

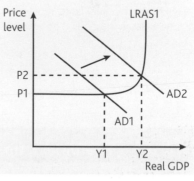

Figure 12.3 *Demand-pull inflation*

Quantity theory of money

The **quantity theory of money** was devised by Irving Fisher in the first part of the 20th century to explain the link between money and the general price level. The quantity theory is based on what is sometimes known as the **Fisher equation** or the **equation of exchange**. This is a mathematical identity which relates aggregate demand to the total value of output (GDP).

$$M \times V \equiv P \times T \text{ (or } MV \equiv PY), \text{ where:}$$

- ■ M is the money supply
- ■ V is the **velocity of circulation** of money
- ■ P is the general price level
- ■ T stands for transactions and is equivalent to output
- ■ Y is the real value of national output (that is, real GDP).

The velocity of circulation is the number of times that a unit of currency, for example, a £20 note, is used in a year to buy goods and services. Monetarists argue that the velocity of circulation of money is broadly predictable and therefore assumed to be constant. T and Y (real GDP) tend to increase slowly over time and are thus also assumed to be constant in any one year. If V and T (Y) are held constant, then changes in the rate of growth of the money supply will lead directly to changes in the general price level.

Consequences of inflation

> 'It is clear that very high inflation, in extreme cases hyperinflation, can lead to a breakdown of the economy. There is now a considerable body of evidence that inflation and output growth are negatively correlated in high-inflation countries. For inflation rates in single figures, the impact of inflation on growth is less clear.'
>
> *Mervyn King, Governor of the Bank of England*

Rapid, unpredictable changes in the price level can have significant economic and social costs. Margaret Thatcher (British Prime Minister 1979–1990) became famous for saying that the control of inflation must be any government's primary economic objective. Whilst low and stable inflation is often seen as an indicator of a healthy economy, **hyperinflation** indicates an economy which is out of control.

High and volatile inflation can impose a variety of consequences on individuals, firms and the economy as a whole.

International competitiveness

Where inflation is higher in the UK than with its international competitors, UK goods and services will become less price competitive, *ceteris paribus*. Since around 30 per cent of UK GDP is generated by exports, and that a similar value is imported, the potential effect is significant, threatening employment, growth and the balance of payments. Exporting firms will eventually make redundancies if they are no longer competitive internationally and revenues fall. Since net exports are a component of aggregate demand, reduced international competitiveness will thus worsen the current account of the balance of payments, reduce the growth of aggregate demand and lead to an output gap.

Key terms

Quantity theory of money: the theory that increases in the money supply will lead to increases in the price level.

Fisher equation or **equation of exchange:** the mathematical identity $MV \equiv PY$ (or $MV \equiv PT$), where M is the money supply, V is the velocity of circulation of money, P is the price level and Y is real output (T is the number of transactions in a year, also equivalent to output).

Velocity of circulation: the number of times the money supply changes hands in a year.

Hyperinflation: very large, rapid increases in the general price level.

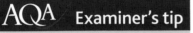

Effect on investment

Investment by firms thrives on certainty and optimism about the future. The problem with inflation is that it creates uncertainty about the future costs, revenues and hence the profitability of long-term investment projects, and so investment levels may fall. Poor investment will, over time, affect growth, employment and the balance of payments.

Unanticipated inflation

An important distinction to make is the difference between anticipated and unanticipated inflation. **Anticipated inflation** is where people correctly predict the rate of inflation in the near future. **Unanticipated inflation** is where they do not. For example, if people predict inflation of 2 per cent and actual inflation turns out to be 4 per cent, there is unanticipated inflation of a further 2 per cent. It is unanticipated inflation that causes problems, since it leads to the uncertainty that undermines investment. Unanticipated inflation is especially likely to arise when the rate of inflation is high and unstable, as it was in the UK in the 1970s and 1980s. Governments are especially keen not to return to these 'bad old days'.

Menu costs

Menu costs are the largely administrative costs to businesses of having to frequently change prices of goods and services, as well as reprogramming computerised accounting systems. This will use scarce resources and could worsen matters if firms attempt to pass on these administrative costs through higher prices – contributing to cost-push inflation.

Shoe-leather costs

If prices are stable, consumers and businesses have some certainty about reasonable prices. When prices are rising, especially when rapidly, consumers and businesses will be unclear about what constitutes a fair price, and have to spend more time, effort and possibly money, 'shopping around' for competitive deals. **Shoe-leather costs** are thus the search costs for consumers gathering information about price changes, and interest rates which banks offer to maximise the real return on their savings. The term evokes images of people pacing up and down the high street to discover the best deals, literally wearing out the soles of their shoes. However, consumers and firms are more likely to use the telephone or Internet to carry out their searches these days.

Effect on distribution of income

This can be an important source of economic injustice and social unrest. Inflation creates winners and losers in ways that are difficult to guard against, especially if it is unanticipated. The winners will be borrowers of money, whose future repayment is fixed in money terms, for example, fixed rate mortgages. The losers will be savers who have a fixed return in money terms or those with fixed money incomes, for example, some pensioners, who will see their effective purchasing power fall over time. In order to protect the real income of these groups, the government could 'index-link' pensions and benefits, that is, ensure that pensions and benefits increase in line with inflation.

Worsening industrial relations

The monetarist economist Milton Friedman famously said that inflation 'tears at the fabric of society, and sets up groups of workers against one another in increasingly violent conflict'. Whilst this sounds rather melodramatic, it is certainly true that strikes can be widespread during periods of inflation as workers feel they are losing out and push for higher pay.

Key terms

Anticipated inflation: where economic agents correctly predict the future rate of inflation.

Unanticipated inflation: where economic agents do not accurately predict the future rate of inflation.

Shoe-leather costs: the time and money spent 'shopping around' by consumers to find the best deals when prices are rising throughout the economy.

Figure 12.4 *Zimbabwean holding a new 10 million Zimbabwe doller (ZWD) note*

Fiscal drag

Fiscal drag is where people pay a higher percentage of their income in tax when there is inflation, as tax thresholds do not move in line with inflation. For example, if an individual's tax-free allowance is £5,000, with any income above this taxed at 20%, an individual earning £5,000 will therefore pay zero income tax. However, if prices rise by 10 per cent, and the individual's income rises in line with this, that is, to £5,500, he or she will now pay £100 in tax and be worse off in terms of real spending power.

To take account of inflation, the Chancellor can increase the tax-free allowance in line with inflation, that is, to £5,500 in this case.

Hyperinflation

Hyperinflation is difficult to define, but is usually regarded as being inflation in excess of 1000% per year. In post-World War I Germany, the price level rose by 100 billion %, whilst in post-World War II Hungary, inflation peaked at 42,000 billion %. Zimbabwe recently suffered inflation of over 100,000%. Inflation in the UK is unlikely to become this serious again, but if it did it would lead to even more severe problems. The currency is effectively destroyed, and can be used neither as a medium of exchange or a store of value. The economic system would increasingly resort to barter.

Case study

Inflation in Zimbabwe

Official figures show that inflation in Zimbabwe hit an annual rate of just under 165,000 per cent in February 2008. Continued shortages of food and fuel tipped inflation up from 100,000 per cent recorded in January 2008.

Staple goods are scarce and the government has responded to shortages by increasing the supply of money. The central bank has recently issued new banknotes to cope with the rapidly increasing prices, including a 10 million Zimbabwe dollar note.

Can inflation ever be a good thing?

The economist G. C. Allen believes that 'creeping inflation lubricates the wheels of industry', that is, low, predictable levels of inflation provide psychological incentives for firms and individuals. At inflation rates of around 2 per cent, workers see some rise in their pay packets in money terms, and firms see revenues increasing. This may be pure **'money illusion'**, but is felt to be preferable to no price increases. In real terms 0 per cent inflation and a 0 per cent wage increase is no different to 2 per cent inflation and a 2 per cent wage increase, but psychologically the second option is preferred.

The inflation target is currently 2.0% (+/− 1%), which suggests that first, it is difficult to hit an inflation target with perfect accuracy, and second, that there must be reasons why governments prefer some gentle inflation rather than total price stability, or deflation. Note too that the target for CPI inflation is symmetrical, that is, it is seen as equally undesirable to undershoot and overshoot the central target.

Deflation

If rising prices are a problem, should falling prices be a good thing? Would it not mean that the cost of living would fall and we would be better off?

First of all, we need to be clear as to what we mean by deflation. It is a fall in the general price level and must not be confused with falls in a few specific prices, such as for computers or TVs. Economists distinguish between **benign deflation** and **malevolent deflation**. The former stems from technological advances which bring down the prices of certain products. Computer chips are a good example. 'Malevolent' deflation is the real problem. Here, aggregate demand falls, the money supply falls and serious economic consequences may result. Unemployment is likely to increase, bringing about further reductions in spending in the economy. This can bring about a downward multiplier effect and tip the economic cycle towards recession.

The last serious world deflation occurred between 1929 and 1933. Prices fell by about 30 per cent in many leading economies and the UK, along with other countries, suffered very badly. Output fell, bankruptcies were widespread and unemployment soared. In recent decades we have seen falling consumer prices in Japan. Banks collapsed because of bad debts and disastrous investments in their own stock market. This had a deep psychological effect and made people build up precautionary savings balances in case they lost their jobs, which depressed consumption and hence aggregate demand. Interest rates were cut to 0.25 per cent in a bid to encourage consumer spending, but this did little good. Psychologically, and economically, the damage had been done and consumer and business confidence crumbled with people and firms reluctant to spend.

AQA Examiner's tip

Make sure you do not confuse a fall in the rate of inflation with deflation. Deflation occurs when the general level of prices actually falls.

Key terms

Benign deflation: falling prices resulting from technological advances across the economy.

Malevolent deflation: falling prices resulting from a significant downturn in economic activity.

Activities

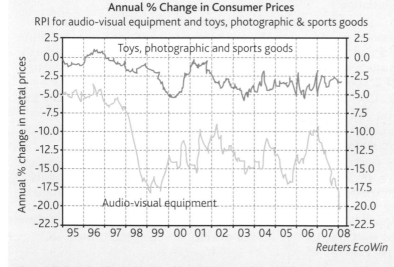

Figure 12.5 *Annual percentage change in consumer prices*

1 Compare the changes in prices of toys, photographic and sports goods with audio-visual equipment between 1995 and 2008.

2 What type of deflation seems to be in evidence with toys, photographic and sports goods and audio-visual equipment over the last decade? Justify your answer.

3 For what reasons might these prices have fallen?

After completing this chapter you should be able to:

■ understand how index numbers are calculated and are used to measure changes in the price level

■ analyse and evaluate the causes of changes in the price level and the consequences for both individuals and the performance of the economy, including the potential impact of a rising or falling price level

■ understand Fisher's equation of exchange and the quantity theory of money

■ appreciate the relevance of expectations in relation to the price level.

Extract A

UK shop price index, December 2005 – February 2008

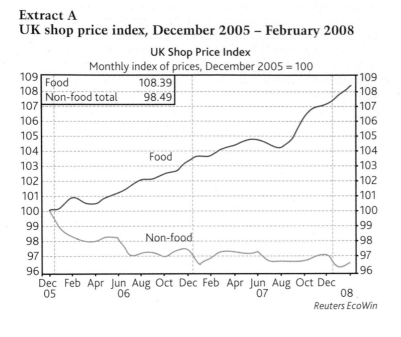

UK Shop Price Index

Monthly index of prices, December 2005 = 100

| Food | 108.39 |
| Non-food total | 98.49 |

Reuters EcoWin

Extract B

Household energy bills forcing up inflation

Soaring household energy bills sparked another sharp jump in inflation last month, worsening the Bank of England's quandary over how to respond to conflicting pressures from rising price pressures and faltering growth. A massive 10.5 per cent jump in the cost of gas and electricity pushed through by utilities groups lifted overall consumer prices by 0.7 per cent last month, driving their annual pace of increase to a nine-month high of 2.5 per cent, up from 2.2 per cent in January and far above the Bank's 2.0 per cent target.

The steep increase in inflation was expected by the Bank and the City, after a change in policy by the Office for National Statistics that means such price rises are added to the figures all at once, rather than being phased in over several months, as in the past practice.

Amid continuing hopes that the Bank's Monetary Policy Committee (MPC) will cut interest again either next month, or in April, there was some reassurance for the MPC as yesterday's anticipated surge in inflation was smaller than expected, thanks to the offsetting impact of an easing in rampant food price inflation. The MPC's anxieties will also be soothed as so-called 'core inflation', excluding volatile food and energy costs, dropped back last month to 1.2 per cent, its lowest rate since August 2006. The annual rate of price gains for food and non-alcoholic drinks dropped back a little, to 5.6 per cent last month, from a heady 6.1 per cent in January.

But the good news was dampened by details showing that this was mainly due to a surprise fall in the cost of seasonal food, while non-seasonal food prices continued to rocket upwards, climbing at an annual pace of 7.4 per cent in February, the fastest for 10 years. The cost of cheese, milk and bread prices rose by 17.6 per cent, the largest rise since records began in 1997. The MPC will welcome the decline in core inflation reported yesterday. This was mainly driven by slower increases in the cost of services, with inflation in the sector falling back from 3.3 per cent in January to 3.1 per cent last month, the lowest for 18 months. In a bigger headache for the Bank, however, goods price inflation on the consumer price index accelerated to 1.9 per cent, from 1.3 per cent.

Hopes that the MPC will press ahead with an expected cut in borrowing costs in the next two months will be reinforced as yesterday's figures confirmed that inflation is falling some way short of the Bank's central forecast for the first quarter of the year (Q1). Geoffrey Dicks, of RBS Global Banking, noted that the Bank's forecasts called for average Q1 inflation of 2.53 per cent and that, for this to be met, inflation would have to accelerate to 3 per cent next month.

The Bank is set to remain on high alert over inflation risks, however, with the further increases in price pressures expected in coming months fuelling its worries that households and businesses will come to expect higher inflation, push up wages and prices, and make this a self-fulfilling prophecy. Those concerns are heightened by the high level of inflation on the retail prices index, closely followed by the public, which was stuck at 4.1 per cent in February for a second month. The MPC's inflation anxieties are being inflamed by record oil prices, now firmly above $100 a barrel, commodity prices at all-time highs, and recent steep drops in the pound, which raise Britain's import bills.

The MPC's headache has been made worse by the Chancellor's big increases in alcohol duties announced in the Budget. Rises in tobacco and alcohol duties will add 0.17 percentage points to the inflation rate for March, and higher fuel duty will add another 0.1 percentage points in October.

Adapted from Grainne Gilmore and Gary Duncan, The Times, 19 March 2008

1 (a) Using Extract **A**, compare the change in food and non-food shop prices during 2007. *(5 marks)*

 (b) Explain, with the use of an example, how a weighted price index is calculated. *(10 marks)*

 (c) With reference to the data and your own knowledge, assess the consequences of rising food and commodities prices for the UK economy. *(25 marks)*

2 (a) Explain how a fall in the rate of inflation might be achieved by both demand-side **and** supply-side factors. *(15 marks)*

 (b) Evaluate the possible consequences of a falling rate of inflation for the performance of the UK economy. *(25 marks)*

AQA, January 2006

AQA Examiner's tip Question 2, part (b) is quite a subtle question, requiring you to be able to appreciate the significance of low inflation, falling inflation and deflation. As ever, the 'performance of the UK economy' requires an analysis of the implications in relation to economic growth, inflation, unemployment and the balance of payments.

Figure 13.4 *Facing seasonal unemployment*

Key terms

Deindustrialisation: a fall in the proportion of national output accounted for by the manufacturing sector of the economy.

Technological unemployment: unemployment due to the introduction of labour-saving technology.

Cyclical or **demand-deficient unemployment**: unemployment due to a lack of aggregate demand.

Involuntary unemployment: when a worker is willing to accept a job at the going wage rate but is not offered one.

Classical or **real-wage unemployment**: results from real wages being above their market-clearing level, creating an excess supply of labour.

Structural unemployment

Structural unemployment occurs when there is a long-run decline in demand for labour relative to its supply, leading to redundancies. Structural unemployment arises due to changes in the structure of the economy, that is, the declining relative importance of primary and secondary sectors of the economy, whilst new job opportunities emerge in the tertiary sector, a process known as **deindustrialisation**. This creates a mismatch of skills, as workers in declining sectors do not have the skills to secure the 'new' jobs, for example, in finance and Information and Communication Technology (ICT), leading to occupational immobility. This problem has tended to be concentrated in certain regions of the UK, reflecting the location of extraction and heavy industries such as coal-mining and shipbuilding. The growth of international competition is an important cause of structural unemployment, as countries such as China and India utilise their comparative labour advantages.

> ### Skills are required to cope with structural changes in output and employment
>
> Structural change is a constant feature of a flexible economy. As some sectors decline, so other sectors – requiring different skills – will expand. The pace of technological change and global integration will increase demand for a more highly skilled workforce with the ability to adapt to changing technologies and shifting product demand.
>
> *HM Treasury, the Benefits of a Flexible Economy, April 2004*

Technological unemployment is a form of structural unemployment, arising as groups of workers in particular industries are substituted by labour-saving technology. Note that automation, that is, machines operating other machines, tends to reduce the demand for labour, whilst mechanisation, or workers operating machines, tends to increase the overall demand for labour.

Cyclical unemployment

Cyclical unemployment or **demand-deficient unemployment** arises during the recession phase of the economic cycle due to a lack of aggregate demand. This will lead to rising unemployment as firms close and make redundancies. The fall in AD from AD1 to AD2 shown in Figure 13.5 leads to a greater negative output gap where actual GDP lies below potential GDP. Because of the derived demand for labour, falling real national output leads to increased unemployment.

Voluntary and involuntary unemployment

Voluntary unemployment occurs when a worker chooses not to accept work at existing wage rates, for example, a frictionally unemployed worker. **Involuntary unemployment** occurs when a worker would be willing to accept work at the going wage but cannot get a job offer. Cyclical unemployment is therefore classed as involuntary unemployment.

Classical unemployment

Classical, or **real-wage unemployment** is the result of real wages being above their market-clearing level leading to an excess supply of labour. In Figure 13.6, the market-clearing wage, at which aggregate demand for labour (ADL) equals the aggregate supply of labour (ASL), is W1. If wages are fixed at a higher real rate, W2, employers wish to hire fewer, QD, of workers, but QS workers are willing to supply their labour. So, the higher wage W2 encourages supply but discourages hiring. There is excess supply of labour in the market, of QS – QD.

Consequences of unemployment

Economic consequences

Unemployment is a waste of scarce resources and leads to the opportunity cost of lost potential output. The economy is operating below the maximum output it could achieve, which could be illustrated by making use of a PPB diagram. Increased unemployment is likely to reduce consumer spending. As consumer confidence falls, the willingness of people to spend will decline and they will tend to build up their savings. Reduced consumer spending will, *ceteris paribus*, reduce aggregate demand.

Strong growth in 2007 caused a reduction in unemployment levels, as can be seen in Figure 13.2 (p146).

Redundancies also waste resources invested in training and educating workers. The longer people spend out of work, the greater the loss of skill and motivation, too. When people are out of work, the government finances will worsen due to higher spending on Jobseeker's Allowance, whilst revenues from income tax, national insurance and VAT will fall.

The longer a person remains out of work, the more difficult they are likely to find getting a job, as their skills and confidence can become eroded. They have fewer incentives to keep searching for work, which can result in increased structural unemployment and a rise in the **natural rate of unemployment**. The **hysteresis** effect is the term used to describe the tendency for unemployment to generate longer-term unemployment, because of the damage that unemployment does to the skills and employability of those out of work.

Social costs of unemployment

There is evidence of links between the level of unemployment and crime, along with increased divorce rates, poorer health and lower life expectancy. Areas and regions of persistently high unemployment see falling real incomes and widening inequalities of income and wealth. Financial worries can contribute to poor mental and physical health, breakdown of relationships and even suicide. Unemployment may thus lead to a range of negative externalities.

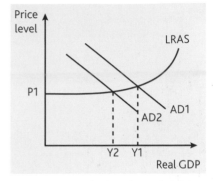

Figure 13.5 *Cyclical, or demand-deficient unemployment*

■ **Key terms**

Natural rate of unemployment: the unemployment that exists when aggregate demand for labour equals aggregate supply, that is, voluntary, frictional unemployment.

Hysteresis: the tendency for a variable not to return to its original value or state when changed; for example, unemployment can lead to higher unemployment.

■ **Case study**

The social costs of unemployment in Sheffield

Britain's most commercially successful film, *The Full Monty* (released in 1997), raised the international profile of Sheffield and South Yorkshire. In the week that *The Full Monty* won its Oscar, the European Union designated South Yorkshire as one of the continent's most deprived regions. The area was ranked alongside Sicily and parts of Eastern Germany. Since the 1980s the region has suffered a considerable decline:

■ Over 177,000 manufacturing jobs have been lost and South Yorkshire has one of the poorest records in England of generating new jobs.

■ Unemployment is 11 per cent above the national average.

■ Earnings have fallen to 12 per cent below the national average.

■ One third of the population receives housing benefits.

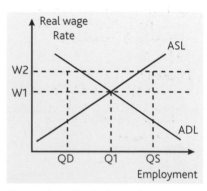

Figure 13.6 *Classical or real-wage unemployment*

■ Some 72,000 people in Sheffield live in areas suffering from poverty, where at least 30 per cent of residents are dependent on state benefits.

■ Twenty-four poverty areas have 40 per cent or more of families with children and no wage earner.

■ Eighteen poverty areas have 17 per cent or more households with no access to a car.

■ Twenty-two areas have 25 per cent unemployment. Two areas have levels approaching 50 per cent.

■ Acute areas of poverty have levels of preventable deaths 55 per cent above the national average.

■ The city has numerous drug-related deaths, mainly due to heroin overdose.

Within Sheffield, in impoverished Burngreave, 44.1 per cent of residents rely on state benefits, compared with 4.1 per cent in affluent Ecclesall. This is due in part to high unemployment levels, but employment has also changed radically. Low paid, part-time, temporary and casual labour has replaced skilled work in industry.

Sheffield Health Authority recently published their annual Public Health Report. It highlighted the deep divides in health rates across the city. Those in areas of high unemployment have poorer facilities and are most likely to be ill at an earlier age. They suffer higher rates of heart disease, depression, mental health issues and certain cancers.

Activities

Long-term unemployment is often linked to structural unemployment. The long-term unemployed tend to be older males. They are also less likely to have higher qualifications. They are more likely to have a disability. Also, lone parents are more likely to be long-term unemployed than heads of family in a married or co-habiting couple. The long-term unemployed are more difficult to get back into work than the short-term unemployed.

Adapted from Labour Market Trends, April 2004,
Office for National Statistics

1 Explain why long-term unemployment is linked to structural unemployment.

2 What are the possible consequences of long-term unemployment?

Possible benefits from unemployment

Whilst most economists and politicians believe the costs of unemployment are likely to outweigh any benefits, firms may find rising unemployment helpful in keeping wage rates down due to the reduced power of workers to bargain for higher wages and salaries. This may also help reduce inflationary pressure. There might also be reduced environmental damage and pressure on non-renewable resources if unemployment leads to slower growth of consumption and production.

■ Government policies to reduce unemployment

The causes and types of unemployment outlined earlier in this chapter can be divided into demand-side and supply-side in nature. The appropriate policy response to cyclical, or demand-deficient unemployment might thus be to stimulate aggregate demand. The other types of unemployment are supply-side in nature and therefore need to be tackled with supply-side policies.

Demand-side policies

Macroeconomic policies designed to increase AD could be used in order to generate increased national income and employment. The government could use fiscal policy to reflate the economy if it was experiencing a recession, for example, by increasing its own expenditure, or reducing income tax rates. It could also urge a 'loosening' of monetary policy by making credit more readily available. The government could also use regional policy to stimulate economic activity in those areas and regions where unemployment tends to be above the national average, for example, offering employment subsidies or tax reductions to firms relocating their operations in such areas.

Supply-side policies

Policies aimed at reducing occupational immobility of labour and structural unemployment seek to provide the unemployed with the skills that they need to find work and also to improve the incentives to find work. Improved education and vocational training will increase the skills-base of the unemployed and make them better-placed to secure available job opportunities. Geographical immobility of labour can be reduced by improving the process of job search, for example, by improving job databases, and by ensuring that there is affordable accommodation available where the jobs are.

Supply-side economists believe that reducing welfare benefits increases the incentive for the unemployed to accept paid work. This may not be the sole cause for the long-term unemployed not securing employment, however, and lower marginal tax rates could be offered to those who enrol on appropriate training courses, for example.

The Phillips curve

In 1958 Professor A. W. Phillips plotted data from 1861–1957 that seemed to illustrate a short-run trade-off between unemployment and wage inflation. It suggested that falling unemployment might cause inflation to rise, whilst reduced inflation might only be possible at the expense of higher unemployment. The line of best-fit showing this inverse relationship, which came to be known as the **Phillips curve,** is shown in Figure 13.7.

The Phillips curve implied that a particular level of unemployment could be traded off against a particular rate of inflation. The Phillips curve also played a role in identifying the causes of inflation. For example, inflation will rise when unemployment falls since, to reduce unemployment, aggregate demand must be strong. Any excess demand may create inflation. At low levels of unemployment, trade unions and other groups of workers may become over-confident about their job security and push for higher wages, leading to higher cost-push inflation. Conversely, inflation will fall as unemployment rises due to weak demand and a weaker bargaining position of trade unions.

Key terms

Phillips curve: an economic model that shows a trade-off between inflation and unemployment.

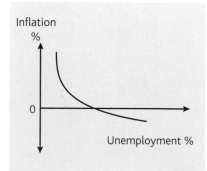

Figure 13.7 *The Phillips curve*

Activity

On graph paper, or using a graphing tool such as in the Excel spreadsheet package, plot the following data for unemployment and inflation from 1970–1985. Does there appear to be any obvious relationship, or had the Phillips curve trade-off truly broken down?

Table 13.1 *Unemployment and inflation 1970–1985*

Year	Unemployment (% of workforce)	Inflation (% change)
1970	2.2	5.9
1971	2.7	8.7
1972	3.1	6.5
1973	2.2	8.4
1974	2.0	17.0
1975	3.2	23.5
1976	4.8	15.7
1977	5.1	14.7
1978	5.0	9.5
1979	4.6	13.7
1980	5.6	16.3
1981	8.9	11.2
1982	10.3	8.7
1983	11.1	4.8
1984	11.1	5.0
1985	11.5	5.3

The Phillips curve trade-off can also be examined with Keynesian AD/AS analysis. As an economy moves towards full capacity, inflationary pressure is likely to arise, and vice-versa.

The expectations-augmented Phillips curve (EAPC)

In the 1970s, the original Phillips curve relationship seemed to break down, as high levels of inflation co-existed with high unemployment in the UK economy, as **stagflation** set in. Some economists argued that the relationship still existed, but that the curve had shifted to the right, indicating that a higher level of unemployment was compatible with any level of inflation. It was suggested that in the 1970s workers had got used to higher levels of unemployment and so did not modify wage claims to the same extent when unemployment rose.

Monetarist economists, particularly the late American economist Milton Friedman, accepted that a short run Phillips curve existed, but that in the long run, the Phillips curve should be drawn as vertical, meaning there was no stable trade-off between unemployment and inflation. Friedman suggested that it is impossible to reduce unemployment in the long run by, for example, increasing the money supply; the job market will simply return to the previous level of unemployment, but with a higher rate of inflation. Friedman introduced the **adaptive expectations** hypothesis. This states that if economic agents, that is, workers, trade unions and firms, experience increased inflation in the current period, they will naturally expect higher inflation in the future. Price inflation will thus prompt higher wage claims, increasing labour costs and subsequently higher consumer prices.

The result may be that higher unemployment is required to keep inflation at a certain target level. Monetarists believe that the best control for inflation is tight control of money and credit. Credible monetary policy can also have the desirable effect of reducing inflation expectations, causing a leftward shift of the short-run Phillips curve.

Free-market economists argue that it is impossible to reduce unemployment below the natural rate of unemployment (NRU), except at the cost of ever-accelerating unanticipated inflation. This is because the original explanation of the Phillips curve wrongly took into account only the *current* rate of inflation and ignored the important influence of the *expected* rate of inflation. The theory of the expectations-augmented Phillips curve importantly brings in the role of expectations to the inflationary process, and is illustrated in Figure 13.8.

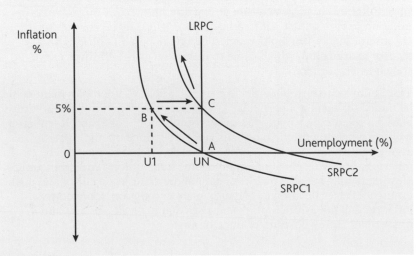

Figure 13.8 *The expectations-augmented Phillips curve*

In Figure 13.8, the economy is initially at point A, with unemployment at the natural rate, UN. At point A, the rate of inflation is zero. We assume that people form expectations of *future* inflation on the basis of the *current* rate of inflation. Thus at point A, since current inflation is zero, workers expect the future rate of inflation also to be zero.

If the government stimulates aggregate demand, we move along the short-run Phillips curve SRPC1, to point B, with unemployment below the natural rate at U1, and inflation rising to, say, 5 per cent. Point B is, however, unsustainable. For workers to supply more labour, the real wage rate must rise. In the short run, more workers may enter the labour market suffering from money illusion, that is, holding the false belief that a 5 per cent increase in money wages is also a real wage increase. Similarly, firms also suffering from money illusion may believe that rising prices mean that sales revenues are rising faster than labour costs. Workers and firms eventually see through their money illusion and refuse to supply labour and demand labour respectively. The economy now moves to point C, but with inflation expectations of 5 per cent now built in. Any further expansion of aggregate demand moves along SRPC2 and to higher rates on inflation. Each time the government attempts to reflate demand in this way, the economy will tend to the NRU. The EAPC suggests that there is no long-run trade-off between inflation and unemployment, as highlighted by the vertical long-run Phillips curve (LRPC) at UN. Any attempt to reduce unemployment below the NRU by stimulating aggregate demand is ultimately futile, and governments will thus need to tackle the root supply-side causes if they wish to reduce unemployment.

The NAIRU

The **NAIRU,** or non-accelerating inflation rate of unemployment, is defined as the rate of unemployment when the rate of wage inflation is stable. It is equivalent to the concept of equilibrium unemployment, outlined at the start of this chapter, and consists of frictional and structural unemployment. If unemployment falls below this level, perhaps because a government stimulates aggregate demand in a bid to reduce unemployment, the rate of inflation increases. Conversely, if unemployment rises above NAIRU, for example, following government policies to reduce inflation, the wage rate and inflation rate will fall. Although the NAIRU is difficult to observe and measure, it is estimated that the NAIRU has fallen from nearly 10 per cent of the labour force in the early 1990s to around 5 per cent in the last few years.

The natural rate of unemployment

The natural rate of unemployment (NRU) consists of voluntary frictional unemployment. Economists often treat the NRU and NAIRU as interchangeable terms, though NAIRU seems to be preferred today, partly because the term 'natural' implies that a certain level of unemployment should always exist.

The long-run Phillips Curve

The long-run Phillips Curve is normally drawn as vertical, as in Figure 13.8, but can shift inwards over time, perhaps due to supply-side improvements to the economy. Labour market reforms which successfully reduce frictional and structural unemployment may lead to a reduction in the natural rate of unemployment by improving the occupational mobility of labour.

■ Key terms

NAIRU: the non-accelerating inflation rate of unemployment, that is, the level of unemployment at which there is no tendency for inflation to accelerate.

What has happened to the inflation/unemployment trade-off for the UK?

■ Case study

The disappearing Phillips Curve

Conventional economic wisdom suggests that higher economic activity measured by rising real GDP growth and falling unemployment will lead to higher inflation and, furthermore, that any attempt to hold activity above its sustainable long-run level indefinitely is likely to result in inflation accelerating. But, over the last decade, consumer price inflation has been both subdued and unusually stable, fluctuating between just 0.8 per cent and 2.6 per cent, while the unemployment rate has fallen from double-digit levels to just 4.6 per cent of the labour force today. So, as unemployment has fallen, inflation has remained low and stable, suggesting that any positive relationship between economic activity and inflation has all but disappeared.

Charles Bean, Chief Economist of the Bank of England, November 2004 speech

From the early 1990s until 2007, Britain enjoyed a long period of falling unemployment and stable, low inflation. Some of the key factors that may explain the UK's apparently improved trade-off up to 2008 are outlined below.

■ **UK labour market flexibility**. A flexible labour market is one in which firms find it relatively easy to hire and fire labour, and for workers to move between jobs. The systematic reduction in the power of trade unions has also reduced collective bargaining power.

■ **Immigration**. A rise in the size of inward migration, from the new EU member states and elsewhere, seems to have helped to relieve labour shortages in some sectors of the economy and therefore mitigated wage inflation pressures.

■ **Setting credible inflation targets**. Inflation targeting has helped to reduce inflation expectations, and has had the effect of establishing a credible monetary policy framework, hence building in low-inflation expectations in the UK economy.

■ **Low inflation in the global economy**. Up until 2007, cost and price inflation in many parts of the world economy had been falling. Rapid **globalisation** has increased the competition between nations whilst reducing the prices of many imported products.

■ **Technological change and innovation**. has improved the efficiency of both the British and international economy, raising labour productivity and cutting production costs.

By 2008, however, the outlook for the trade-off became gloomier as largely external sources of inflation put upward pressure on pay claims, and the threat of economic downturn holds poor prospects for unemployment. Will we see a return of stagflation?

■ Key terms

Globalisation: worldwide growth of multinational companies, international integration, the spread of free markets and policies of liberalisation and free trade.

After completing this chapter you should be able to:

- analyse and evaluate the causes of unemployment and the consequences for individuals and the performance of the economy
- explain possible policy measures to deal with unemployment
- understand the concept of, and the factors which determine, the natural rate of unemployment and both the short-run and long-run Phillips curves, and be able to discuss the implications of these for economic policy.

Qualms over unemployment among young

The numbers claiming unemployment benefit have fallen to the lowest level for more than a quarter of a century but the Government is still struggling to reduce long-term youth joblessness, according to official figures. Recent data paint a benign picture, with wage growth under control despite a tight jobs market. But economists noted that unemployment figures, published by the Office for National Statistics, are a lagging indicator and that a rise is expected later this year.

Another concern was a 35 per cent increase in the past year, to more than 100,000, in the number of 18- to 24-year-olds who have remained unemployed for more than 12 months. The increase reflects the difficulties ministers face in reducing hard-core, long-term unemployment and the even larger number of economically inactive people who may not be claiming unemployment benefit but are still out of work. A key concern about 18- to 24 year-olds is that many have not achieved the qualifications required to either secure employment, or places at colleges or universities. As the pattern of demand moves more towards relatively high-skilled service sector output, people need to show they have the relevant skills and qualifications if they are to be employed.

The total number of people claiming unemployment benefit dipped just under 795,000 last month, the lowest level since June 1975. The number of people in work rose to a record 29.4m, during the three months to the end of December, while total unemployment fell by 61,000 to 1.6m – the biggest quarterly decline for five years. Vacancies totalling more than 680,000 remained close to record levels in January.

Despite the tight labour conditions, average annual earnings growth, including bonuses, dipped by 0.2 of a percentage point to 3.8 per cent, which is below the level that the Bank of England considers a serious threat to its inflation target.

Adapted from Andrew Taylor, FT.com, 14 February 2008

1 (a) Outline the **two** main measures of unemployment in the UK. *(5 marks)*

   (b) Explain **two** types of unemployment that are suggested in paragraph two. *(10 marks)*

   (c) With reference to the Phillips curve model, discuss whether or not the last paragraph of the article supports the theory. *(25 marks)*

2 (a) Explain the possible demand-side **and** supply-side causes of unemployment. *(15 marks)*

   (b) Discuss the view that, as any economy approaches full employment, inflation will inevitably accelerate. *(25 marks)*

AQA, January 2006

 A good answer to Question 2, part (b) will require well thought-out analysis, probably including diagrams such as the basic Phillips curve and its expectations-augmented version. AD/AS analysis could also be used.

14 Fiscal policy and supply-side policy

In this chapter you will learn:

- the main objectives of the UK tax system

- more about direct and indirect forms of taxation, including their relative merits

- the principles of a 'good' taxation system

- the significance of the government's budgetary or fiscal stance

- the government's fiscal rules

- the microeconomic and macroeconomic effects of fiscal policy

- the relevance of various supply-side policies in achieving macroeconomic policy objectives.

Figure 14.1 *Taxation can be used to correct market failures such as negative externalities*

Key terms

Direct taxes: taxes levied directly on the income of an individual or organisation.

Fiscal policy was introduced at AS. This chapter looks in more detail at taxation and government expenditure and examines the relationship between the level of government spending and taxation. It also covers several of the key issues of fiscal policy, including the relative merits of direct and indirect taxes and the government's fiscal rules. As outlined at AS, government supply-side policies are largely fiscal in nature, and in this chapter we analyse and evaluate a range of policies linked to achieving the government's macroeconomic policy objectives.

Fiscal policy

Fiscal policy may be defined as the manipulation of public spending, taxation and borrowing to achieve the government's macroeconomic objectives. An increase in government expenditure, or a reduction in taxation, should boost aggregate demand and national income. However, as noted at AS, fiscal policy can also be used to influence supply-side economic performance. For example, fiscal policy changes can have important effects on the incentives for individuals to offer themselves for employment and for entrepreneurs to invest.

Taxation

The main objectives of the UK tax system

The UK government's objectives for the tax system may be outlined as:

- **Funding government spending**: Governments must raise finance for their various expenditures. They are able to borrow money up to a certain extent, but the majority of the finance must come from taxation, in order to avoid inflationary pressure.

- **Managing the economy as a whole**: Taxation can be used to influence the UK's macroeconomic performance. The government may alter taxes and their rates in order to influence economic growth, inflation unemployment and, to a lesser extent, the balance of payments. Governments also appreciate that reducing certain taxes can lead to important microeconomic supply-side improvements.

- **Redistribution of income**: If a government judges the distribution of income to be unfair, or inequitable, it may levy taxes to reduce the income and wealth of some groups in society, in order to boost the income and wealth of other groups.

- **Correcting market failure**: At a microeconomic level, the UK government often uses taxes to improve the workings of markets. For example, indirect taxes may be increased on demerit goods, or on fuel to reduce negative externalities.

Direct and indirect taxes

In the UK it is traditional to divide taxes into two broad categories. **Direct taxes** are largely taxes on income paid directly to Her Majesty's Revenue and Customs by the individual taxpayer. Direct taxes logically include income tax, inheritance tax, capital gains tax and also corporation tax. Tax liability cannot be passed onto someone else. **Indirect taxes** are largely taxes on spending, including VAT and a range of excise duties on oil, tobacco and alcohol. Depending on the price elasticity and supply for a good, firms may be able to shift the burden of an indirect tax onto the consumer. In recent decades there has been a shift away from using direct taxation as part of discretionary fiscal policy.

The principles of taxation

Whilst most taxpayers would view paying taxes as inherently 'bad', most would also appreciate the need for taxation in order to raise revenues to pay for essential goods and services provided by the government. In making an assessment of whether a tax is 'good' or 'bad' from an economic point of view, a useful starting point is to use the set of principles developed by classical economist Adam Smith known as the **canons of taxation**. Adam Smith suggested that taxes should be economical, equitable, convenient and certain. Two more modern **principles of taxation** that we may wish to add to these are efficiency and flexibility.

1 **Economical**. A tax should be simple and cheap to collect, so that the revenue is maximised compared to the cost of collection.

2 **Equitable**. Taxes should be fair and based on the taxpayer's ability to pay. This is a key justification for the progressive nature of income tax, that is, that the the proportion of tax paid rises with income. **Horizontal equity** occurs when people or firms with the same income and financial circumstances pay the same amount of tax. **Vertical equity** occurs when the amount that people and firms pay is based on their ability to pay, so that people with high incomes pay more than those with low incomes.

3 **Convenient**. The payment method and timing should be convenient to the taxpayer.

4 **Certain**. Taxpayers should understand how the system works and should be clear about what, when and how to pay. Taxes should also be difficult to evade.

5 **Efficient**. An efficient tax system meets its aims whilst minimising negative distortions such as reducing individual incentives to work or for firms to invest.

6 **Flexible**. The structure and rates of taxation must be capable of easy alteration in response to changing economic conditions.

Hypothecation

Hypothecation of taxes means that taxes are raised for a specific purpose, that is, the revenue is earmarked for a specific use. In the last decade, for example, the government has announced that a large proportion of tobacco duty would be used by the National Health Service (NHS) for tackling smoking-related diseases. Hypothecation gives some choice to consumers, and can reveal how much people are prepared to pay for particular services. It can also be used to take money from those creating negative externalities to be spent on compensating those who suffer the spillover consequences. The argument that taxes should be linked to the benefits that taxpayers receive from the tax is known as the **benefit principle**.

The relative merits of direct and indirect taxes

As well as using the principles of taxation outlined above, we can also examine the following arguments about the relative merits of direct and indirect taxation.

Figure 14.2 *Her Majesty's Revenue & Customs are responsible for collecting the bulk of UK taxation*

Key terms

Canons of taxation: the characteristics of a 'good tax', after Adam Smith.

Principles of taxation: a modern list of characteristics of a 'good tax' system.

Horizontal equity: when people or firms with the same income and financial circumstances pay the same amount of tax.

Vertical equity: when the amount that people and firms pay is based on their ability to pay.

Hypothecation: when taxes are earmarked for a specific purpose.

Benefit principle: the argument that taxes should be linked to the benefits received by taxpayers.

Arguments for indirect taxation

■ **Influencing spending patterns**. Indirect tax changes are arguably more effective in changing the overall pattern of demand for particular goods and services, by changing relative prices.

■ **Correcting externalities**. Indirect taxes can be useful in correcting the spillover effects of economic transactions, for example 'making the polluter pay' by 'internalising' the external costs of production and consumption.

■ **Incentive effects**. Indirect taxes have less impact upon individual work versus leisure choices. Therefore, governments could levy higher indirect taxes to allow a reduction in direct taxation.

Flexibility. Indirect taxes can be changed more easily than direct taxes, since direct taxes can only be changed once a year at the time of **The Budget**.

■ **Choice**. People have a choice about whether to buy products that attract indirect taxes whereas direct taxes inevitably leave people with less of their take-home pay in their pockets, plus they are hard to avoid.

Arguments against indirect taxation:

■ **Distributional effects**. The regressive nature of many indirect taxes means that they can make the distribution of income more unequal.

■ **Inflationary effects**. Increases in indirect taxation can trigger cost-push inflation, and a subsequent rise in expectations of inflation.

■ **Crime**. High levels of indirect taxation create incentives to avoid them.

■ The lack of **'announcement effect'** means that many people are unaware of how much they are paying in indirect taxes, which goes against the 'certainty' principle of a good tax system.

Progressive, proportional and regressive taxation

A **progressive tax** system means that the proportion of a person's income paid in tax increases as income increases. A **regressive tax** system sees the proportion paid in tax falling as income increases. A **proportional tax**, or flat tax, means that proportion of income paid in tax stays the same as income increases. Progressivity can be applied to a specific tax or the tax system as a whole. Progressive and regressive taxes can affect supply-side incentives, the distribution of income and the action of automatic stabilisers.

How progressive is the income tax system in the UK?

In a progressive tax system people pay a higher proportion of their income in tax as their income increases. Table 14.1 shows that the UK income tax system is indeed progressive. In 2006, the average rate of tax paid increased from around 2 per cent on incomes of £5,000–£7,499 to almost 18 per cent for people in the £30,000–£49,999 income bracket. People earning over £100,000 per year paid over a third of their income in tax.

> ■ **Key terms**
>
> **The Budget**: the government's annual announcement of changes to its planned levels of spending and taxation.
>
> **Progressive tax**: where the proportion of a person's income paid in tax increases as income increases.
>
> **Regressive tax**: where the proportion paid in tax falls as income increases.
>
> **Proportional tax**: where the proportion of income paid in tax stays the same as income increases.

Table 14.1 *Income tax payable by income bracket, 2006*

Annual income (£)	Number of taxpayers (millions)	Total tax liability (£m)	Average rate of tax (%)	Average tax liability (£)
4,895–4,999	0.1	1	0.1	5
5,000–7,499	2.9	369	2.0	126
7,500–9,999	3.5	1,580	5.1	445
10,000–14,999	6.1	7,560	9.8	1,220
15,000–19,999	5.1	11,500	13.0	2,260
20,000–29,999	6.4	24,000	15.4	3,760
30,000–49,999	4.3	28,900	17.9	6,690
50,000–99,999	1.5	25,900	25.7	17,000
100,000 and over	0.5	34,200	33.4	71,100
All incomes	30.5	134,000	18.2	4,390

Office for National Statistics

But the system is not as progressive as it might be and as it was over twenty years ago. The extent of the 'progressivity' of the income tax system has been reduced over the years. Before 1979, the top rate of income tax was 83 per cent, with a 15 per cent supplement for investment income. Now most taxpayers face a similar marginal tax rate of 22 per cent compared with a top rate of 40 per cent but on top of the basic rate there is National Insurance Contributions (NICs) at 11 per cent and 1 per cent extra on NICs for higher earners, making the overall rates 33 per cent, and 41 per cent. This is not such a great progression. If a government wanted to use the income tax system to achieve a more even final distribution of income, it could:

- raise the top rate of income tax above 40 per cent
- increase the tax free allowance for people
- introduce lower marginal rates of tax for lower-income households.

Case study

Chancellor accused of widening poverty trap for poorest workers

More than 1.8 million low-paid workers face losing 60p more for every extra £1 they earn as a result of tax changes that come into effect next month. Gordon Brown and Alistair Darling were accused of worsening the poverty trap by scrapping the 10p starting rate of income tax and clawing back tax credits from those earning more than £6,420.

The measures would affect low-paid workers, while millionaires were taxed at 40 per cent, said Stephen Byers, the former Transport Secretary. Figures included in the 2008 Budget showed that the numbers subject to tax rates equivalent to 60 per cent or more will exceed 1.8 million in the coming year, compared with 760,000 a decade ago. 'Poorly paid people are facing a reduction in their income of over 60 per cent, higher than millionaires who are paying 40 per cent income tax. For a progressive government this is not an acceptable situation,' Mr Byers told MPs.

The close ally of Tony Blair and a long-time critic of Mr Brown's tax credit system called for large increases in the national minimum wage to help to release more people from the poverty trap.

Ministers said that they were right to concentrate on meeting the Government's target to halve the number of children in poverty. Poorer parents are to be offered £200 to take up free nursery places and could receive further cash payments to meet targets set for their child.

Francis Elliot, The Times, *14 March 2008*

Government expenditure

Government, or public, expenditure includes spending by both central and local government and the remaining public corporations. It can be divided into:

Capital expenditure on hospitals, schools, roads etc.

Current expenditure on the day-to-day running of public services, including the pay of teachers and the purchase of medicines for NHS use.

Transfer payments, that is, money transferred from taxpayers to receivers of benefits, for example, pensioners and the unemployed.

The budget balance

The Chancellor's annual Budget was outlined at AS. Using the symbols G and T for government spending and taxation respectively, the three possible budgetary positions for the economy as a whole are:

G = T (balanced budget)
G > T (budget deficit)
G < T (budget surplus)

Figure 14.3 *Government spending might include building a new hospital*

■ **Key terms**

Capital expenditure: government spending to improve the productive capacity of the nation, for example, on schools and hospitals.

Current expenditure: government spending on the day-to-day running of the public sector, including raw materials and wages of public sector workers.

Transfer payments: government payments to individuals for which no service is given in return, for example, state benefits.

Balanced budget: where government receipts equal government spending in a financial year.

Budget deficit: where government spending exceeds government receipts in a financial year.

Budget surplus: where government receipts exceed government spending in a financial year.

Key terms

Fiscal stance: whether the government is seeking to increase or decrease aggregate demand through its fiscal policy measures.

Neutral fiscal stance: where the government runs a balanced budget.

Expansionary fiscal policy: where the government runs a large budget deficit.

Contractionary or deflationary fiscal policy: where the government runs a large budget surplus.

Demand management: use of macroeconomic policy to manipulate the level of aggregate demand in the economy.

Cyclical budget deficit: a budget deficit resulting from fluctuations in the economic cycle.

Automatic stabilisers: features of government spending and taxation that minimise fluctuations in the economic cycle.

Structural budget deficit: a budget deficit resulting from fundamental changes in the structure of the economy.

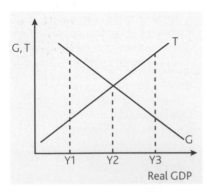
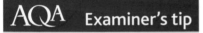

Figure 14.4 *The budgetary position*

AQA Examiner's tip

Ensure you understand the difference between the cyclical and structural elements of a budget deficit.

Expansionary and contractionary fiscal policy: measuring the fiscal stance

A government's **fiscal stance** refers to whether it aims to increase or reduce aggregate demand through its fiscal policy tools. A **neutral fiscal stance** is where the government runs a balanced budget, designed to have a benign impact on the level of economic activity. **Expansionary fiscal policy** occurs when the government uses a budget deficit (that is, $G>T$) in order to boost aggregate demand and economic activity. A government may implement an expansionary fiscal policy by increasing government expenditure and cutting taxation during a recession. Once the economy starts to pick up it is likely to try to seek to reduce its level of spending and/or raise taxes. **Contractionary** or **deflationary fiscal policy** occurs when the government runs a budget surplus (that is, $G<T$) in order to depress the level of aggregate demand and economic activity.

Influencing the level of aggregate demand in the economy is referred to as **demand management**. Governments do this to create greater stability, smoothing out fluctuations in the economic cycle, injecting extra demand when private sector demand is considered too low and reducing its own demand when private sector demand is too high. In the past, governments attempted 'fine-tuning', altering government spending and/or taxation, aiming to make precise adjustments to the level of aggregate demand. Governments now accept that fiscal policy cannot be used so precisely, however.

Figure 14.4 shows how tax revenue rises and government expenditure falls as Gross Domestic Product (GDP) rises. At income level Y1 there is a **cyclical budget deficit**, at income level Y2 there is a balanced budget and at income level Y3 there is a cyclical surplus. As briefly outlined at AS, some categories of government expenditure and taxation adjust automatically with economic activity to minimise any fluctuations in the economic cycle. These features are referred to as **automatic stabilisers**. For example, spending on unemployment benefits fall when economic activity is buoyant.

The cyclical and the structural budget deficit

We can examine the links between the government's budgetary position and the level of economic activity, distinguishing between the cyclical and the structural components of a budget deficit. The cyclical budget deficit is the component of the overall budget deficit which rises and falls with the fluctuations of the economic cycle, as automatic stabilisers take effect. In the downturn and recession phases of the economic cycle, tax revenues fall but public spending on unemployment and other welfare benefits increases, resulting in a deterioration of government finances. Conversely, in the upturn and boom periods, tax revenues rise and spending on unemployment benefits falls. Over the course of an economic cycle, then, a growing budget deficit would be cancelled out when economic growth occurred, providing growth was sufficiently robust.

However, more powerful structural changes may work in the opposite direction. A growing **structural budget deficit** in the UK has resulted from fundamental changes in the structure of economic activity such as deindustrialisation and the growth of single parent families increasing the numbers of households that are dependent on welfare benefits. The growing structural deficit suggests that governments wishing to improve public finances will need to significantly increase taxes and/or reduce public spending.

The public sector net cash requirement

The **public sector net cash requirement** (PSNCR) is the term given to the excess of the various types of government spending over revenue, that is, a budget deficit. To finance the gap between revenue and spending, the government will borrow either from the banking sector (high street banks or the Bank of England) or the non-bank private sector (insurance companies and individuals). The government borrows by selling, for example, Treasury bonds and National Savings certificates. A negative PSNCR means that revenue exceeds expenditure, that is, there is a budget surplus. This would enable a government to repay past debt.

Does a budget deficit pose a problem?

A persistent, substantial budget deficit can present problems for the government and the economy as a whole, for the following reasons:

1 Financing the deficit. A budget deficit has to be financed, which will incur interest. Persistently high levels of debt will thus incur substantial interest payments which will be a leakage from the circular flow of income.

2 A growing **national debt**. Over time, government borrowing increases the national debt. The Government will have to spend more money each year in debt interest payments, which might have been used in more valuable ways, for example, on building schools and roads.

3 Fiscal **'crowding-out'**. The term 'crowding out' refers to the extent to which an increasing budget deficit leads to higher interest rates and taxation, thereby reducing private sector expenditure, as consumption and investment spending are adversely affected.

Possible benefits of a budget deficit

1 A stimulus to growth: If a budget is used to finance additional capital spending, for example, on building new roads or schools, this can boost the long-run supply-side capacity of the economy.

2 Demand management: Keynesian economists would advocate running a budget deficit to boost aggregate demand, avoiding a large negative output gap.

The UK government's fiscal rules

Although monetary policy is currently the dominant policy used to influence the level of aggregate demand, fiscal policy does still have a role, especially in improving the supply-side efficiency of markets, helping to foster macroeconomic stability. In 1998, the government was concerned that the level of national debt should not become excessive as a proportion of GDP and hence established the Fiscal Policy Framework, which includes a **Code for Fiscal Stability**.

The Code has two main rules. The **golden rule** states that the government could only borrow money to invest in new social capital, such as schools and hospitals, over the course of an economic cycle. If it needs to finance current spending, such as welfare benefits in a recession, it would have to repay any increased borrowing in a boom. **The sustainable investment rule** states that over the economic cycle public sector debt is to be held at a 'stable and prudent' level of less than 40 per cent of GDP.

The publication of the Code for Fiscal Stability signalled the government's recognition that fiscal policy should not generally be used as a demand management tool. However, the growth of the structural budget deficit has caused the government to introduce new **'stealth' taxes** that it hopes people won't notice, in order to raise revenue. Future governments need not adhere to these fiscal rules, however, and it is worth noting that the

Labour government temporarily relaxed its fiscal rules in the Pre-Budget Report in November 2008.

During the formation of plans for the European Monetary Union (EMU), the potential problems created by member countries running substantial budget deficits and amassing subsequent national debts were recognised. A condition of membership was thus set that government borrowing could not exceed 3 per cent of GDP, and that the national debt of a country could not exceed 60 per cent of GDP. This agreement is known as the Stability and Growth Pact. As the UK is not participating in the single currency, it is not currently bound by the terms of the Pact, which gives more flexibility in terms of how much the UK government can borrow. However, future applicant countries do need to meet the conditions of the Pact.

Activities

The national debt is the total amount owed by the UK government, and has hit an all-time high of £500bn. But is this really a cause for concern? As a percentage of GDP it stands at 38.1 per cent, lower than the 40.6 per cent of GDP that the Labour government inherited in 1997. However, with rising government budget deficits, the figure is likely to grow further, so is it sustainable? Read the case study article 'National debt hits record £500 bn mark' and answer the following questions:

1 Explain the relationship between the budget deficit and the national debt.

2 Examine the likely impact of the rising budget deficit on (a) interest rates, (b) the level of investment and (c) economic growth.

3 Assess the impact that an economic downturn would have on the level of national debt in (a) the short term and (b) the long term.

Case study

National debt hits record £500bn mark

The national debt has broken through the £500bn level for the first time ever as a result of several years of big government deficits and in spite of record stamp duty receipts last month. Government figures showed that at the end of 2006, government net debt stood at £504.1bn, up from £467bn at the end of 2005. Public sector net borrowing – the Government's preferred measure of its deficit – ran at £7.2bn last month which was enough to push overall debt above £500bn.

'Today's figures show that as each month passes Gordon Brown is losing control of the public finances. The Chancellor needs to stop dreaming about Number 10 and concentrate more on the economy,' said Liberal Democrat Treasury Spokesman Vince Cable.

As a percentage of the economy, however, the national debt is far lower than it has been in the past. It is currently at 38.1 per cent of gross domestic product, lower than the 43.6 per cent that Labour inherited in 1997 but well up from the trough of 30.1 per cent seen in 2002 after the government had run budget surpluses for several years and used £22bn of receipts from an auction of mobile phone licences to bring down debt levels. But since the low point the Government has run several years of large deficits which have pushed the national debt up towards the 40 per cent of GDP level that Mr Brown has pledged not to bust. The current 38 per cent figure is the highest since December 1999.

'At a time when the economy is experiencing sustained economic growth, these figures highlight the problem the Chancellor will have in the future in the event of a downturn,' said Mr Cable. The Office for National Statistics (ONS) figures showed that in December, government fiscal receipts were 9 per cent up on the same month of 2005 while spending was up only 4.8 per cent. But over the first nine months of the fiscal year, spending and receipts both grew 6–7 per cent, which experts at the Institute for Fiscal Studies said meant Mr Brown may struggle to reduce the public deficit as planned this year.

January, however, will be a key month as receipts of income tax are usually very strong because of self assessment tax payments and Christmas bonuses in the City, which this year hit record highs of close to £10bn. Therefore, January's public finances could swing Mr Brown back on course and even push the national debt back below the £500bn mark. One bright spot for the Chancellor was that receipts of stamp duty hit a record high of £1.3bn last month thanks to strong house prices and rising share prices.

Ashley Seager, The Guardian, *19 January 2007*

The microeconomic effects of fiscal policy

As was noted at AS, fiscal policy measures can be used to improve the supply side of the economy, through their various microecenomic effects. Thus there is considerable overlap here with the supply-side policies that follow later in this chapter.

Incentives to work

Considerable debate surrounds the links between tax changes and impacts upon incentives to work. For example, whilst a reduction in the basic rate of income tax will increase the take-home pay of those in work, this may have the undesirable effect of encouraging the individual to work less, since they will need to work fewer hours to maintain their target level of income. Alternatively, the individual may be encouraged to work more hours, since the lower tax might act as an incentive to work, since he or she can gain more post-tax income per hour worked. In reality, however, many workers have little choice about the number of hours that they work.

The negative effects of the 'poverty trap', where households on low incomes gain little net financial benefit from supplying extra hours of their labour, can also be reduced with reforms of the tax and benefit system.

The pattern of demand

Increasing indirect taxes and government subsidies can be used to influence the pattern of demand for goods and services, for example, reducing the demand for various demerit goods, or increasing the quantity of merit goods demanded.

Business investment

Lower rates of corporation tax and business rates will increase potential profitability and hence boost firms' spending on fixed capital. Increased tax allowances can be used to stimulate increases in research and development and encourage entrepreneurship. Relatively low rates of corporation tax could also be used to attract new **foreign direct investment** (FDI). The Irish economy is often cited as an example of how a favourable tax regime can attract large amounts of FDI.

The macroeconomic dimension

Keynesian economists would emphasise the importance of fiscal policy to macroeconomic demand management. This is where changes in government spending, taxation and the budget balance can be used to smooth out some of the fluctuations in the economic cycle.

Discretionary or active fiscal policy is the deliberate manipulation of government spending and taxes to influence the economy. A government deciding to cut income tax rates is an example. However, some fiscal changes are built-in to occur automatically as the economy moves through the different phases of the economic cycle. These changes are also known as automatic stabilisers. Government spending and taxes can both be automatic stabilisers. If an economy moves into recession and national income falls, the amount of tax revenue falls, whilst spending

Key terms

Foreign direct investment: investments in the domestic economy in new manufacturing plants by foreign multinational companies.

Discretionary or active fiscal policy: deliberate changes in government spending or taxation to influence the economy as a whole.

on means-tested welfare benefits rises, meaning disposable income and aggregate demand is held at a higher level than it would otherwise have been.

Limitations of fiscal policy

One of the reasons that fiscal policy is not predominantly used at the moment to manage aggregate demand may be that it is seen by many economists as a less precise demand-management tool than monetary policy. The two main problems with fiscal policy are the time-lags involved and the potential for 'crowding out' the private sector. In addition to the time taken for the government to recognise that aggregate demand is slowing or accelerating, it then takes time to implement active or discretionary fiscal policy; government spending plans may take years to initiate, whilst income tax changes can normally only be changed once a year at the time of the Budget. In addition, the multiplier effects will also take several years to work through the economy. The inability to accurately predict these time lags arguably makes it impossible to use fiscal policy for fine-tuning aggregate demand, as demonstrated by destabilising 'stop-go' cycles of the past.

■ Supply-side policies

As outlined generally at AS, improvements to the efficient workings of the economy have not all come about as a direct result of economic policies. Many supply-side improvements come increasingly from the private sector, although there is certainly a role for government in creating the ideal conditions for these supply-side improvements to flourish.

Throughout the 1980s and after, there have been many attempts by governments to influence the supply-side of the economy. The aim of supply-side policies, which are largely microeconomic and fiscal in nature, is to shift the long-run aggregate supply curve to the right, enabling expansion of output without additional inflationary pressure, as shown in Figure 14.7. Supply-side policies can be divided into labour market measures and product market measures.

Labour market measures

Lower rates of income tax

Marginal rates of income tax may be reduced to create incentives to work, or tax thresholds or personal tax allowances may be raised. There is increasing support for the UK to adopt a flat-rate, or proportional, income tax, following their introduction in other EU countries.

Supply-side economists argue that high income tax rates and a high overall burden upon taxpayers create disincentives to work which have negative impacts upon national income and the government's total tax revenue. This effect is illustrated by the **Laffer curve** in Figure 14.5. The Laffer curve, named after the supply-side economist Arthur Laffer, shows how the government's total tax revenue changes as the average tax rate increases from 0 per cent to 100 per cent. Tax revenue, logically, is zero when the average tax rate is 0 per cent, but the diagram also shows that total tax revenue is again zero when the tax rate is 100 per cent. With an average tax rate of 100 per cent, all income is paid to the government in tax. Clearly there will be no incentive to work in paid employment in this case, so the government ends up collecting no tax revenue.

Between the extreme tax rates of 0 per cent and 100 per cent, the Laffer curve shows tax revenue first rising and then falling as the average rate

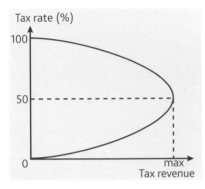

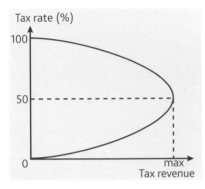

AQA Examiner's tip

Free-market economists believe government spending crowds out private sector spending, whilst Keynesian economists believe that government spending can encourage private sector spending.

■ Key terms

Laffer curve: a model that shows the theoretical relationship between tax rates and tax revenues.

Figure 14.5 *The Laffer curve*

of taxation increases. Tax revenue is maximised at the highest point on the Laffer curve, which in Figure 14.5 occurs at an average tax rate (for all taxes) of 50 per cent. Beyond this point, any further increase in the average tax rate has a negative effect on total tax revenue.

Reducing state welfare benefits, and 'welfare to work'

Reducing benefit levels creates incentives to choose low-paid employment rather than claiming unemployment-related benefits. Welfare benefits can also be made more difficult to claim. Employment programmes such as the New Deal are part of the government's **'welfare to work'** strategy to increase levels of employment and labour participation. 'Welfare to work' is the term used for a range of approaches, also including the Working Families' Tax Credit (WFTC) and introduction of a national minimum wage, designed to increase incentives to supply labour rather than live off benefits.

Education and training

Increasing educational attainment and relevant training have the effect of boosting the productivity of labour. In turn, this should increase the supply capacity of the nation and also reduce the unit labour cost per unit of UK output, thereby helping to improve our international competitiveness. Training agencies and City Technology Colleges have been established to develop vocational and technical education. However, UK governments have rejected the proposal to impose a 'training tax' on all employers to prevent 'free-riding' by firms with no training schemes which 'poach' trained workers from firms that do train their workers. Educational Maintenance Allowances (EMA) are means-tested benefit payments designed to encourage students from less wealthy households to continue with post-16 education.

Trade union reforms

As noted at AS, and in more detail in Chapter 8 of this book, trade unions seek to increase the wages of their members by restricting the supply of workers. Such action increases unit labour costs, reduces efficiency and labour market flexibility, and reduces international competitiveness. The 1980s saw vigorous moves by the Conservative government to reduce the power of trade unions through a series of Acts of Parliament. New Labour has not done anything to increase the power of trade unions.

Product market measures

Supply-side policies in product markets are designed to increase competition and efficiency. If the productivity of an industry improves, it will be able to produce more with a given amount of resources, shifting the Long Run Aggregate Supply (LRAS) curve to the right. As already outlined in Unit 3 of this book, private ownership of formerly public-owned organisations has been advocated by supply-side economists as leading to greater productive efficiency, and a reduced drain on the public purse. In addition, deregulation, the removal of barriers to entry in an industry, has arguably led to the creation of much more competitive markets where there had previously been a state monopoly.

Tougher competition policy has arguably forced companies to become more dynamically efficient, and reduced the ability of firms to abuse a dominant market position.

Measures to encourage entrepreneurship and capital spending, such as loan guarantees for new start-ups, reducing rates of corporation tax for small businesses, allowing tax relief on capital spending, and regional policy assistance in depressed areas are all important supply-side policies.

Figure 14.6 *Professor Arthur B. Laffer, sometimes referred to as the 'Father of supply-side economics'*

Key terms

'Welfare to work': a series of policies designed to increase incentives to gain employment.

Supply-side growth and macroeconomic policy objectives

Supply-side growth offers the possibility of steady, non-inflationary, sustainable growth and job creation, possibly with improvement in the current account of the balance of payments. Even when aggregate demand is rising, expansion in the productive capacity of the economy can keep inflation and current account problems under control, as shown in Figure 14.7. The increase in equilibrium national income from Y1 to Y2 will create more jobs without upward pressure on prices. Whilst there may be more demand for imports, a low inflation environment in the UK may mean that our exports can be price competitive. Supply-side growth occurs when the quantity and/or quality of the factors of production (land, labour, capital and, to an extent, enterprise) increase, and can also be illustrated with a PPB diagram, as in Figure 14.8.

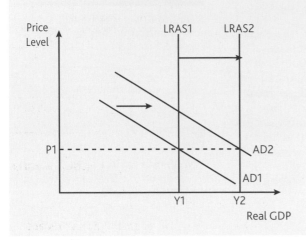

Figure 14.7 *Non-inflationary growth*

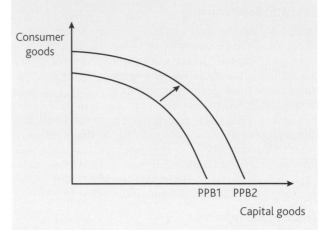

Figure 14.8 *An increase in the productive capacity of the economy*

After completing this chapter you should be able to:

■ discuss the issue of the budget balance and be able to evaluate the possible economic consequences of a budget deficit or budget surplus and the possible corrective measures

■ assess the economic significance of changes in the level and distribution of public expenditure

■ analyse and evaluate the microeconomic significance of taxation and the various roles and relative merits of the different UK taxes

■ understand the taxation principles likely to underlie a taxation system, such as the ability to pay and the impact on incentives

■ understand the introduction of fiscal rules: the UK Code for Fiscal Stability and the Stability and Growth Pact within the Euro area

■ analyse and evaluate supply-side policies such as education and training, welfare to work and tax incentives and be able to explain the relevance of these to achieving macroeconomic policy objectives.

Fiscal Policy in the United Kingdom

Extract A

Changes, actual and estimated, for the public sector net cash requirement (PSNCR) and public sector net debt in the UK, 2001–2009

Per cent
of GDP

	Actual		Estimate	Projections				
	2001–02	2002–03	2003–04	2004–05	2005–06	2006–07	2007–08	2008–09
Public sector net cash requirement*	0.3	2.1	3.6	2.6	2.3	2.2	1.8	1.6
Public sector net debt	30.2	30.9	32.8	33.8	34.6	35.1	35.4	35.5

* A positive (+) number for the public sector net cash requirement is a fiscal deficit.

UK Government Pre-Budget Report, The Treasury, December 2003

Extract B

Public sector finances and the economic cycle

The economic cycle, with its associated changes in unemployment and GDP growth, has significant short term effects on public sector finances. This means it is important to distinguish between the effects on public sector finances resulting from the economic cycle and those resulting from underlying, 'structural' changes in the economy. UK experience suggests that serious mistakes in fiscal policy can occur if purely cyclical improvements are treated as if they were structural, or if a structural deterioration is interpreted as cyclical.

Adapted from UK Government Pre-Budget Report, The Treasury, December 2003

Extract C

Take the politics out of fiscal policy

Around the world today, there is quiet satisfaction with the management of monetary policy but it is impossible to feel similarly comfortable about fiscal policy. Although recently Britain has seemed to manage its public finances well, politics, as in other countries, interferes with honest budgeting. There is a growing case for setting up a fiscal policy commission, similar to the Monetary Policy Committee at the Bank of England, to bring to fiscal policy the detachment that has worked so well for monetary policy.

Is this conceivable? The right to tax is the fundamental prerogative of democratic government. However, on more careful analysis, the idea is less radical than it seems. Britain has declared adherence to the golden rule of neutral fiscal policy over the whole economic cycle. And the purpose of the European Stability and Growth Pact is to rein in irresponsible financing by individual states.

The fiscal policy commission's job would be to assess the overall level of taxation needed to meet the government's declared goals: fiscal stability, cyclically adjusted budget balance, consistency with the policies and practices of a common currency zone. The assessment would probably best be expressed as a recommendation on the required standard rate of VAT.

The creation of a fiscal policy commission is not a new idea: according to the Governor of the Bank of England, the aim is to make fiscal policy as boring as he hopes monetary policy will soon become. The fiscal policy commission should, in the first instance, be a purely advisory body. However, if it acquired expertise and reputation, as it should, it would become increasingly difficult for government to ignore it without political damage and adverse reaction from financial markets.

Adapted from John Kay, Financial Times, 27 February 2003

1   (a)   Explain the relationship shown in Extract **A** between the UK's
            public sector net cash requirement (PSNCR) and public sector net debt.   *(5 marks)*

    (b)   Extract **B** states that 'serious mistakes in fiscal policy can occur if
            purely cyclical improvements are treated as if they were structural,
            or if a structural deterioration is interpreted as cyclical'. Explain this statement.   *(10 marks)*

    (c)   Discuss the case for and against setting up a fiscal policy
            commission to assist the implementation of fiscal policy in the UK.   *(25 marks)*

AQA, June 2005

2   (a)   Explain the main economic reasons for government spending.   *(15 marks)*

    (b)   The UK government indicated in 2003 that it needed to borrow
            £37bn to finance the budget deficit. To what extent, if any, is it
            important for a UK government to restore and maintain a balanced budget?   *(25 marks)*

AQA, January 2006

Question 2, part (b) will require a detailed explanation and evaluation of the circumstances in which a budget deficit is beneficial, or at least not problematic.

15 Monetary policy

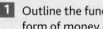

Activities

The 'death of cash' has been forecast for many years, but it has not yet happened. But will new technology finally lead to the demise of notes and coins? With the advent of prepaid cards, for example the Oyster card for public transport in London, payment via mobile phones and the continued growth of 'plastic', it may be that cash is on the way out.

1 Outline the functions that any form of money has to fulfil.

2 Assess the extent to which 'plastic' can fulfil the functions of money.

Figure 15.1 *An oyster card*

This chapter builds on the concepts introduced at AS. In order to facilitate a better understanding of monetary policy, the chapter begins with an outline of the functions of money. The chapter then explores the objectives and instruments of current UK monetary policy, along with a focus on the factors considered by the Monetary Policy Committee of the Bank of England (BoE) when making their monthly interest rate decisions. This chapter also takes a closer look at the so-called 'transmission mechanism' of monetary policy.

Money

Most people living in the UK would agree that money comprises coins and banknotes issued by the Bank of England, along with deposits in high street banks and building societies. In a modern economy, people and businesses are prepared to accept what are essentially 'tokens' such as banknotes and coins, with little intrinsic worth, as payment because they are confident that these will be accepted when they decide to spend them.

The functions of money

There are four functions that money performs in an economy:

A medium of exchange. Money is an asset which is accepted in exchange for goods and services, rather than having to resort to barter. Without a suitable medium of exchange, trade could only take place if there was a double coincidence of wants, which is unlikely.

A store of value or wealth. Because we can exchange money for goods and services, it is a convenient way of holding purchasing power into the future if we choose not to spend it today.

A unit of account. Money provides a means of expressing value, which allows people to compare the relative values of goods and services via their quoted prices.

A standard of deferred payment. In a developed economy, goods are frequently purchased on credit, with the amount repaid in the future. This function allows people to delay paying for goods or settling debts, since we can be reasonably confident about the future value and purchasing power of money.

The problem of defining the money supply

The money supply is the total amount of money circulating in the economy. Arguably, no single financial asset possesses all the required functions of money, and so financial assets tend to be placed along a spectrum of **liquidity** as shown in Figure 15.2. At one extreme are the assets that best fulfil the required functions of money today, that is, cash. At the other extreme are assets that are much less liquid, for example, shares and property.

Figure 15.2 *The liquidity spectrum*

Cash shares	Current accounts	Deposit accounts	Treasury bills	Property

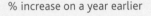

Key terms

Liquidity: the degree to which financial assets can be easily converted into money.

Narrow money: notes, coins and balances available for normal financial transactions.

Broad money: money held in banks and building societies that is not immediately accessible. This money is held in accounts for which notice is required to make withdrawrals, for example, some types of savings accounts.

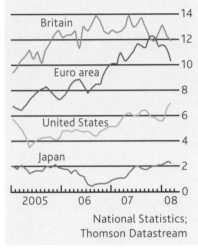

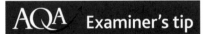

Figure 15.3 *Broad money supply, % increase on year earlier*

AQA Examiner's tip

The Bank of England uses a number of money supply measures, for example M0 and M4. Whilst specific knowledge of the components of these will not be tested at A2, it is useful to know that M0 constitutes cash, whilst M4 is 'broad money'.

Because there is no single financial asset which perfectly possesses all the functions of money, the Bank of England uses more than one definition of the money supply. However, there are two general types of money supply definition; **narrow money** and **broad money**. The term narrow money restricts the measure of money to cash and bank and building society current accounts, which are most readily used as a medium of exchange.

Broad money supply

Many central banks keep an eye on broad measures of the money supply as an indicator of overheating or cooling in the economy. Linked to the quantity theory of money, an annual increase in the money supply above 5 per cent in a developed country would give an early warning sign of inflation, that is, of too much money chasing too few goods. A rate below 5 per cent may signal a downturn in economic growth or falling prices. However, money supply growth has proven to be an unreliable indicator, because the velocity of circulation varies. In times of economic uncertainty, as in 2007/8, firms and households prefer to keep more of their wealth in cash or more liquid bank accounts. This explains why, as shown in Figure 15.3, broad money has either picked up or stayed strong despite weaker economic growth.

Adapted from The Economist, *10 May 2008.*

For a few years from the mid-1970s to the mid-1980s, during the so-called 'monetarist era', control of the money supply became an important part of economic management in general, and monetary policy in particular. During this period, monetarist economists devoted considerable attention to the problem of precisely which assets to include and exclude when defining the money supply. Targets were set in relation to growth of various sections of the money supply, in a bid to control inflation, linked to a reliance on the quantity theory of money, as explained in Chapter 12. However, it became difficult to control specific sections of the money supply, and subsequently money supply targeting was abandoned as a tool of economic management.

Demand for money

Individuals and firms tend to hold a variety of financial assets, which can be divided into **financial assets** and **physical assets**. Financial assets include cash, bank accounts and shares, while physical assets include property, consumer durables, art and fine wines.

The demand for holding money is determined by two key factors:

1 **Income**. The higher the level of income, the greater the demand for money, in order to facilitate spending.

2 **The rate of interest**. Money could be used to buy financial assets such as bonds, which yield interest. The higher the rate of interest, the higher the opportunity cost of holding money.

Figure 15.4 highlights the relationship between interest rates and the demand for money, and also the impact of a change in income on the demand for money. The demand for money curve slopes downwards because a rise in the rate of interest increases the incentive to hold interest-bearing financial assets such as bonds. A rise in income will shift the demand for money curve to the right (DM1 to DM2) at any given rate of interest, because the requirement to hold money for spending transactions increases.

The rate of interest

The rate of interest is effectively the price of holding money. Figure 15.5 shows the demand and supply curves for money. As outlined above, the demand curve for money is downward-sloping because a rise in the rate of interest rate increases the attractiveness of holding interest-bearing financial assets such as bonds, and vice-versa. It is usual to draw the money supply as a vertical line, as we assume that a central bank such as the Bank of England can control the supply of money in the economy independently of its price. The equilibrium rate of interest is at re, where the demand for money equals the supply of money.

If the demand for money increases, for example, following an increase in income, more money will be demanded at any given interest rate (DM1 to DM2) and, as shown in Figure 15.6, the equilibrium rate of interest will increase from r1 to r2.

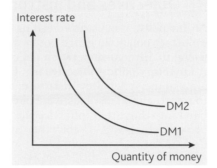

Figure 15.4 *The demand for money*

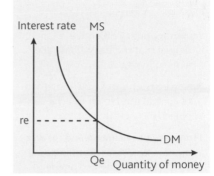

Figure 15.5 *The equilibrium rate of interest*

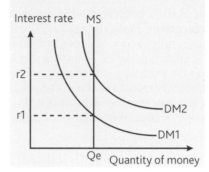

Figure 15.6 *An increase in the demand for money*

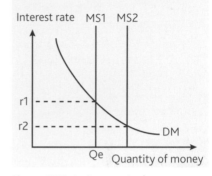

Figure 15.7 *An increase in the money supply*

A fall in demand for money will lead to a fall in the rate of interest. If the government or central bank increases the money supply, the MS curve will shift rightwards (MS1 to MS2), as shown in Figure 15.7. This will lead to a fall in interest rates from r1 to r2. A reduction in the money supply will lead to an increase in interest rates.

Whilst we have assumed here that there is one market for money and thus one equilibrium rate of interest, it is worth clarifying that, in reality, there are many different money markets and subsequent rates of interest. Rates of interest for government bonds differ from those for credit cards and mortgages, for example. However, interest rates tend to move in the same direction. For example, if the Bank of England cuts the **base rate** of interest, then we expect to see lower mortgage rates and lower rates on savings accounts offered by banks and building societies. With the effects of the '**credit crunch**' continuing in 2008, and several high street banks and building societies in financial difficulty, it is fair to say that this link has been slow to materialise recently. When these institutions face difficulties, they tend to be much more reluctant to pass on lower interest rates.

It is also worth pointing out the difference between nominal and real interest rates. **Nominal interest rates** are those not adjusted for inflation, whilst **real interest rates** are those that have been adjusted for inflation. The real interest rate is more important for businesses and consumers to consider when making spending and saving decisions. The real rate of return on savings, for example, is the nominal rate of interest minus the rate of inflation. So, if a saver is receiving a nominal rate of interest of 5 per cent on his savings, but price inflation is 2 per cent, the real rate of return on these savings is only 3 per cent.

Key terms

Base rate: the interest rate a bank sets to determine its lending and borrowing rates. It will tend to offer interest rates below the base rate to savers, whilst charging rates above the base rate for borrowers.

Credit crunch: a recently coined term used to refer to the reduced willingness of financial institutions to lend to households and to one another.

Nominal interest rates: interest rates not adjusted for inflation.

Real interest rate: the nominal rate of interest minus the rate of inflation.

■ Key terms

Monetary policy objective: a target or goal that the Bank of England aims to meet.

Policy instrument: a tool or method of control used to try to achieve an objective.

Monetary base control and reserve asset ratios: restrictions imposed by the Bank of England on the ability of high street banks to supply credit and bank deposits.

■ Link

Look back at Chapter 12, p140 for the quantity theory of money.

■ Objectives and instruments of monetary policy

At this point, it is worth rereading the chapter in your AS textbook on monetary policy. To gain a better understanding of monetary policy, it is useful to distinguish between policy objectives and policy instruments. A **monetary policy objective** is a target or goal that the Bank of England aims to meet. A **policy instrument** is a tool or method of control used to try to achieve an objective. Policy instruments are divided on the one hand into those that influence the supply of new credit and creation of bank deposits, and, on the other hand, those that influence the demand for loans or credit.

Monetary policy objectives

Controlling inflation has been the main objective of UK monetary policy since the late 1970s. Before 1992, however, the Bank of England attempted to control inflation using **intermediate monetary policy objectives**. From the mid-1970s until 1985, underpinned by monetarist economic theory, the money supply was used as the intermediate target of monetary policy. This was replaced from 1985 until 1992, by a focus on the exchange rate. Intermediate policy objectives were eventually abandoned in 1992 when the pound was forced out of the European exchange rate mechanism (ERM). Since then, the target of monetary policy has been on control of inflation directly.

The 'monetarist era'

Monetarists believe that inflation arises directly from an increase in the quantity of money in the economy. This is the essence of the quantity theory of money, outlined earlier. The quantity theory of money predicts that if the quantity of money holdings increases, this leads to excess demand for goods and services economy-wide, leading to demand-pull inflation.

From the late 1970s until 1985, monetary policy involved announcing a target rate of money supply growth and then implementing policy to achieve this target. The 'monetarist experiment' ended in 1985, when Margaret Thatcher's Conservative government abandoned these formal money supply targets. The reasons for abandoning the targets were the realisation that the growth of the money supply proved extremely difficult to control, and that the relationship suggested by the quantity theory of money seemed to break down in the 1980s.

The exchange rate and monetary policy

From 1985 to 1992, the exchange rate was adopted as the monetary policy objective. This involved first attempting to achieve a high exchange rate, and then maintaining the exchange rate at a high level, latterly within the exchange rate mechanism. The government believed that a high exchange rate creates a source of external discipline, reducing inflationary pressure in the UK economy. A high exchange rate reduces the relative prices of imported food and consumer goods, and the cost of imported oil and raw materials falls, which helps to reduce cost-push inflationary pressure.

Monetary policy instruments

There are two groups of monetary policy instruments: those that affect the money supply, and those that affect the general public's demand for money.

Controlling the supply of money

Monetary base control. Historically, the Bank of England limited the ability of commercial banks to supply more credit and bank deposits in two main ways. The first method involved imposing **reserve asset ratios** on banks, meaning they were obliged to hold a certain proportion of their total assets in reserve. The Bank of England has also imposed direct controls on bank lending. Both quantitative and qualitative controls were used. Quantitative controls impose maximum limits on the amount that banks can lend, or on the rate at which banks can expand total deposits. Qualitative controls instruct or persuade banks to lend only to certain types of customer, for example, business customers.

Open market operations (OMOs). The Bank of England can issue government bonds, which, if purchased by the non-financial sector, passes money to the central bank. This reduces the available money supply, because money lodged at the Bank of England is not usually counted as part of the money supply.

Influencing the demand for money

Modern monetary policy primarily involves manipulating interest rates. To influence the demand for money, the Bank of England raises or lowers its official rate of interest, which rations the demand for bank deposits. For example, an increase in the Bank of England's lending rate or **repo rate** means that high street banks must increase the interest rates charged to their own customers, meaning bank loans become more expensive. Consequently, households and firms will reduce their demand for credit, and seek to repay existing loans. This reduces overall bank deposits, along with the size of the money supply.

Current UK monetary policy

While control of inflation remains the policy objective, interest rates, rather than the control of the banks' cash and liquid asset ratios, are now the principal instrument of monetary policy, and changes in interest rates affect the demand for bank loans or credit rather than the supply of bank deposits. Since 1992, UK monetary policy has involved meeting a published inflation rate target. The Monetary Policy Committee (MPC) of the Bank of England estimates what the inflation rate is likely to be around 18 months ahead, if interest rates remain unchanged. If this forecast rate of inflation is different from the government's central target rate, the Bank will change interest rates accordingly.

After 1997, this inflation target-setting approach was maintained, though the incoming New Labour government made some crucial changes. The most significant alterations were giving operational independence for meeting the inflation target to the Bank of England, and the creation of the Monetary Policy Committee (MPC) within the Bank to implement monetary policy. The inflation rate target was also made symmetrical. This means that it is as undesirable to undershoot the central target as it is to overshoot it. Thus the Bank of England should seek to stimulate aggregate demand, tending to raise the rate of inflation, if actual inflation falls, or is predicted to fall, below the target rate. Similarly, the Bank should reduce aggregate demand and hence inflation if it is above the target rate, or predicted to rise above it. The MPC was also made accountable for any deviations from the central target rate of inflation. If inflation is more than 1 per cent higher or lower than the target, the Governor of the Bank of England is required to write an open letter to the Chancellor, explaining why the divergence has occurred, and what the Bank intends to do to bring inflation back into target range. Whilst the primary objective of monetary policy is price stability, the Bank of England is also obliged to support the government's other macroeconomic policy objectives.

Critics argue that the New Labour government relies too much on monetary policy and interest rates to manage aggregate demand. They

Key terms

Open market operations (OMOs): the buying and selling of government bonds in exchange for money to either increase or decrease the money supply.

Repo rate: the interest rate set by the Monetary Policy Committee of the Bank of England in order to influence inflation. Short for 'sale and repurchase' rate.

 Examiner's tip

The Bank of England implements the government's monetary policy, while fiscal policy is implemented by the Treasury.

Figure 15.8 *The MPC of the Bank of England in 2008*

■ Key terms

Eurozone: the countries in the EU that have adopted the single currency.

Transmission mechanism of monetary policy: the process by which a change in interest rates affects aggregate demand and inflation.

believe the Chancellor should be prepared to use fiscal policy in a more active way to manage aggregate demand. Currently, however, fiscal policy is used primarily to create a beneficial supply-side environment.

The Monetary Policy Committee

The nine members of the MPC are required to consider a large volume of economic information ahead of each monthly meeting. Whilst some of the charts and terminology presented seem quite technical, much of the theoretical background will have already been covered in the Economics course. The data considered is summarised in the minutes published two weeks after each decision and includes the following:

Financial markets. This will include share prices, which are both an indicator of investor confidence and a determinant of household wealth and consumer confidence.

The international economy, including recent macroeconomic developments in the US, **Eurozone** and Asia. Trends in the pound's exchange rate against the euro or US dollar will also be considered. A weakening pound may lead to cost-push inflationary pressure through imports of raw materials, for example.

Money and credit. Bank lending and consumer credit figures will be analysed including the levels of mortgage equity withdrawal (MEW) from the housing market along with monthly data on unsecured lending. Movements in narrow and broad money measures will also be analysed.

Demand and output. Consumption and planned investment survey figures are analysed here. The rate of growth of real GDP along with estimates of the size of the output gap will also be considered.

The labour market. Figures for employment and unemployment will be presented here. Labour market data can be key indicators of demand-pull and cost-push inflationary pressure. High annual rates of wage inflation might eventually feed through into a rise in consumer prices, for example.

Costs and prices. Manufacturer surveys of input costs and 'factory gate' prices are used as an indicator of whether firms are passing inflation along the 'pipeline' to the high street, a good signal of cost-push inflationary pressure.

Many of these areas of analysis are reinforced by surveys from the Bank's own team of Regional Agents.

The problems of accurately forecasting inflation

In practice, it is extremely difficult to forecast inflation with great accuracy, and the consumer price index itself contains errors and omissions. In addition, the economic effects of unforeseen external shocks such as a natural disaster, terrorist attack or outbreak of war can make forecasts inaccurate. Indeed, the Bank of England's economists do not even attempt to forecast inflation precisely. In its Inflation Report, published quarterly, the Bank of England produces a 'fan chart', as shown in Figure 15.9, which shows the Bank's central forecast for inflation for the next two years, along with paired bands of probabilities of inflation falling within certain ranges.

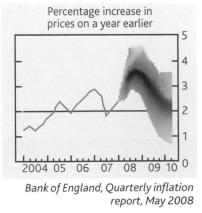

Percentage increase in prices on a year earlier

Bank of England, Quarterly inflation report, May 2008

Figure 15.9 *CPI inflation fan diagram*

■ The transmission mechanism of monetary policy

The link between a change in the Bank of England's official interest rate and subsequent changes in inflation is referred to as the **transmission mechanism of monetary policy**. Monetary policy influences aggregate demand and inflation in several ways. The flow diagram in Figure 15.10 shows how an interest rate change feeds through to inflation.

The Bank's interest rate decisions affect interest rates set by mortgage-lenders, commercial banks and financial institutions. These same decisions and announcements influence the confidence and expectations of firms and households, as well as asset prices and the exchange rate.

Aggregate demand $(C + I + G + (X - M))$ is subsequently affected. The domestic component of demand will be stimulated by lower market interest rates as spending, and investment by individuals and firms is boosted. Conversely, higher market interest rates would tend to reduce domestic demand. Further, a fall in the official interest rate will lead to a rise in asset prices and subsequent 'wealth effect' meaning people generally become more confident about the future. This leads to an increase in consumption. In addition, lower interest rates cause reduced demand for holdings of pounds, which in turn causes the exchange rate to fall. This reduces the prices of UK exports, while raising the price of imports. Demand for UK goods and services increases.

Changes in aggregate demand can affect demand-pull inflationary pressures if there is little spare capacity. Cost-push pressures may also arise from the effects of changes in aggregate demand on wage rates. Changes in the relative prices of imports affect inflation in two ways. Increasing prices of imported food and consumer goods affect inflation directly, while increasing prices of imported raw materials affect cost-push inflationary pressures. The Bank of England estimates a time lag of up to two years between a change in the official rate of interest and subsequent changes in the rate of inflation.

Monetary policy stance

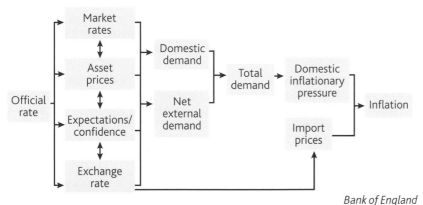

Bank of England

Figure 15.10 *The transmission mechanism of monetary policy*

The monetary policy stance refers to whether interest rates are intended to either stimulate or depress aggregate demand, or else allow aggregate demand to grow in line with the economy's long-term underlying growth rate. Expansionary monetary policy is thus aimed at reflating aggregate demand, whilst contractionary monetary policy is used to depress aggregate demand. A neutral monetary policy is one in which interest rates neither increase or decrease aggregate demand, that is, where there are intended to be no positive or negative output gaps. A negative output gap occurs when actual output is below the potential output, whilst a positive output gap, which occurs in the boom phase of the economic cycle, is where actual output is above the level of the sustainable trend rate of growth.

Economic analysts have argued that monetary policy is expansionary when the official interest rate is 4 per cent and that the neutral interest rate is in the range of 5 per cent to 5.5 per cent. If this is indeed the case, monetary policy would be deemed contractionary when the Bank's lending rate is above 5.5 per cent.

After completing this chapter you should be able to:

■ build on your knowledge of the role of the Monetary Policy Committee (MPC) of the Bank of England from AS and be able to discuss how the Bank can influence the money supply and the rate of interest

■ show an awareness of the objectives of monetary policy

■ identify and explain the instruments of policy which are currently employed by the Bank of England to achieve the inflation target set by the government

■ understand how the demand for, and supply of, funds in different markets affect interest rates

■ understand the factors that are considered by the MPC when setting interest rates.

Extract A

In the early days of monetary policy, money supply targeting was a core element of anti-inflation policy. This approach was slowly dropped during the 1990s, but the underlying growth of the money supply has remained an important issue for policy-makers and recent growth in the money supply has led to concern from some commentators that higher inflationary pressures may yet emerge.

Extract B

Bank's inflation controllers leave the NICE decade to enter the not-so-nice. Threadneedle Street's rate setters are having to work harder to tame the economy

The call came to Mervyn King as he returned home after a game of tennis on bank holiday Monday 10 years ago this week. Eddie George, the Governor of the Bank of England, was on the line in a state of high excitement after being told that Gordon Brown, freshly appointed to the Treasury in Tony Blair's government, was proposing to hand over day-to-day control of interest rates to Threadneedle Street.

'I received a call from Eddie asking me to meet him in the Bank as soon as possible. That was the last I saw of the sun for quite some time,' Mr King recalled in a lecture last night to mark 10 years of Bank independence. Mr Brown, Labour's first chancellor in almost 20 years, dropped his bombshell the next morning, leaving King to burn the midnight oil over the subsequent weeks to flesh out the plan for a nine-strong monetary policy committee.

Since Mr Brown's announcement on 6 May 1997, there have been 120 meetings of the 9 member monetary policy committee. Mr King is alone in having attended all of them, first as chief economist, then from 1998 as deputy governor, and since 2003 as governor after 'Steady Eddie' retired. The Bank has set interest rates for the second half of the 'NICE' decade – non-inflationary constant expansion – and is now trying to keep the economy on an even keel in what Mr King calls the "not-so-bad" decade.

Last month, for the first time since independence, inflation rose to a level more than a percentage point above the 2 per cent target set by the Chancellor. As a result, the Governor was obliged to write to Mr Brown explaining why the situation had been allowed to develop and what the Bank intended to do about it. The City believes the remedy will be exactly the same as that applied when there were signs of incipient price pressure in May 1997 – higher interest rates. A quarter-point increase is seen as a done deal; some analysts say the first half-point increase since Bank independence could be in prospect. A half-point increase would be painful for Britain's hard-pressed borrowers, but Brown considers the decision to free the Bank from political control to be one of Labour's great achievements. The public, he believes, accepts that the Bank does what is necessary to ensure price stability and that his model for independence is better than that in either the US or the Eurozone. Mr Brown believes the Fed is over reliant on the personality of its chairman while the European Central Bank remains obsessed by data on the money supply.

Coincidentally, Mr King and his colleagues are under fire from economists – including one of the original members of the committee, Charles Goodhart – who say the Bank's decision to ignore the large amounts of cheap credit swilling round the economy is the reason inflation is flashing amber warning signals. While acknowledging the criticism last night, the Governor said it was difficult to know what signals about inflation changes in the money supply were sending. Attempts to target it in the past had been unsuccessful but the Bank would devote more resources to analysing the money supply. Lord George made clear in a newspaper interview yesterday, that while the handing of interest rates to the Bank was a bolt out of the blue for the public and most of the Bank's staff, he had been discussing it with Mr Brown and his aide, Ed Balls, for two years before the announcement. Lord George was also careful to praise the setup that was put in place five years previously. 'I think the big step for monetary policy was adopting inflation targeting in 1992 [under then Chancellor

Norman Lamont].' Mr King argued last night that 'granting independence to the Bank of England was the dramatic constitutional change that convinced financial markets of the UK's conversion to stability as the basis of macroeconomic policy'. And that stability, by most measures, has been impressive. Growth has averaged 2.8 per cent – slightly above the postwar average – and there has not been a single quarter of negative growth. The deviation of inflation from its Treasury-set target has been a mere –0.08 per cent.

The Governor pointed out that the last 10 years, in spite of a considerable number of economic shocks ranging from the dotcom bust to the recent spike in energy prices, have seen not only a good economic performance in Britain but a better one than any of its partners in the Group of Seven leading economies. 'The fact that the UK improved not only its absolute but also its relative performance – moving from last to first in the G7 league table – is encouraging.' But, he said, the Monetary Policy Committee (MPC) could not take all the credit. The faster than average growth performance of the last decade was probably down to the far-reaching economic reforms of previous governments which have made the economy more flexible. The MPC, though, could take credit for the greater stability the economy had enjoyed, he said. 'All this amounts to a revolution in the way interest rate decisions are made in this country. It is hard now to imagine policy being set in any other way.'

Ashley Seager and Larry Elliott, The Guardian, 3 May 2007

1   (a)   Briefly explain the theoretical relationship between money supply growth and inflation. *(5 marks)*

    (b)   How could money supply targeting be used as an instrument of monetary policy? *(10 marks)*

    (c)   Discuss the extent to which the Monetary Policy Committee of the Bank of England should be concerned about the growth of the money supply. *(25 marks)*

2   (a)   Explain the possible causes of a rise in the rate of inflation in the economy. *(15 marks)*

    (b)   In recent years, the priority in UK macroeconomic policy has been the control of inflation. Evaluate the likely economic consequences of this for the UK's economic performance. *(25 marks)*

AQA, January 2006

AQA Examiner's tip   Evaluation in Question 2, part (b) will require some judgement about whether or not it is beneficial for overall macroeconomic performance to focus on just one objective.

16 Globalisation

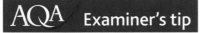

In this chapter you will:

- learn the causes and characteristics of globalisation

- understand the reasons for international trade

- understand the pattern of UK trade and how it has changed

- learn the theories of international trade and their limitations

- appreciate why and how some countries restrict trade.

AQA Examiner's tip

Make sure you keep up to date with current examples of globalisation by using newspapers or magazines such as *The Economist*.

This chapter marks the commencement of the final aspect of the specification the international economy. We are going to consider the development and growth of international trade, the theories that underpin it, the winners and losers from it and the progress, via the World Trade Organization, toward freer trade.

A term which has become increasingly used about the international economy in recent years is globalisation. This is the growing integration of the world's economy where businesses increasingly produce all or part of their product in areas other than their country of origin, or source their raw materials in the cheapest parts of the world and increasingly market their products on a worldwide basis. A business may make parts for a product in several different countries and assemble them in another because this is the most cost effective and efficient method to get the product to its consumers. They will tend to make use of their business's competitive advantage by locating production wherever it is most efficient. This means that decisions taken in one part of the world affects other parts; for example, the decision taken by the management of PSA Peugeot/Citroen to make the Peugeot's 206's successor in a new factory in Trnava, Slovakia led to 2,300 jobs being lost at Ryton near Coventry. Firms base their decisions on what is happening in the 'world market' rather than national markets.

You may think that the increasing use of the term 'globalisation' heralds something new in the international economy. This is untrue as the world economy was extremely well integrated before the First World War and subsequently until the worldwide slump (or Great Depression) of the 1930s led to increasing levels of protection and a diminution of world trade.

Figure 16.1 *The Wall Street Crash of 1929 led to millions of people being out of work throughout the 1930s*

Important aspects of globalisation

There are a number of aspects which indicate and have affected globalisation:

- The growing importance of international trade as the volume of world trade has increased and world imports and exports have increased annually by 10 per cent between 2000 and 2006 (WTO world trade report 2007).

- The growth of companies that can be referred to as **multinational corporations (MNCs)** whose familiar products and brand names appear worldwide and are probably best illustrated by McDonald's and Coca-Cola but include others like Ford and Sony. The businesses are not all from the developed world; increasing numbers are from the BRICs (Brazil, Russia, India and China).

Multinational corporations

The speed of globalisation has been increased by a number of factors:

- Technological change, as communications technology has enabled easy, secure and relatively cheap transfer of information between the head office and its global sites. The Internet allows consumers to compare prices on a worldwide basis before they decide to purchase products.

- A revolution has occurred in transportation with containerisation, which has allowed firms to pack their products on site, and has removed the bottleneck formerly caused by the inefficient labour-intensive and inflexible dockside techniques of loading and unloading freight. This has reduced the costs of sea transport which is the way in which most goods are transported internationally.

- The growth of East European market-based economies, since the opening up of the former satellites of the Union of Soviet Socialist Republics (USSR), has increased the markets available to global businesses as the new open markets are available to foreign competition. These markets, with their lower costs of production, attract inward investment from multinational companies.

- Trade is gradually becoming more liberated as protection has been reduced due, formerly, to the activities of the General Agreement of Tariffs and Trade (GATT) and now to the activities of the World Trade Organization (WTO). While the Doha Round appears to have stalled, the end of the MultiFibre agreement has increased multinational trade in textiles.

These factors have allowed firms to organise their production in such a way that reduces their costs and has led to a general reduction in the price of many manufactured goods.

Globalisation has increased competition in all markets and has led to a number of outcomes:

- Foreign competition has entered markets previously the prerogative of domestic businesses, for example, E.ON, formerly Powergen, is a German energy company that supplies around 9 million gas and electricity customers in the UK while Vivendi, a French company, supplies some UK water customers. BT is one of the world's leading providers of communications solutions, serving customers in Europe, the Americas and Asia Pacific.

- Unemployment and deindustrialisation occurs as MNCs move production out of developed countries and into newly industrialising

Link

See *AQA Economics AS*, Chapter 15 p172, for more on the economic growth of BRICs.

countries. For example, vacuum cleaner manufacturer Dyson moved its production to Asia and the power tool maker Black & Decker cut 1,000 jobs when it switched work to the Czech Republic. When relocating its operations, a business may consider how it can reduce its costs or access skilled labour to improve product quality, for example, Microsoft locating its research laboratories in Cambridge.

- Globalisation has meant greater economies of scale as businesses operating worldwide are able to spread their fixed costs over a larger volume of output and reduce unit costs.

- Mergers and joint ventures. Business are increasingly merging or forming alliances with others, often in other countries, to reduce costs and increase supplies of goods or services to a global market. For example Volkswagen, Ford and PSA have developed a diesel engine that they all use in their people carriers.

Role of multinational corporations

The role of MNCs has been crucial in the development of globalisation as they originated in developed countries and provided most of the foreign direct investment into developing countries, where they either locate production processes or generate raw materials. Their impact on the developing country will depend upon a number of points.

- Their willingness to accommodate to the needs of the local economy in terms of employment, training, environmental protection and health and safety considerations. Often multinationals have moved to reduce their levels of costs and may not relish increasing them by undertaking expensive policies even though these may confer positive externalities on their host economies. This may be balanced by the fact that they are extremely conscious of adverse publicity in the Western press.

- The ability of the host governments to regulate their activities effectively and not to be prepared to forgo safety or human rights considerations to attract foreign direct investment (FDI). For example Friends of the Earth accuse Shell of following unsustainable policies and ignoring regulations in numerous countries where it is extracting oil and gas.

- Multinationals may expect incentives, such as the abolition of trade restrictions, special tax rates, subsidies and dispensations from labour laws (for example, minimum wage legislation). Evidence from the World Bank suggests that when other factors – such as infrastructure, transport costs, and political and economic stability – are more or less equal, the taxes in one location may have a significant effect on investors' choices. Such tax incentives are not only likely to reduce the level of fiscal revenues but also frequently create opportunities for illicit behaviour by tax administrators and companies. This issue has become crucial in emerging economies, which face more severe budgetary constraints and corruption than industrial countries.

- While it is frequently alleged that MNCs are extremely mobile, in that if they see cheaper production opportunities they may decide to relocate closing their facilities with consequent increase in unemployment for the host country, research by Holger Görg and Eric Strobl, presented at the Royal Economic Society's Annual Conference, suggests that the argument is not as clear-cut as critics of multinationals make it seem. While a comparison of foreign multinationals and domestic plants shows that the former are about 40 per cent more likely to exit an industry than comparable domestic plants, new jobs created in multinationals are about 10 per cent more likely to survive than jobs created in similar domestic plants.

Link

For further information on this topic go to www.foe.co.uk/campaigns/corporates/case_studies/shell/index

Activities

1. Outline the causes of globalisation.

2. What are the advantages of rapid globalisation to a MNC?

3. What benefits do (a) developed and (b) developing countries get from globalisation?

Link

For further information on Royal Economics Society's Annual Conference go to www.res.org.uk/annualconference.asp

The influence of globalisation

Globalisation has allowed a better communication flow amongst More Developed Countries (MDCs) and Less Developed Countries (LDCs). It has enabled trade to grow, capital and education flows to increase and a better allocation of resources to be met around the world. There are many gains from globalisation for companies around the world, some Multinational Enterprises (MNEs) that locate themselves in LDCs bring along growth and development, like, for example, employment, technology knowledge, profit reinvestment among other factors to host countries.

Nevertheless, there are several negative aspects about globalisation as well. For instance, MDCs have a tendency to profit from globalisation in various ways when negotiating with LDCs. MNEs that go to LDCs for example, gain from cheaper labour force, cheaper land and tax rates. In the end, however, some MNEs end up negatively affecting the host country's economy by taking all profits back home, socially, by polluting the environment and finally also politically by paying bribes to the local governments to reduce tax rates or other fees.

In spite of its controversial position in different regions, some countries like the Asian tigers or the Asian New Industrial Countries (NICs) have gained incredibly from globalisation in the past 30 years. Other continents however, have proved themselves not yet ready for such a change. An example of the latter is Africa and South America, where due to different factors like corruption, low education level, weak political policies and poor transport infrastructure globalisation hasn't been able to benefit them in the same way as the NICs. It is therefore up to each county to decide and control Foreign Direct Investment (FDI) and gain from it or not.

*Contributed by **Chun Lie** and posted on Global Envision 21 February 2005*

Figure 16.2 *An example of globalisation*

It should be noted that China's rapid growth has led to a massive search to acquire resources and raw materials, China has become an extremely important source of FDI for a large number of developing countries.

■ International trade

The Pattern of UK trade

The European Union is the largest market for the UK and supplier of goods to the UK and accounts for a large percentage of UK exports (see Table 16.1). The importance of Europe as a trading partner has increased steadily since 1945. Within the EU, Germany is Britain's major market and supplier of imports, mainly machinery and manufactured goods including cars and chemicals. Next is France, which exports to the UK manufactures and food, followed by the Netherlands, which sends dairy produce and other foodstuffs.

Trade with the USA and Canada increased after 1945 but has now fallen and accounts for about 13 per cent of UK exports and imports. The USA exports machinery and other manufactures to the UK, plus natural resources including cereals, tobacco, cotton, non-ferrous metals and ores. Canada is still an important supplier of wood and pulp, metals, ores and foodstuffs.

Japan, Hong Kong, Australia, New Zealand and South Africa are less than half as important as North America as markets for UK exports, though they supply a slightly higher proportion of UK imports. Japan heads the list as it is the fourth largest supplier of imports into the UK after Germany, USA and France, almost entirely of manufactured goods such as machinery and motor vehicles.

Imports from Australia consist primarily of foodstuffs and minerals; from South Africa they include manufactured goods as well as cereals, metals, fruit and vegetables; from New Zealand they are substantially foodstuffs.

As for the developing countries, China was the UK's 11th largest export market in December 2007 while the UK is India's largest trading partner in Europe with 6.4 per cent market share.

Table 16.1 *UK export and import destinations*

	Exports		Imports	
Destination	Goods %	Services %	Goods %	Services %
EU27	63	41	58	54
France	12	5	9	10
Germany	11	7	13	7
USA	13	22	8	16
Americas including USA	16	27	11	21
China	1	1	5	<1
China including Asia	12	17	17	13
Australasia	1	3	<1	3
Africa	3	3	3	3

Table 16.2 *UK categories of goods traded 2006*

Types of goods	Exports %	Import %
Food, beverages and tobacco	5	8
Crude oil and oil products	9	8
Semi-manufactures	27	21
Finished goods	56	58

Table 16.3 *UK categories of services traded 2006*

Types of services	Exports	Imports
Transport, air, sea	13	20
Travel and tourism	15	35
Communications	3	4
Insurance	3	1
Financial	23	6
Computers and Information	5	3
Other business	29	20

■ **Key terms**

Semi-manufactures: products beyond the raw material stage that are used in the production of finished products, for example chemicals, stone and metals.

Trade between developed and developing countries

Developed countries

- Developed countries have often seen developing countries as a source of cheap raw materials that could be used by developed countries in the production of goods. But the focus has now shifted as the developing countries industrialise and exploit their comparative advantage of cheap labour. Over the past decade this has been a benefit to the developed countries as the availability of cheaper products has reduced inflationary pressure and allowed the developed countries to experience lower interest rates.

- The reduction in the price of manufactured goods has increased the real incomes of consumers in developed countries and allowed them to have a higher standard of living.

- The movement of manufacturing to the developing world has allowed developed countries to experience cleaner environments as their tertiary sectors have grown and manufacturing has shrunk.

- The movement of manufacturing and the growth of outsourcing in terms of call centres and information technology services has led to calls for job protection from developed countries. This has been especially marked in the USA which has experienced a loss of jobs and increasing structural unemployment as firms have relocated to developing countries.

Developing countries

- Increasing levels of trade should assist developing countries to become more integrated into the world economy which should lead to successful domestic firms establishing contacts with the international capital markets.

- Increasing levels of trade should lead to a foreign trade multiplier effect which should reduce both the levels of unemployment and poverty.

- The terms of trade for primary products tends to fluctuate according to movements in demand from developed countries, which means that if the developed countries experienced a recession, demand for primary products would fall, leading to adverse terms of trade for the developing world. At present, with increasing world demand, the prices of primary products are rising rapidly. This is moving the terms of trade in favour of the primary producers increasing their export income and making necessary imports less expensive.

- The agricultural sectors of developing countries face tariffs imposed by developed countries, which reduce their potential to exploit their comparative advantage, for example, the EU's Common Agricultural Policy. The EU has pledged to discontinue all agricultural subsidies by 2013.

A common view among anti-globalisers is that the developed countries have written the international trade rules so that developing country subsidies to their industries are banned, while developed country subsidies to their agricultural sectors/farmers, are permitted. An example of this is the EU agricultural export subsidy.

Benefits of free international trade

International trade exists because firms can see the opportunity of making profits by importing and exporting goods and services. Though trade takes place to make profits for individuals it does lead to certain advantages for the economy as a whole and if trade is allowed freely between countries these benefits can be maximised:

- Specialisation leads to resources being used more efficiently (productively in terms of firms reducing costs to their lowest level to remain competitive; allocative in terms of producing/modifying goods so that consumers wish to buy them; and dynamic in terms of developing new products). With greater efficiency the prices of goods should fall and falling import prices will put pressure on domestic producers to improve their efficiency and lower their prices.

- Worldwide selling opens up larger markets for countries with the lowest comparative costs. Firms will have access to larger markets, which will enable them to produce on a larger scale and achieve the minimum efficient scale. This increase in output should bring lower costs, improve competitiveness and increase profitability.

- For the UK, international trade is essential to achieve full employment and the exploitation of economies of scale as the UK market is too small in isolation. The expansion of firms should bring with it economic growth and rising living standards for the country.

The case for specialisation and trade is based on the idea that all countries in total will gain in terms of increased production, economic efficiency, and welfare. But there is no guarantee that the gains are fairly distributed and, although restrictions will reduce economic welfare, some countries may consider protective measures to be in their best interest. As a result many countries have resorted to protecting their industries.

The theory of absolute advantage

Assume that there are two countries, A and B, and they produce just two commodities, bread and bananas. Each country has 10 units of resources. Using all of their resources they can produce the output shown in Table 16.4.

It is clear from Table 16.4 that A has an **absolute advantage** in the production of both bread and bananas as it can produce more than country B given the same resources. If each country was self-sufficient and did not trade the output would be as shown in Table 16.5.

Table 16.5 *Self-sufficiency*

	Country A	Country B	Total
Bread	200	160	360
Bananas	200	80	280

The theory of comparative advantage

While B has an absolute disadvantage compared to A, it still benefits countries to specialise even if they do not have an absolute advantage in the production of a good or a service. The theoretical basis for free trade is the theory of comparative advantage. The theory indicates that global resources can be used more efficiently when countries specialise in producing those goods and services in which they have a **comparative advantage**. Comparative advantage means that the opportunity cost of producing the good is less in a country than elsewhere.

The following ratios can be drawn up:

In country A	In country B
1 bread = 1 banana	1 bread = 0.5 of a banana
1 banana = 1 bread	1 banana = 2 bread

These opportunity cost ratios show that country B has a comparative advantage in bread as to produce an extra unit of bread it only has to give

Activities

1. Account for the reasons of the changing pattern of UK trade.

2. Explain what advantages both developed and developing countries obtain from trading with each other.

3. Explain how trade increases efficiency.

Table 16.4 *Absolute advantage*

	Country A	Country B
Bread	400	320
	or	or
Bananas	400	160

Key terms

Absolute advantage: where a country using a given resource input is able to produce more than other countries with the same input.

Comparative advantage: where a country can produce a good with a lower input cost than other countries.

up half of a banana compared to one for country A. However, country A has a comparative advantage in bananas as to produce an extra banana it only has to give up one unit of bread compared to two units for country B.

Differences in comparative advantage and opportunity costs can give rise to international trade where countries specialise in the area where they have the greatest comparative advantage. In terms of A and B this is shown in Table 16.6.

Table 16.6 *Specialisation on the basis of comparative advantage*

	Country A	Country B	Total
Bread	0	320	320
Bananas	400	0	400

From Table 16.6 you can see that the output of bananas has significantly increased from 280 to 400. However, the output of bread has fallen from 360 to 320. To rectify this situation partial specialisation can be used as can be seen in Table 16.7.

Table 16.7 *Partial specialisation*

	Country A	Country B	Total
Bread	60	320	380
Bananas	340	0	340

The final production table shows that the total output of bread has increased from 360 to 380 whilst the production of bananas has also increased from 280 to 340. International trade has led to an increase in the total supply of both products and both countries will benefit from an increase in economic welfare.

It still benefits countries to specialise even if they do not have an absolute advantage in the production of a good or a service. The theory of comparative advantage indicates that global resources can be used more efficiently when countries specialise in producing those goods and services in which they have a comparative advantage. Comparative advantage means that the opportunity cost of producing the good is less in a country than elsewhere. For example, the UK could produce bananas by growing them in heated greenhouses but the opportunity cost would be high. Efficiencies can be obtained by importing from countries where the opportunity cost is lower and concentrating on exporting goods/services in which a country has a comparative advantage.

Global specialisation should increase both allocative and productive efficiencies and competition should lead to dynamic efficiencies. If there is no trade, and countries try to be self-sufficient, these benefits will be lost. Without trade some firms will not be able to fully exploit the economies of scale and reach the minimum efficient scale.

Trade between two countries

The example above indicated how specialisation and trade would increase output. The following example considers the terms of trade between two countries.

Table 16.8 *USA and Asia*

	USA	Asia
Products	Units per hour	Units per hour
1 unit of food	6	2
1 unit of clothing	3	1.5

While the US can produce more of both goods in less time than Asia and so has an absolute advantage, Asia has the least comparative disadvantage in the production of clothing. The US has an absolute advantage in both products but in clothing the US does not have such comparative superiority as it is only twice as productive as opposed to three times as productive in food.

The US is three times as productive in food compared to Asia (six units per hour compared to two units per hour). With clothing the US is also more productive and can produce three units of clothing per hour, while Asia can only produce 1.5 units per hour.

Given this comparative advantage, the US should specialise in food, the country's greatest comparative advantage, and Asia in clothing, that continent's least comparative disadvantage.

So, if there was free trade and these two areas specialised in accordance with the theory of comparative costs, both would benefit and production would be more efficient. If the US took six units of food to Asia (it would forego three units of clothing) where 1.5 units of clothing are exchanged for two units of food and it would recieve 4.5 units of clothing (3×1.5 as the ratio in Asia is 1.5 food to clothing). Output would increase and appear as follows:

Table 16.9 *Benefits of trade*

Products	USA	Asia
	Units per hour	Units per hour
1 unit of food	6	2 (3)
1 unit of clothing	3 (4.5)	1.5
Overall gain	1.5	1

While this is a fairly simple example, the realities of the theory are more complex:

■ The original **Ricardian theory** assumes perfect competition and free trade. In reality, multinational oligopolists exist and countries operate protective policies.

■ The theory assumes constant costs and perfectly mobile factors of production. However, specialisation should lead to economies of scale as output increases and factors are not perfectly mobile. When it becomes obvious that another country has a comparative advantage in the production of a particular product, resources employed in that industry should gradually shift elsewhere. But this may happen quite slowly and during the transition period resources may remain unemployed. This is illustrated in the UK by the closure of the coal industry where miners remained unemployed for a long period of time.

■ The theory ignores the problems that are caused by a fluctuating currency. A country could have a comparative advantage in production that could be eliminated by a movement of the currency, which could cause prices and costs to change. This would lead to inefficiencies and a reduction in the amount of trade taking place.

■ In reality, countries are likely to protect goods or services which they consider to have a **strategic value** to their economy, and political considerations such as **trade embargoes** may lead to countries producing goods with high comparative costs.

Activity

Write a paragraph using Table 9 to explain why Asia will gain from trade.

Key terms

Ricardian theory: David Ricardo was a UK economist 1772–1823; outlined the theory of comparative advantage.

Strategic value: of extreme importance to a country – may be required in circumstances like war.

Trade embargoes: prohibition of the export and import of certain types of products.

- The time period is ignored – comparative advantages do not remain static they may change over time with technology and dynamic efficiencies. Deindustrialisation has occurred in the major developed economies as the newly industrialising countries have gained a comparative advantage.

- The theory ignores transport costs and while these have fallen as a result of bulk carriage and containerisation, the level of costs could eliminate the benefits of specialisation and exchange.

The terms of trade

In Table 16.9 the USA will find it advantageous to trade if its terms of trade are three units of clothing for every six units of food exported. Asia will only trade if it receives two units of food for every 1.5 units of clothing exported. In Figure 16.3 the terms of trade will lie somewhere between the two possibility boundaries.

The rate of exchange between food and clothing, or the terms of trade, will determine the benefits of trade for the two trading partners. The **terms of trade** (TOT) are the ratio between export prices and import prices. Movements in the TOT will be caused by inflation, or changes in the value of the currency.

A nation's average TOT are measured with index numbers

$$= \frac{\text{index of export prices}}{\text{index of import prices}} \times 100$$

If the UK's TOT improves or moves in the country's favour, more imports are received for a given number of exports. For this to occur either the country's export prices have risen or the prices of the country's imports have fallen.

The effect of this improvement in the terms of trade on the total amount spent on imports and exports (the trade balance) depends on the price elasticity of demand for imports and exports.

If the UK's TOT improves and foreign demand for UK exports is elastic then less will be spent on them as their prices have risen. If at the same time UK demand for imports is elastic then more will be spent on imports as their price has fallen. Under these conditions the overall effect of an improvement in the TOT could be an increase in the deficit on the balance of payments. However an improvement in the TOT will make imports cheaper and will reduce inflationary pressure in the UK.

If the TOT moves against us or becomes adverse, then fewer imports are received for the same quantity of exports. For this to occur, export prices have fallen or the prices of the country's imports have risen.

Once again the overall effect of this will depend on elasticity. In the UK's case, the balance of payments should improve as long as the price elasticity of demand for both imports and exports is greater than one or elastic. Export prices will have fallen so foreign trading partners should spend more on UK exports and import prices have risen so customers in the UK should spend less. This position over elasticities is summed up in the **Marshall-Lerner condition** – a reduction in the value of sterling will improve the UK balance of payments as long as the sum of the price elasticities of demand for imports and exports is greater than one

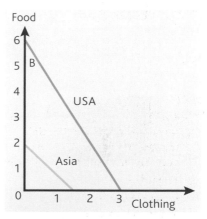

Figure 16.3 *Trading possibilities*

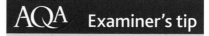

While the UK is in the position where an adverse movement of the TOT should lead to an improvement in the balance of payments, imports will be more expensive and this will exert inflationary pressure on the UK economy.

Restrictions on trade

As has been mentioned above, there is no guarantee that the gains of trade are equally distributed, and although restrictions on trade will probably reduce world welfare, individual countries may feel that it is in their interest to do so.

Arguments for protection

1   The infant industry argument. This argument is based on the premise that the industry will be of great importance to the country, either economically in terms of having a comparative advantage or strategically, but it is unlikely to develop unless it is protected from foreign competition. Korea used this technique in the development of the Kia range of cars and it has been used widely by governments of developing countries.

2   To maintain domestic employment – The theory of comparative advantage assumes that all factors are mobile and full employment will occur. In reality, labour is immobile and unemployment is likely to occur. To avoid the high economic and political costs of unemployment, countries may employ policies that maintain employment levels even though the labour is used inefficiently. An example is the European Union which has imposed quotas, since the MultiFibre agreement was phased out in 2005, to protect employment in Italy, France and other countries with large textile sectors. The costs of structural unemployment are seen as too high and domestic industries need time to adjust to the increased flow of cheaper imports.

3   To prevent dumping – Some countries subsidise firms to produce goods that can then be exported and sold below the price of non-subsidised firms in competitor countries. This is considered to be unfair and other countries are likely to stop these cheap imports, as they will adversely affect domestic industry. Dumping may be motivated by the need to obtain foreign currency or to gain a foothold in a foreign market, or in the hope of achieving economies of scale. The case study on page 191 is an example of retaliatory action.

4   To avoid 'unfair' competition – It is sometimes claimed that developing countries will often exploit their labour by paying low wages, employing child labour, not installing proper safety procedures and not having to pay the levels of tax, and National Insurance that occur in existing, high wage industrialised countries. On this basis, protection from such 'unfair' competition is advocated often by the supporters of the domestic industry that is unable to compete. Interpretation of the rights and wrongs of such cases is often extremely difficult and economists do not always see them as a legitimate reason for protection. An alternative view is that these countries are specialising in those goods where their plentiful supply of labour gives them a comparative advantage and trade will lead in the future to increased development, an increasing standard of living, and an improvement in economic and social conditions.

Case study

China slams EU anti-dumping charges on shoes

China on Friday denounced the European Union for imposing anti-dumping duties on its leather shoe exports, the latest in a series of disputes that have strained trade ties.

The Commerce Ministry said in a statement on its website that China was not dumping shoes in the European Union, and that the EU's charges were groundless. EU Trade Commissioner Peter Mandelson on Thursday announced punitive anti-dumping duties for imports of leather shoes from China and Vietnam. The duties, to be introduced between 7 April and 15 September, will range up to 19.4 per cent for Chinese shoes and 16.8 per cent for Vietnamese shoes. In announcing the decision, Mandelson said he had to counter 'disguised subsidies' and 'state-supported dumping'. 'We are not targeting China and Vietnam's natural advantages. We are targeting anti-competitive behaviour,' he said. Chinese Commerce Ministry spokesman Chong Quan dismissed Mandelson's claims. 'It's well known that shoemaking is a labour-intensive industry, and China, with its low labour costs, has a comparative advantage in this industry,' he said. This was the latest incident, he said, in a long history of unfair treatment of China's leather shoe makers, which had long faced quotas in the EU until they were annulled at the beginning of 2005. 'This smacks of protectionism and is completely out of line with the overall trend of free trade represented by the Doha Round,' he said, referring to the World Trade Organization's latest round of trade negotiations. Chong said that leather shoe manufacturing was one of the most market-orientated industries in China, with 98 per cent of such firms being privately owned. 'The European Union ignored this fact and denied the market economy status for China's leather shoe manufacturers, which is full of strong discrimination and goes against the principles of fair trade,' he said. Chong said the EU's investigation was full of problems and was not objective. He urged his European counterpart to reconsider, saying, 'We ask the EU to treat Chinese shoemakers fairly and to re-evaluate the issue comprehensively and reasonably.' The shoes case is one of a proliferation of anti-dumping actions involving China, whose exporting prowess is raising political hackles in Europe and the United States.

(Reuters) Updated: 24/02/06 17:02 Copyright by chinadaily.com.cn.

Arguments against protection

1 Welfare losses will occur due to economic inefficiency as countries are not specialising in those goods where they have the lowest opportunity cost. This can be seen in terms of domestic consumers paying higher prices as a result of EU protection for textiles and shoes. Figure 16.4 illustrates the welfare loss as supply falls.

The demand and supply curve before protection are shown as D and S. The consumer surplus is shown by the area ABC and the producer surplus by the area ACE. Protection shifts the supply curve upwards and the consumer surplus falls to BFG. The producer surplus falls to HFG and there is a deadweight loss shown by the arrowed triangle. The upper part of the triangle labelled C shows deadweight loss to the consumer the lower part to the producer. We may also argue that protection will limit consumers' access to goods and services which are produced domestically, thus restricting access and reducing choice. Domestic goods may be more expensive or inferior to their imported counterparts.

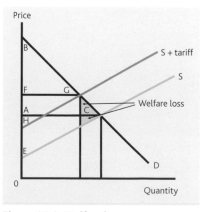

Figure 16.4 *Welfare loss*

Specific tax: a tax levied at a fixed rate per unit.

Ad-volorem: a tax which is a percentage of the price of the unit.

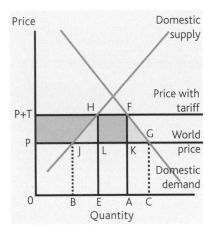

Figure 16.5 *The imposition of a tariff*

2 Retaliation – Countries who feel that their domestic industries will be harmed by protection are likely to retaliate, which will just reduce world trade to the detriment of all. China threatened to retaliate against the levy of additional duties by the EU on its exports of shoes.

3 Protection props up inefficient and monopoly producers as they do not face efficient competition. For example, Italian firms may delay restructuring to compete with Chinese imports and reap monopoly profits while the protection is in place.

4 Protection redistributes income in favour of the protected, which means that if one country stays with free trade while its major trading partners are turning to protection it is likely to suffer increasing current account deficits and rising unemployment.

Techniques of protection

1 Tariffs – These may be **specific** or **ad-valorem**, and are taxes placed on imported, but not domestic, goods. The ability of the tariff to reduce imports depends on its size and the price elasticity of demand.

In Figure 16.5 the world price before the imposition of a tariff is 0P. After the tariff is imposed the price increases to P+T. Before the imposition of the tariff domestic demand was 0C, while domestic suppliers were producing 0B so imports were BC. The tariff increases price to P+T and domestic demand falls to 0A and domestic output rises to 0E. Imports are now EA.

■ Total consumer welfare has fallen by P, P+T, F, G.

■ Domestic suppliers have gained P, P+T, H, J at the expense of consumers (gain from the higher price P, P+T multiplied by the increased output E).

■ HFKL represents the revenue from the tariff – the amount imported multiplied by the price.

■ The overall net loss is shown by the triangles JHL and FGK indicating that the tariff has reduced welfare as a whole.

2 Subsidies – These could be shown in Figure 16.4 by shifting the supply curve downwards rather than upwards. Subsidies have to be hidden to avoid WTO restrictions or the scrutiny of the EU. They could take the form of cheap finance, tax breaks or non-market land rent or regional aid given to reduce the costs for exporters.

3 Embargoes – The prohibition of commerce and trade with a certain country, in order to isolate it and to put pressure on its government to change its policies. Embargoes are often used to stop armaments being supplied to a particular country but are likely to lead to smuggling and black markets.

4 Quotas – This restricts the number of imports allowed into the country by the use of a licence. The quota may be numerical or based on value. Quotas, like other trade restrictions, are used to benefit the producers of a good in a domestic economy at the expense of all consumers of the good in that economy. Critics argue that quotas often lead to corruption, in the form of bribes to officials in order to obtain the quota allocation, or smuggling to obtain more of the restricted goods and higher prices for consumers.

5 Administrative restrictions which make it difficult to export to a country, together with a complex set of documents and procedures that have to be followed, can be used by countries as a technique of protection. Often such procedures can be spuriously legitimised on health and safety grounds.

6 Voluntary export restraints (VER) – One government may try to persuade another to pressurise its exporters into limiting supplies into certain markets. The EU had a VER with Japanese car makers during the period 1991–1999. The effect of such agreements is to reduce competition and lead to consumers paying higher prices than they otherwise would.

■ The World Trade Organization (WTO) and trade liberalisation

The World Trade Organization's (WTO) predecessor, the General Agreement on Tariffs and Trade (GATT), was established after the Second World War to monitor international trade and to seek to reduce levels of protection between trading countries.

The World Trade Organization (WTO) is the only global international organisation dealing with the rules of trade between nations. At its heart are the WTO agreements, negotiated and signed by the bulk of the world's trading nations and ratified in their parliaments. The goal is to help producers of goods and services, exporters and importers conduct their business. The aim is to reduce tariffs and other types of protection and this is accomplished through 'rounds' where countries try to agree to reduce tariff levels. One essential component is multi-lateral agreements using the principle of 'most favoured nation status' where if a country agrees a tariff reduction with one country it has to accept the reduction with all others. This can be contrasted with bi-lateral agreements where the country only agrees trading terms with another country and does not extend it to others.

The Doha Round is a new round of trade talks under the WTO initiated at Doha, Qatar in 2001. Its primary aim is to help the developing countries expand their trade, and in order to achieve this, developed countries need to open up their markets to exports from the developing countries. The developing countries are not expected to liberalise their markets to the same extent. In the latest meeting of the Doha Round the EU declared it will eliminate agricultural export subsidies by the year 2013, but an agreement was not reached on liberalising market access for non-agricultural products and services. For the developing countries the elimination of European farm subsidies will improve their chances of selling agricultural products in developed countries.

At the end of this chapter you should:

- ■ appreciate the effects of globalisation and its implications for the UK economy
- ■ understand why international trade is necessary and beneficial
- ■ understand the reasons for changes in the patterns of trade
- ■ appreciate why some countries resort to protection.

Davos meet urges new push for Doha deal, amidst economic uncertainty

Some of the world's leading economies have called for another push for a deal in the long-running Doha Round of global trade negotiations, motivated this time by growing anxiety about the world economy.

Meeting on 26 January in the Swiss alpine resort of Davos, trade ministers from the US, the EU, Brazil, India, and a dozen other countries called for a 'mini-ministerial' meeting in March or April to strike a framework accord on cutting tariffs and farm subsidies, paving the way for concluding the struggling talks by the end of the year.

Ministerial exhortations about the Doha Round have almost become an annual feature of the World Economic Forum's annual summit in Davos, with little discernible effect. Nevertheless, the ongoing turmoil in global financial markets and concerns that the US economy may be headed into a recession contributed to a heightened sense of urgency about concluding an accord. The Davos group recognised the importance of reducing protectionism in terms of exploiting comparative advantage and resource allocation plus the dangers of bi-lateral agreements.

Cello Amorim, Brazil's foreign minister, said that the 'window of opportunity' he had referred to a year ago had now become a 'window of necessity' for a Doha agreement. Pointing to the financial market instability that has followed the sub-prime mortgage crisis in the US, he expressed hope that 'this is a moment that will bring to us a sense of urgency that this has to be done now'.

With a gloomy outlook in the developed countries the conclusion of this round will be a shot in the arm for the global economy as it will presage a very large increase in demand which would have massive repercussions added Indian Commerce minister Kamal Nath.

Indian minister Nath called for understanding of his country's 'sensitivities', a term he has repeatedly used when claiming New Delhi's inability to remove quotas and 'expose hundreds of millions of subsistence farmers to the full force of international competition.' The US and other farm exporters – including some developing countries – have staunchly opposed demands from India, Indonesia, and the other members of the G33 group to shelter some farm products from tariff cuts arising from the Doha Round.

Nath said that it was in rich countries' self-interest for a Doha deal to be good for developing countries, since emerging nations were now important drivers of the global economy. 'The content of this round must deliver to healthy economies in Asia, in Africa, in the Pacific and in Latin America because that's the goose that's laying the golden egg,' he said, according to the Inter Press Service news agency.

Adapted from Bridges weekly trade news digest, 27 January 2008

1   (a)   Explain what the Indian Commerce minister means by 'a shot in the arm for the global economy as it will presage a very large increase in demand which would have massive repercussions'.   *(5 marks)*

    (b)   With the aid of a diagram explain the effect on the Indian economy of a removal of quotas in the agricultural sector.   *(10 marks)*

    (c)   Using the passage and your own knowledge evaluate the consequences, both positive and negative, of WTO trade negotiations aimed at reducing protectionism.   *(25 marks)*

The theory of comparative advantage suggests that countries benefit from specialisation and free trade.

2   (a)   Explain what you understand by the term 'comparative advantage' and the likely benefits of free trade.   *(15 marks)*

     (b)   Discuss the economic arguments for and against trade protectionism.   *(25 marks)*

The balance of payments

AQA Examiner's tip

Candidates are required to be aware of the composition of the current account, as per AS module 2. However, a detailed knowledge of the remainder of the accounts is not required, although knowledge of the nature and significance of short-term and long-term capital flows (that is, the financial account) is required.

Key terms

Current account: the part of the balance of payments that primarily records trade in goods and services.

Capital account and **financial account:** the part of the balance of payments that records capital flows in and out of the country.

Current account deficit: when imports of goods and services exceed exports.

In this chapter we will look again at the current account of the balance of payments introduced at AS, and also introduce the other two accounts, namely the capital and financial accounts. The chapter considers in more detail the significance of a current account deficit, as well as a current account surplus, and presents possible corrective solutions. Given that the City of London is arguably now the world's most important centre for global capital flows, the chapter also considers the significance of this for the UK's balance of payments.

Balance of payments accounts

As noted in Chapter 17 of the AS book, the balance of payments records financial transactions between Britain and all other countries. The AS specification requires a detailed look at the **current account** of the balance of payments, which measures trade in goods and services, net investment incomes and transfers. At A2, you are expected to have knowledge of the two other accounts of the balance of payments, namely the **capital account** and the **financial account**. The capital and financial accounts record flows of financial capital arising from saving, investment and currency speculation.

Table 17.1 *Selected items, UK economy 'Pink book' 2007, all figures in £m*

The current account	
Balance of trade in goods	−83,631
Balance of trade in services	+29,194
Net income flows	+18,555
Net current transfers	−11,899
Balance of payments on current account	**−47,781**
The capital account	**+830**
The financial account	
Net direct investment	+7,395
Net portfolio investment	−43,487
Net financial derivatives	−7,449
Other investment	+61,022
Reserve assets	−426
Financial account balance	**+17,055**
Overall balance of payments	**−29,896**

Office for National Statistics

The current account of the balance of payments

The current account of the balance of payments records payments for the sale and purchase of goods and services, and hence the country's net income from trade. In general, if the value of exports of goods and services is less than the value of imports of goods and services, we say there is a **current account deficit**. A **current account surplus** occurs when the value of exported goods and services exceeds the value of imports. There are, however, other items in the current account, known as net income flows and net current transfers, though the trade balance is regarded as the most crucial aspect since it gives an indication of an economy's international competitiveness.

The balance of trade in goods

The **balance of trade in goods** is often referred to as the visible trade balance and includes the value of goods exported minus the value of goods imported, converted into the domestic currency. As noted in *AQA Economics AS*, Chapter 17, p193–4, if the UK exports more than it imports, this is known as a trade surplus, whereas if the UK imports more than it exports, this is known as a trade deficit. The UK has tended to run a trade deficit in recent decades, linked to the reduction in the size of our manufacturing sector. Also, a modern, developed economy such as ours gives rise to a growing demand for a sophisticated range of products that we may not be able to produce domestically. The UK's net trade deficit in goods is highlighted in Table 17.2.

The balance of trade in services

Formerly known as 'the workshop of the world' during our industrial age, services are nowadays much more important to the UK economy than manufacturing. The UK's comparative advantage in financial, insurance and Information and Communication Technology (ICT) services has led to an overall balance of trade surplus in services, as shown in Table 17.2. Trade in services is also referred to as trade in invisibles, since services are an intangible item.

Although the UK exports more services than it imports, a growing number of services that were previously produced within the UK are now imported, linked to the process of globalisation. Many UK companies now outsource or buy-in services from outside suppliers, often based in cheap labour countries, for example, call centres in India.

Table 17.2 *An analysis of the UK's balance of payments current account*

Year	Trade in goods (£bn)	Trade in services (£bn)	Total trade (£bn)	Total income (£bn)	Current transfers (£bn)	Current account balance (£bn)
1997	−12.3	+14.1	+1.8	+3.3	−5.9	−0.8
1998	−21.8	+14.7	−7.8	+12.3	−8.4	−3.2
1999	−29.1	+13.6	−15.5	+1.3	−7.5	−21.7
2000	−33.0	+13.6	−19.4	+4.5	−10.0	−24.8
2001	−41.2	+14.4	−26.8	+11.7	−6.8	−21.9
2002	−47.7	+16.8	−30.9	+23.4	−9.1	−16.5
2003	−48.6	+19.2	−29.4	+24.6	−10.1	−14.9
2004	−60.9	+25.9	−35.0	+26.6	−10.9	−19.3
2005	−68.8	+24.6	−44.2	+25.7	−12.0	−30.5
2006	−83.6	+29.2	−54.4	+18.6	−11.9	−47.8

Office for National Statistics

Net income flows and current transfers

Not all flows of money are from trade in goods and services. Income flows arise out of the use of factors of production overseas. Reflecting the former dominance of the British Empire, most of this income is from interest, profits and dividends on UK assets abroad, for example, profits earned by a UK multinational firm with a branch in Singapore. Equally, interest, profits and dividends also flow out of the country, to the overseas owners of assets located in the UK, for example, a Japanese multinational company which owns a subsidiary in the UK. Therefore, **net income flows**

Key terms

Current account surplus: when exports of goods and services exceed imports.

Balance of trade in goods: visible exports minus visible imports.

Balance of trade in services: invisible exports minus invisible imports.

Net income flows: the difference between inward and outward flows of interest, profits and dividends.

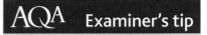

AQA **Examiner's tip**

You are not required to have a detailed knowledge of all the different individual components of the balance of trade.

Figure 17.1 *A call centre in Bangalore, India*

■ Key terms

Net current transfers: mainly government transfers to and from overseas organisations.

'Hot money': volatile capital movements which take place in the foreign exchange markets due to the interst rate changes.

are the difference between these inward and outward flows of interest, profits and dividends. The fact that the UK's net income flows are typically positive seems to indicate that UK companies own more profitable assets in the rest of the world than foreign multinationals own in the UK. Some of this is also due to aspects of the overseas earnings of the City of London.

Net current transfers consist mainly of government transfers to and from overseas organisations including the European Union.

The current balance is thus the difference between total exports and total imports, or the sum of the balance of trade in goods, the balance of trade in services, and the balance of income flows and current transfers.

■ Case study

Key UK deficit widens to a record level

The UK's current account deficit, a key economic indicator, widened to a record level in the three months from July to September, official data shows. The deficit was £20bn, or 5.7 per cent of gross domestic product, compared with £13.7bn in the previous three months, the Office for National Statistics said. This is a record, largely due to a worsening trade gap and wider deficit in investment income between Britain and other countries. As the dollar has weakened against other key currencies, this has increased demand for US goods and services. While the pound remains relatively strong against the dollar, sterling has continued to weaken against the euro, falling to a six-year low.

Adapted from news reports, December 2007.

Questions

1 What are the main determinants of the increase in the UK's current account deficit?

2 Assess the likely impact of a weaker pound on the UK's balance of payments.

The capital and financial accounts

The capital account of the UK's balance of payments is relatively unimportant, and consists largely of repatriation of financial capital from people entering or leaving the UK, along with government transfers including some types of foreign aid.

The UK's financial account records the vast majority of flows of financial capital into and out of the UK, and consists of three main components:

■ Net **foreign direct investment (FDI)**, that is, the net acquisition of productive assets by UK firms overseas, and by foreign firms in the UK. The purchase of a production facility for Dyson vacuum cleaners in Malaysia would be an example of outward direct investment, whilst the building of a car factory in Sunderland in the north east of England by Nissan is inward direct investment.

■ Net **portfolio investment** involves the purchase of financial assets, for example, shares, rather than physical or productive assets.

■ Other capital flows. These are mainly short-term capital movements, for speculative purposes, also called **'hot money'**.

Short-term and long-term capital flows

The largest component of international capital flows is made up of short-term items. The short-term is usually defined as a period of time up to one year, and short-term capital flows arise predominantly from speculating companies, banks and wealthy individuals seeking quick profits. They do this by moving capital around the globe, for example buying and selling currencies they predict will appreciate or depreciate, also referred to as 'hot money'. Short-term flows are also triggered by differences in interest rates. Funds tend to flow into currencies with high interest rates and out of currencies with lower interest rates.

Long-term capital flows are divisible into **direct investment** and **portfolio investment** flows, and are made for longer than one year, often much longer. For example, a UK firm may buy a foreign subsidiary, which it intends to own indefinitely, or a government may make a loan which is repayable in 10 years or more.

International capital flows have grown very rapidly in recent decades, reflecting the process of globalisation. This growth brings both benefits and disadvantages. Benefits include:

- It promotes growth of world trade.

- It generates a source of finance for firms that would otherwise be unable to obtain finance within their own country. This may be particularly crucial for firms in less developed countries.

- Foreign direct investment facilitates the transfer of technology, information and 'best practice' between firms and countries. This can bring important supply-side improvements.

However, there may be disadvantages:

- As highlighted recently, difficulties in one sector of the financial system can affect the global financial system. The 'sub-prime' mortgage crisis in the USA that materialised in 2007 led to a tightening of lending criteria, and 're-pricing of risk', on both sides of the Atlantic, leading to the so-called 'credit crunch'.

- Foreign direct investment may lead to the global dominance of multinational firms buying up companies around the globe. This may lead to exploitation of a country's consumers and resources.

- Large-scale 'hot money' flow of funds between currencies can destabilise exchange rates, the current account of a country's balance of payments and domestic economies as a whole.

Financial services and the City of London

The financial services industry has grown to become one of the UK's largest industries. The financial services industry, much of which is focused in the headquarters of specialist firms in the City of London, makes a considerable contribution to the current account of the balance of payments, and to capital flows in and out of the UK economy. Growth of the financial services industry has created both income and employment, with over a million people in the UK employed directly or indirectly in the industry. Financial services are particularly important to the local economy of London, with nearly a quarter of London's contribution to Gross Domestic Product (GDP) coming from financial services. Further, in 2006, nearly 10 per cent of the UK's exports of goods and services consisted of financial and insurance services, contributing to the surplus on the balance of trade in services.

Key terms

Direct investment: the acquisition of productive assets, for example, factories and offices.

Portfolio investment: the acquisition of financial assets, for example, shares and financial derivatives.

Figure 17.2 *The City of London is an important centre for financial and capital flows*

The golden gateway

Only 9,000 live in the City of London, but trillions of pounds, euros, dollars and yen flow in and out of it. The 325,000 workers who come into it every day have turned London into the world's favourite bank. This year the City has overtaken New York to become the world's money capital, and nearly £9 billion in bonuses will be shared. So how did London overtake Wall Street, and what does the future hold?

London is going from strength to strength and is outperforming the rest of the world. London is now more international than New York. It attracts the best financial talent and is overtaking New York in terms of the size of funds managed. Although official studies show that London has only 7 per cent of global funds under management, this does not take into account its importance as an offshore centre. There are billions of pounds held offshore that are perfectly legally managed here but never appear on any City balance sheets.

London dominates foreign-exchange trading, and volumes are growing at 39 per cent a year, faster than New York. Almost 80 per cent of all European hedge funds are managed here and the average UK fund made returns of over 16 per cent last year, about twice the US average. The value of European corporate takeovers, led by London, is on course to eclipse the US market this year for the first time in four years. With only a few weeks before the end of the year, European-targeted takeovers have totalled $1.15 trillion, just ahead of $1.14 trillion of deals involving US companies. Over the past 12 months, £20 billion of new capital has been raised by UK private-equity firms. Throw in the almost £11 billion worth of fees each year generated by City law firms – London is home to three of the four biggest commercial law firms in the world – and it's easy to see why London has become the global capital of global capital.

The causes of London's success are complex and include 9/11, Enron, cluster theory, time zones, the decline of the dollar and the rise of the pound, India, China, Russia, the Middle Eastern petrodollar boom, the legal system, private equity, hedge funds and many other local and global changes. Twenty years ago, Margaret Thatcher, encouraged by her Industry Secretary, Cecil Parkinson, set off the Big Bang, which involved the radical deregulation of the financial markets.

The market liberalisation created by the Big Bang attracted a new wave of immigrants – the world's biggest financial-services groups. America's Citigroup, Goldman Sachs, Merrill Lynch, Morgan Stanley and the Bank of America opened vast offices there. Deutsche Bank moved the global headquarters of its investment banking division from Frankfurt to London.

The City is in the right place. Halfway between the Asian markets and the US, traders can work virtually 24 hours a day. London does business in the right language. 'English is the international language of business,' says the equity-derivative dealer Roger Heaton. Throw in Britain's phenomenally generous non-domicile tax laws – work in the States and you get taxed on your global earnings; work or live in Britain and you only pay tax on what you earn here. Britain's refusal to join the euro has not, as europhiles predicted, damaged London's status as a financial centre. Frankfurt, home of the European Central Bank, was supposed to take over from the City as Europe's financial hub following the introduction of the new currency. Canary Wharf is a larger financial centre than the German city, with almost 80,000 working there for companies such as HSBC, Lehman Brothers, Credit Suisse, Barclays, Morgan Stanley, Citigroup and Bank of America. More euros are traded each day in London than in the rest of Europe combined.

London's success is producing startling effects in the form of super-expensive cars and soaring property prices. Retailers and service providers are busy redefining the lifestyle benefits of being seriously rich. One consequence of the spending boom is that the new money is keeping old craftsmanship alive. Savile Row tailors who have been struggling in their traditional Mayfair home have recently started opening branches in the City. But it's the property market that is the most dazzling beneficiary of the bonus system.

But can the boom last, and would it be a good thing for Britain if it did? There are political risks. New Labour has in the past indulged the City and allowed its markets to operate freely. But City chiefs argue that a growing burden of tax and the threat of EU regulation risk stopping the financial-services boom in its tracks. They point out that while Revenue and Customs has stepped up regulation of markets, rival financial centres in Europe, Asia and the Middle East have reduced red tape and improved their international tax treaties. Recently, HSBC, which moved its HQ from Hong Kong to London in 1993 to take advantage of UK tax laws, said it might move back overseas owing to waning tax competitiveness and the threat of increased corporation tax.

Critics point out that although London may be booming, the most successful firms in the Square Mile are not actually British. Indeed, most are American or Swiss. Then there are the social costs. Rich young people – the average City worker is 31 and earns £110,000 a year – are very annoying. They price the middle classes out of the market for the goods and services they thought they could take for granted – a home in a fancy(ish) neighbourhood, quality childcare, private school. A recent Halifax Bank survey found that only nine professions can now 'comfortably' afford private-school fees in London. First-time buyers are now being forced to buy with friends or take out risky 100 per cent mortgages to get on the property ladder. The concentration of wealth – especially wealth that is tied up in property – in the capital is creating an economic isolation zone. The more successful London becomes, the more we are in danger of becoming two nations: a rich south-eastern core, and the rest.

Critics tend to ignore that much of what the City does is good. Investment funds sink capital into forward-looking companies that may well end up enriching all our lives. EmPower and Ceres Power, both leading-edge British fuel-cell companies, and Windsave, which makes micro-turbines, would not exist if it were not for investment from the hedge fund RAB Capital. The Square Mile also bolsters cultural life. It may be rooted in self-interest, but the City sponsors the 'high' arts to the tune of more than £60m a year. If this sounds insignificant, the City is the only thing keeping Britain's macroeconomy in the black. The sector has filled the gap left by declining manufacturing. By 2005, trade in manufactured goods had slumped to a record deficit but exports of financial services had risen to a record surplus of £23 billion. Financial services provide over a quarter of corporation taxes for the Treasury and account for one-fifth of the country's corporate profits – around £10 billion. A staggering one in six jobs in the capital is linked to the City.

Activities

Read the case study 'The golden gateway' and answer the following questions:

1 Produce a list of the key activities that the City of London seems to specialise in.

2 Outline the reasons stated in the case study accounting for the City's global dominance as a centre for financial services.

3 How does the dominance of the City of London as a global financial centre affect:

■ the UK's balance of payments

■ overall UK macroeconomic performance?

Put simply, the City has saved our nation's bacon. The Centre for Economics and Business Research, an independent consultancy that monitors the London economy, predicts that jobs in financial services, which hit a record high of 335,000 this year, up from 324,000 in 2005, will grow by another 10 per cent next year.

*Adapted from an article by **John Arlidge**, Sunday Times, 3 December 2006*

Balance of payments equilibrium

Balance of payments equilibrium, or external equilibrium, occurs when exports are equal to imports over a number of years. Balance of payments equilibrium tends to be narrowly defined, referring only to the current account, since it is argued that this gives a good impression of a country's international competitiveness. The balance of payments is in equilibrium when the current account more or less balances over a period of years and thus balance of payments equilibrium is compatible with short-term current account deficits or surpluses. A balance of payments disequilibrium exists when there is a persistent tendency for the value of imports to be greater or less than the value of exports over several years.

Does a current account deficit matter?

Running a sizeable deficit on the current account leads to a net outflow from the circular flow of income and suggests an underlying lack of international competitiveness. Note, however, that the current account does not have to balance because the balance of payments also includes the capital and financial accounts, which tend to record surpluses, as outlined earlier.

While the government need not be worried about a short-run deficit or surplus on the current account, a persistent or long-run deficit or surplus suggests a more fundamental disequilibrium. However, the extent of the problem depends upon the size and cause, as well as the type of exchange rate system in use. If the deficit is caused by a lack of competitiveness of the country's industries, this is a fundamental weakness that must be addressed.

A current account deficit is seen as more problematic when the exchange rate of a currency is fixed than in a free-floating exchange rate system. In both types of exchange rate system, the basic cause of a deficit tends to stem from exports being too expensive in overseas markets, while imports are relatively cheap. However, in a free-floating exchange rate system, the exchange rate can simply respond to market forces and fall, restoring competitiveness of exports and hence curing or reducing balance of payments disequilibrium. Exchange rate systems are explained in detail in Chapter 18.

Policies to control or reduce a balance of payments deficit

In deciding upon the most appropriate policies to control or reduce a deficit on the current account, we can isolate demand and supply-side causes of the problem. If the cause of a substantial trade deficit is excessive aggregate demand, the deficit may correct itself in the event of an economic downturn or recession, as real incomes and spending slow down. However, if the deficit arises from supply-side problems, then we need policies designed to improve our international competitiveness by, for example, reducing unit labour costs.

Governments can use two categories of policy to cure a persistent balance of payments deficit. These are known as **expenditure-reducing policies** and **expenditure-switching policies**.

Key terms

Expenditure-reducing policies: policies used to correct current account imbalances by reducing consumer spending power.

Expenditure-switching policies: policies used to correct current account imbalances by encouraging consumers to buy domestically produced output rather than imports.

Expenditure-reducing policies

These are deflationary policies that aim to reduce the real spending power of consumers and aggregate demand:

- fiscal policy, for example, an increase in income tax to reduce disposable income
- monetary policy, for example, increasing interest rates to depress consumer spending.

Expenditure-reducing policies recognise that UK citizens generally have a high **marginal propensity to import**, and thus if people have less money to spend, they will tend to cut back on consumption of both domestically produced and foreign products. Expenditure-reducing policies are unlikely to be used as a long-term solution because of their negative impact upon economic growth and unemployment.

Expenditure-switching policies

These are policies that attempt to encourage consumers to switch their spending away from imports towards the output of domestic firms. Expenditure-switching occurs if the relative price of imports can be raised, or if the relative price of UK exports can be lowered. Measures include **direct controls** and **devaluation**.

Direct controls are basically import controls. Tariffs raise the relative price of imports while quotas directly prevent or reduce expenditure on imports. Such controls do not, however, cure the underlying cause of disequilibrium, that is, the uncompetitiveness of a country's goods and services. Import controls may reduce rather than increase competitiveness, and such protectionist measures tend to provoke retaliation. Unsurprisingly, international trade organisations such as the World Trade Organization (WTO) are thus keen to prevent the use of these measures, since trade protectionism reduces the global welfare gains from free trade. Note that European Union (EU) countries will be unable to use these measures against one another due to the existence of the common external tariff.

Devaluation. Another possible way of tackling a current account deficit is for the government or central bank to devalue the currency. As detailed further in Chapter 18, devaluation means reducing the value of a fixed or semi-fixed exchange rate. This affects the relative prices of imports and exports, and thus their international competitiveness. If the currency operates in a free-floating exchange rate system, the specific term used then is **depreciation**. However, devaluation and depreciation have the same effects. Reluctance by governments to use import controls means that a country must generally choose between deflation and devaluation if it wishes to reduce a current account deficit. The effectiveness of devaluation or depreciation in reducing a balance of payments deficit depends largely on the price elasticities of demand for exports and imports.

Devaluation and price elasticity of demand

Overall, devaluation of the pound should make exports more price competitive and hence lead to more exports being sold, but this may not necessarily lead to a corresponding fall in the value of products imported. Clearly the respective price elasticities of demand for imports and exports will be an important consideration. The Marshall-Lerner condition is a simple rule to judge whether a change in the exchange rate is likely to improve the current account of the balance of payments. The condition states that when the sum of the elasticities of demand for both exports and imports is greater than one, a fall in the exchange rate will lead to an improvement in the current account.

Key terms

Marginal propensity to import: the proportion of an increase in income that is spent on imports.

Direct controls: controls on imports, such as tariffs and quotas.

Devaluation: reducing the value of a currency in a fixed or semi-fixed exchange rate system.

Depreciation: in relation to currencies, reducing the value of a currency in a free-floating exchange rate system.

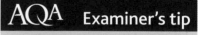

AQA Examiner's tip

Understanding of the Marshall-Lerner criterion and the J-curve effect can greatly improve the quality of your answers on currency depreciation/devaluation.

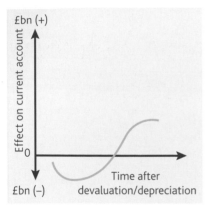

Figure 17.3 *The J-curve effect*

■ **Key terms**

J-curve effect: in the short term, a devaluation or depreciation will lead to a deterioration of the current account before it starts to improve.

The J-curve effect

In the short term there may be a problem with using devaluation as a policy tool to improve the current account, known as the **J-curve effect**. This is because of the low price elasticities of demand for imports and exports immediately following an exchange rate change. At first, the volume of imports will change very little, partly because of the difficulty in altering import contracts. However, depreciation raises the price of imports in pound terms, meaning the value of imports rises. Demand for exports will also tend to be inelastic in response to the exchange rate change in the short term and thus the balance of trade may initially worsen in the months following a devaluation. This is illustrated in Figure 17.3. As predicted by the Marshall-Lerner condition, providing that the elasticity of demand for imports and exports are greater than one, then the trade balance will improve over time. In the medium term, export values will tend to rise while import values may fall, thus improving the current account position. However, even when the benefits of a falling exchange rate are eventually realised, they may not last long. The increased price competitiveness produced by the devaluation may be wiped out due to the inflationary effects of relative increases in import prices.

■ **Activities**

1 One component of the current account of the balance of payments is 'trade in goods'. State two other components of the current account.

2 Discuss the possible consequences for the UK economy of continued growth in its current account deficit.

3 Assess the policies the UK government could use to improve its balance of payments position.

Does a current account surplus matter?

As outlined above, a persistent and substantial current account deficit can be a problem. However, a balance of payments surplus on the current account is not necessarily a good thing. Because a surplus is often seen as a sign of a strong economy, it is often argued that a large surplus indicates excellent economic performance. Whilst a current account surplus can certainly indicate competitive exporting industries, there are reasons why a large current account surplus may also be considered undesirable.

Logically, it is not possible for all countries to run surpluses together. Countries with persistently large surpluses must act to reduce these in order for countries with balance of payments deficits to improve their positions. This may lead to countries experiencing deficits imposing import controls, which penalise all countries.

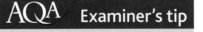
AQA Examiner's tip

Whilst the impact of current account surplus is unusual for the UK, do not rule it out as a potential exam question, particularly in relation to the European and Global Contexts of the exam.

Via the exchange rate, a balance of payments surplus can trigger domestic inflation. A balance of payments surplus is an injection of aggregate demand into the circular flow of income which, via the multiplier effect, increases national income still further. If the economy is close to full capacity, demand-pull inflation is likely to result, as shown in Figure 17.4. An increase in aggregate demand from AD1 to AD2 increases the equilibrium level of real GDP from Y1 to Y2, but also leads to price inflation, rising from P1 to P2.

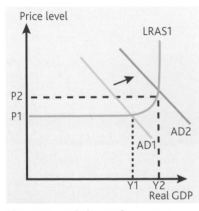

Figure 17.4 *A balance of payments surplus can lead to demand-pull inflation*

Policies to control or reduce a balance of payments surplus

The policies available to a government for reducing a balance of payments surplus are the opposite of those outlined above for correcting a balance of payments deficit. The policy options are reflation, removal of direct controls on imports, and **revaluation**.

- **Reflation** of aggregate demand using monetary policy (for example, reducing interest rates) or fiscal policy (for example, reducing income tax rates), will increase demand for imports.

- **Removing direct controls on imports**. Increasing free trade by removing import controls is likely to win approval from international trade organisations.

- **Revaluation**. This involves increasing the value of a currency in a fixed or semi-fixed exchange rate system. In a free-floating exchange rate system, the specific term would be currency **appreciation**. For a revaluation or appreciation to reduce a current account surplus, the Marshall-Lerner criterion must still hold. A reverse J-curve effect may operate, causing the current account surplus to increase immediately after the revaluation, before it eventually falls in the medium to long term.

After completing this chapter you should be able to:

- understand the difference between the current and capital and financial accounts on the UK balance of payments

- understand the importance of the City of London to the trade in financial services

- understand the possible significance of deficits and surpluses for an individual economy

- analyse and evaluate measures which may be taken to deal with such imbalances.

Key terms

Revaluation: increasing the value of a currency in a fixed or semi-fixed exchange rate system.

Appreciation: increasing the value of a currency in a free-floating exchange rate system.

Global Context

Table 1 shows some indicators of the UK's economic performance compared to those of the USA during 2003. During the same period, there have been changes in the UK's exchange rate against the $US.

Table1 *Performance of UK and US economies (2003)*

	Units	UK	USA
Balance of trade in goods	$bn	−73.5	−548.6
Current account balance	$bn	−36.1	−541.7
Economic growth	%	2.0	3.6
Unemployment	%	4.8	5.7

Table 2 *Performance of UK and US economies*

Sterling exchange rate	USA
14 January 2003	$1.61
14 January 2004	$1.84

1   (a)   Define what is meant by the current account of the balance of payments. *(5 marks)*

       (b)   With reference to Table 1, compare the UK's balance of trade in goods with its current account balance and explain the reason for this difference. *(10 marks)*

       (c)   Table 2 indicates that the pound sterling appreciated against the US dollar between 14 January 2003 and 14 January 2004. Discuss whether a continued appreciation of the value of the pound sterling against the US dollar would improve or worsen the UK's current account balance. *(25 marks)*

2   (a)   The City of London is a world centre specialising in financial services. Explain the importance of the City of London to the UK's balance of payments. *(15 marks)*

       (b)   Discuss the measures a government could take to correct a persistent deficit on the current account of the balance of payments. *(25 marks)*

AQA Examiner's tip   Question 2, part (b) will require you to show judgement about the range of policies available to a government to correct a persistent balance of payments deficit. Each policy or method may have different impacts and several may have constraints upon their use.

18 Exchange rates

In this chapter you will:

- learn how floating exchange rates work and how to represent them diagrammatically
- be able to explain with the aid of diagrams the operation of fixed exchange rates
- appreciate why governments choose managed exchange rate systems.

In this chapter we will consider the transactions between different currencies that have to occur in order to make international trade a possibility. As many countries have their own currency a mechanism is required to ensure that when goods and services are imported or exported currencies can be exchanged in an orderly fashion. In this chapter we will look at floating exchange rates where the value of currencies is determined by demand and supply, fixed rates that are set and maintained by governments, and a managed float where the government accepts the rule of market forces but intervenes periodically to push its exchange rate toward a level it considers desirable.

Floating exchange rates

The exchange rate between two currencies is the price of one in terms of the other, for example, if the price of a dollar ($) expressed in sterling (£) is 50p the rate of exchange between sterling and dollars is £1 = $2 making the price of $ 50p. In order to consider this further we will consider the demand for the currencies of two countries – the UK and the US.

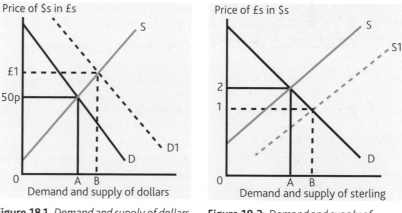

Figure 18.1 *Demand and supply of dollars*

Figure 18.2 *Demand and supply of pounds*

Figure 18.1 shows the demand and supply of dollars. The demand for dollars comes from the UK, for which the UK will offer pounds in exchange, and the supply of dollars to obtain sterling comes from the US. Both countries demand each other's currency for a variety of reasons:

- to purchase each other's goods
- to purchase each other's services
- to invest in each other's firms
- to speculate – buy currencies in the hope that they will rise in value
- to put funds in each other's banks when the rate of interest increases.

The equilibrium price of the dollar in Figure 18.1 is 50p which means that $1 will exchange for 50p. In terms of export prices it means that $1 spent in the US will purchase 50p's worth of UK exports while 50p, spent in the UK will buy $1's worth of US imports – ignoring tariffs and transport costs.

AQA Examiner's tip

When constructing the diagrams the currency whose price you are considering is the one that is being demanded and supplied.

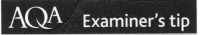

In Figure 18.1, assume that the demand for the dollar increases as a result of a change in taste in the UK toward US goods, the demand curve shifts from D to D1 and the price of the dollar increases from 50p to £1. The dollar is now worth more, it has **appreciated** in relation to the pound while sterling has **depreciated,** in that it is now worth less in terms of the dollar.

This change has also led to a change in the prices of imports and exports; a change in the terms of trade. Previously one dollar spent in the US would buy 50p's worth of UK exports – now the expenditure of a dollar will buy one pound's worth of UK exports as the price of UK goods in the US has fallen.

Previously in the UK, 50p would buy one dollar's worth of US imports; now one pound is required. When a currency appreciates its exports increase in price while its imports fall in price; the reverse is true for a currency that depreciates – its exports decrease in price while its imports rise in price. Thus, assuming that demand for exports is elastic for the UK, currency depreciation could improve the balance of trade while for the US the appreciation could harm its trading position.

Figure 18.2 examines the change indicated in Figure 18.1 but from the aspect of the demand and supply of sterling. If UK demand for dollars increases there has to be a complementary supply of pounds in exchange. The diagram indicates the original equilibrium where two dollars exchanged for one pound. The increased supply of sterling, S to S1 leads to a fall in the price of sterling from $2 to $1 as more sterling will only be purchased if the price falls.

Complementary movements

We could adapt Figure 18.2 to show the effects of an increase in UK exports to the US by shifting the demand curve to the right as demand for sterling will increase. Figure 18.1 could be used to show the complementary increase in the supply of dollars, which would occur as a result of the increase in the demand for pounds.

An increase in the US rate of interest relative to the UK should lead to a flow of hot money from the UK to the US, to take advantage of the higher returns to deposits, shifting demand for dollars from D to D1 in Figure 18.1 and supply of pounds from S to S1 in Figure 18.2.

A rise in UK imports can be shown in Figure 18.1 by an increase in the demand for dollars and in Figure 18.2 by a complementary shift in the supply of pounds.

If speculators think that the value of sterling is likely to fall and the dollar to increase they will sell sterling – in Figure 18.2 supply increases from S to S1 – and buy dollars – Figure 18.1 demand increases from D to D1.

While the global trend is towards exchange rates being determined by market forces, governments are likely to intervene even when they accept the discipline of the market.

Advantages and disadvantages of floating exchange rates

Advantages

Represents the working of the market system:

■ Continuous and automatic adjustment as the foreign exchange (Forex) market changes the rates automatically to reflect the purchasing power of one currency against another. A country with a large balance of payments deficit will find its exchange rate depreciating, its exports falling in price, therefore becoming more competitive, while its imports will be more expensive and less will be purchased.

■ Reduced speculative pressure – under fixed exchange rates speculators can sell the currency, hoping to repurchase when its price has fallen. If there is considerable speculation governments may be forced to reduce the value of their currency and speculators gain by selling at one price and buying back at a lower price. This has effects on the country's import and export prices and on its macroeconomy. Under floating exchange rates countries cannot be forced to devalue and speculators have no idea how far a central bank will allow its currency to fall. This removes some of the destabilising effects of speculation.

■ A floating rate should reduce the need for governments to hold large foreign exchange reserves as they no longer have to maintain the level of a fixed exchange rate.

Disadvantages

■ No guarantee that allowing the rate to float will solve balance of payments problems as the total spent on a country's products depends on the price elasticities of demand for exports and imports.

■ Effect on domestic inflation – when the currency depreciates imports increase in price. Imported raw materials, food and oil become more expensive (as is occurring at the time of writing, 2.6.2008). Firms are likely to raise their prices anticipating that increased costs, higher food and oil prices will register on the consumer price index (CPI) and retail prices index (RPI) leading to employees asking for increased wages.

■ Uncertainty – since the removal of **exchange controls** massive capital flows can occur, which are destabilising and can lead to large changes in a currency's price. Rapid increases in the value of a currency can lead to increasing levels of unemployment as export prices increase and imports become cheaper, while falls in the value lead to increasing inflationary pressure from dearer imports.

■ Foreign currency reserves have not become redundant as most governments buy and sell their currency to maintain what they think should be its optimal value.

Trade weighted index

The sterling Exchange Rate Index (ERI), also known as the effective exchange rate, is an index used by economies to compare their exchange rate against those of their major trading partners. Those trading partners that constitute a larger portion of an economy's exports and imports receives a higher index. The trade weighted index is used to make a complete comparison between one economy's currency and other currencies it interacts with. It measures the average price of domestic goods relative to the average price of goods of trading partners, using the share of trade with each country as the weight for that country. A country whose ERI is falling, is trading internationally on worsening terms; it is costing that country more to buy goods and services from abroad. For the UK the fall in the index means that rising import prices may have implications for monetary policy as it will mean increasing food and oil prices and a knock-on effect on CPI inflation.

Case study

Does the Bank of England want the Pound to weaken?

On Thursday 6 December the Bank of England bowed to the inevitable and cut the UK's base rate for the first time in this cycle, from 5.75 per cent to 5.5 per cent.

Key terms

Exchange controls: restrictions on the ability to trade foreign currencies by a country's central bank.

Activities

1 Construct a diagram showing the demand and supply of euros in terms of dollars.

2 Explain what factors may have caused the increased demand for euros.

3 Analyse the likely effects on the German economy of the increased demand for euros.

Although equities gave back some of the aggressive gains from the previous session on the news the most startling reaction took place in the currency markets where sterling resumed its marked decline against both the euro and the dollar.

Interestingly, for all the reasons cited by the Bank to justify its decision to cut UK base rates, sterling was not one of them. Strikingly, sterling had declined by 3 per cent against a basket of currencies over the seven days prior to the decision and by 6 per cent from the highs reached in the summer.

Indeed the trade weighted index has fallen to 99.2, a more precipitous decline than that envisaged by the Bank's Monetary Policy Committee (MPC) in the November Quarterly Inflation Report.

However, the Bank is unlikely to press the panic button yet. Trade weighted sterling, although at its lowest level since April 2006, is still only just below its average level over the past two years. Secondly, the MPC must have factored sterling weakness into its equations prior to making the decision to cut the base rate.

Two further points need making. Firstly, if sterling is falling because the economy is weakening, the potentially adverse impact of the currency's depreciation on inflation is likely to be muted. Secondly, the MPC may actually encourage sterling to fall further on the basis that at least part of the monetary loosening it now regards as necessary will come in the form of a weaker exchange rate rather than aggressively lower base rates.

Where sterling does become a headache for policymakers is when the currency continues to fall sharply on the foreign exchanges at a time in which the Bank is still concerned about lingering inflationary pressures.

*Adapted from an article by **Jeremy Batstone-Carr**, Director of Private Client Research at Charles Stanley 12 December 2007*

Factors affecting exchange rates

Some of the more important factors likely to affect exchange rates are:

1 Relative interest rates

2 Inflation

3 Foreign direct investment

4 Trade and current account deficits

Exchange rates are influenced by a wide range of economic factors, and the importance of each varies both from country to country and, for any given currency, over time.

Relative interest rates

An increase in the rate of interest in the UK should lead to an increase in the demand for sterling as hot money flows into the UK. This is an enormous pool of money owned by companies and rich individuals that moves around the world seeking the highest interest rates compatible with safety. The money will flow into UK banks to benefit from the higher interest rates. This increase in the demand for sterling will increase its value, changing the relative prices of imports and exports and affecting aggregate demand. It may also lead to a rise in unemployment in the UK economy. The fall in employment will be more likely in exporting firms as, since deindustrialisation, the UK does not provide many substitutes to imported consumer goods. This increase in imports and decrease in exports will have an effect on the balance of payments current account.

Inflation

Figure 18.3 examines the situation where inflation in the UK is rising faster than in the US. This will lead to a fall in US demand and a fall in the supply of dollars, while at the same time the UK will try to import more of the now, relatively cheaper, US goods and the demand for dollars will increase. A fall in the supply of dollars coupled with an increase in demand for them will lead to an increase in their price.

Equilibrium occurs where demand and supply are equal where the exchange rate is $1 = £1. The UK inflation makes UK goods more expensive in the US which will lead to a fall in US demand, and the supply of dollars will shift from S to S1, as less sterling is required. At the same time, US goods will appear relatively cheaper than domestically produced UK goods, and the demand for dollars will increase from D to D1. The overall effect of these changes is that the dollar has appreciated to $1 = £2.

The effect of the inflation is that it has led to a depreciation of sterling, UK exports have become cheaper and imports dearer.

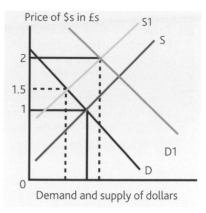

Figure 18.3 *The effect of inflation*

■ Less revenue is received from the sale of exports as they have fallen in price, and the terms of trade move against the UK. To maintain export earnings the UK must increase exports to cover the initial reduction in revenue.

■ For the UK, foreign demand is elastic so a fall in price of UK exports should benefit the balance of payments, as more will be spent. With imports, UK demand appears, at least in the short term, to be inelastic and so more will be spent on imports. But overall depreciation benefits the UK so the Marshall-Lerner condition must hold. If the elasticities were different there is no guarantee that depreciation would be successful.

■ While the balance of payments might benefit, the depreciation will lead to increasing inflationary pressure in the UK and the authorities will have to take steps to deal with it. Consumers will notice an increase in imported food prices, while firms will experience increased prices of imported raw materials. Under certain conditions this could lead to a rising inflationary spiral and if prices are forced up, the benefits of the initial depreciation will be lost.

■ The need for spare capacity – if foreign demand increases, spare capacity is required to produce exports and the government may have to take steps to ensure the products do not get consumed at home now that import prices have risen.

Foreign direct investment

Increasing flows of capital into an economy in the form of genuine long-term investment funds, as opposed to hot money, are referred to as foreign direct investment (FDI) and are usually to set up a factory or purchase shares in a foreign business. This will increase demand for the country's currency and will lead to an increase in its value. Thus the increasing inflows of FDI into Asia should lead to an appreciation of the Asian currencies.

Trade and current account deficits

Countries that have trade and current account deficits are increasing the supply of their currency in relation to the demand for it, and its value is likely to fall. If the deficits become persistent or a large percentage of the

Activities

1. Construct a diagram of the demand and supply of euros in terms of dollars.

2. Assume the price of goods in the Euro area falls relative to US goods. Indicate the effect of this on your diagram.

3. Explain what will happen to import and export prices in both the Euro area and the US as a result of question 2 above.

country's gross domestic product, speculators may feel that the value of the currency is likely to depreciate and they may transfer out of it and into currencies where countries have a surplus. This speculative pressure may have destabilising effects on both the creditor and debtor countries.

Fixed exchange rates

While fixed rates have fallen out of fashion with the increased supply-side emphasis on markets, this has not always been true; exchange rates were fixed between 1944 and 1972 and in 1990/91 by our membership of the exchange rate mechanism (ERM).

The major difficulty was that at the time when rates were fixed against other currencies they may have been perfectly realistic, but changes in market pressures meant that the fixed rate did not always correspond with the market rate and serious imbalances occurred. A number of factors can be advanced to explain such misalignment.

- A major reason was different rates of inflation in different countries. For example, if the UK inflated faster than other countries more pounds would be offered to buy imported goods and services while our trading partners would offer less foreign currency as our goods would price our partners out of the market. The pressure on sterling would be for it to fall and it would be difficult to maintain its value.

- Another problem was differential growth rates – some countries grow faster than others reducing the prices of their goods making them technologically superior and increasing demand for them. This would make the exchange rate of these countries appreciate and make it difficult to maintain a fixed rate especially if the pressure on other currencies is to fall in value.

- Fixed exchange rates were also vulnerable to speculation, which could influence market sentiment as to the value of the currency. This often lead to a situation where market forces, the flows of currency, coming from the private sector were so huge that governments were usually forced to change their exchange rate in line with the market equilibrium.

In Figure 18.4, assume the government fixes the exchange rate at 50p to the dollar. Initial equilibrium is where D and S are equal at an exchange rate of 50p to the dollar where 0B dollars are demanded and supplied. An increase in the demand for dollars, D to D1 creates a disequilibrium situation as the demand for dollars is now 0A while the supply has remained at 0B. If the exchange rate was floating, the dollar would appreciate to 60p. As it is fixed, the demand for dollars exceeds the supply. Under a fixed exchange rate system the central bank, in this case the Bank of England, would sell AB dollars out of its foreign currency reserves to stop the dollar appreciating to 60p. It would also be likely to have regulations in place which restricted the exchanges between sterling and other currencies.

While in the short term the Bank of England can supply dollars out of its foreign exchange reserves, if the imbalance were maintained the demand for dollars exceeding the supply, there would be a continuous drain on the reserves – a situation that could not continue indefinitely as reserves would fall to zero and the fixed rate would have to be abandoned. There are a number of possible actions the authorities could take.

- Abandon the fixed rate and allow sterling to find its own level according to market forces, in this case 60p.

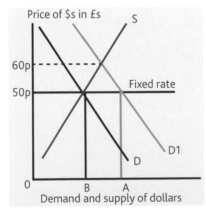

Figure 18.4 *Fixed exchange rates*

■ Take steps to restrict the demand for dollars in the UK by following a deflationary domestic policy. This might be an increase in taxation, but is more likely to be an increase in the rate of interest. This has the effect of reducing disposable income (mortgage costs rise as do the costs of other loans) and will reduce the demand for imports. The increase in the interest rate has a further advantage in that the demand for sterling will rise, increasing the supply of dollars as Americans buy sterling to deposit in UK banks to take advantage of the high interest rates.

You will see from the last bullet point that under fixed rates the focus of the rate of interest was maintaining the value of the currency rather than its present role of targeting inflation, and a return to fixed exchange rates would mean a change in the direction of monetary policy.

In order to overcome some of the problems of misalignment between the fixed rate and market sentiment, variations of the totally fixed rate could be used – the **adjustable peg** where currencies could be changed to new fixed values if required and the **crawling peg** where currency values could be changed weekly or monthly to reflect market conditions.

A further problem with fixed rates was speculation where hot money flows either into or out of a currency could virtually determine whether the currency was **revalued** or **devalued.** Figure 18.6 indicates the possible outcome of what is known as a run on a currency.

A run on the currency

Figure 18.5 shows fixed rates in terms of pounds and Deutschmarks (DMs – the German currency prior to the euro) to illustrate the UK's problem over the exchange rate mechanism. In the diagram, 2.95 DMs to the pound represents the fixed exchange rate. If speculators thought that sterling was fundamentally overvalued and only maintained its value due to high interest rates in the UK they would be likely to sell sterling (S to S1) and receive 2.95DMs for every pound, buying it back at a cheaper price when its value had fallen. Should the UK authorities elect to support sterling the Bank of England would buy AB sterling from its foreign exchange reserves. Should market sentiment still believe that a devaluation was imminent more banks and financial institutions will sell pounds adding to the speculative pressure against it, shifting the supply curve to S2.

There are a number of measures that the authorities could take to relieve the situation.

■ They may raise interest rates in the hope of increasing demand for the currency, but investors are reluctant to buy a currency that they think is fundamentally overvalued and in imminent danger of devaluation.

■ They may decide to raise a loan – to borrow foreign currency in order to purchase sterling and maintain its value.

However governments do not like the stigma of official loans, for example from the **International Monetary Fund**, as conditions might be attached regarding the future economic policy the government has to follow and this might not prove politically acceptable. The Chancellor facing this situation borrowed DMs from the Bundesbank but the speculative flows were too large and the UK was forced to leave the ERM. It appears that the size of hot money flows dwarfs anything that individual central banks can offer and only concentrated action by the world's central banks would be likely to have a result.

The Bank of England may tell the Chancellor that market sentiment is too strong and devaluation, and/or a return to floating, will have to take place.

■ **Key terms**

Adjustable peg: value of the fixed exchange rate can be changed as circumstances require.

Crawling peg: frequent changes in the value of a fixed exchange rate.

Revalued: when the authorities increase the value of their currency against others.

Devalued: when the authorities decrease the value of their currency against others.

International Monetary Fund: a multinational institution set up in 1947 to operate the adjustable peg exchange rate system.

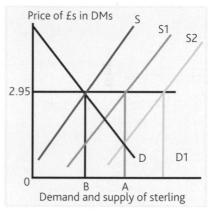

Figure 18.5 *A run on a currency*

Advantages and disadvantages of fixed exchange rates

Advantages

- Increased certainty for businesses as, with fixed rates, the business knows the price that it is likely to receive for the goods that it sells and what it is going to pay for its raw materials, as the currency is stable and not fluctuating. While under a floating system firms can use the Forex markets and buy currency at today's price, for delivery in the future, this imposes a cost on the business.

- Fixed rates were seen as a way of controlling inflation as the government had to follow economic policies that would maintain the rate by restricting the demand for foreign currency and ensuring that inflation was no higher than our major trading partners. This quite often required politically unpopular deflationary policies.

- It was felt that fixed rates would lead to orderly international currencies resulting in price stability and increased trade. The fluctuations of the trade cycle would be reduced as countries would not be able to gain an unfair competitive advantage by allowing their currencies to depreciate making their exports cheaper at the expense of their trading partners, rather than dealing with the problem domestically by, for example, reducing aggregate demand. Adherence to fixed exchange rates would make this technique of remedying a balance of payments deficit far more difficult.

Disadvantages

- Fixed exchange rates need periodic revision, as countries grow at different rates, and differences in the levels of inflation mean that if rates remain the same some countries have permanent surpluses, while others have permanent deficits. Some countries need to devalue while others need to revalue.

- In order to maintain a fixed exchange rate the government might need to run a perpetual deflationary policy. This will reduce the country's rate of economic growth and its standard of living will not be growing rapidly over time.

- Speculation – given the huge capital flows that take place, countries that have persistent balance of payments deficits are going to find that speculation will take place against their currency as international financial opinion will expect it to be devalued.

Case study

Fixed or Flexible?

Analysts agree that 'getting the exchange rate right' is essential for economic stability and growth in developing countries. Over the past two decades, many developing countries have shifted away from fixed exchange rates (that is, those that peg the domestic currency to one or more foreign currencies) and moved toward more flexible exchange rates (those that determine the external value of a currency more or less by the market supply and demand for it). During a period of rapid economic growth, driven by the twin forces of globalisation and liberalisation of markets and trade, this shift seems to have served a number of countries well. The considerations that have led countries to shift toward more flexible exchange rate arrangements vary widely; also, the shift did not happen all at once.

Many countries that traditionally pegged to the US dollar, for instance, adopted a basket approach to managing their rates. Another key element was the rapid acceleration of inflation and countries with inflation rates higher than their main trading partners often depreciated their currencies to prevent a severe loss of competitiveness. This led many countries in the Western Hemisphere, in particular, to adopt 'crawling pegs', whereby exchange rates could be adjusted according to such pre-set criteria as relative changes in the rate of inflation. Later, some countries that suffered very high rates of inflation shifted back to a pegged exchange rate as a central element of their stabilisation efforts.

Many developing countries have also experienced a series of external shocks and often adjustment to these disturbances required not only discrete currency depreciations but also the adoption of more flexible exchange rate arrangements.

The trend toward greater exchange rate flexibility has been associated with more open, outward-looking policies on trade and investment generally and increased emphasis on market-determined exchange rates and interest rates.

Adapted from Fixed or Flexible? Getting the exchange rate in the 1990s, Economic Issues 13, by Francesco Caramazza and Jahangir Aziz, 1998, International Monetary Fund

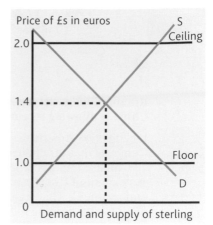

Figure 18.6 *A managed float*

A managed float

In order to be able to concentrate the use of the rate of interest on inflation targeting, which would be impossible under fixed rates, and the fact that 'free floating' can lead to large changes in the price of imports and exports, the authorities may elect a 'managed float' where sterling is free to fluctuate between undisclosed levels. Should the value of sterling appear to be seriously departing from its target, the Bank of England can intervene in order to try to tip the market in the desired direction.

In Figure 18.6 assume the UK government sets, for example, an upper limit, a **ceiling price** of two euros to the pound. At any higher value to the pound UK exports will be too expensive abroad. The lower limit or **floor price** is, for example, one euro to the pound. At any lower value, imports into the UK will be too expensive and exert inflationary pressure on the UK economy. The exchange rate can be seen as a trade-off between too much inflationary pressure from import prices and competitive export prices to improve the balance of payments.

In addition to targeting inflation by the use of interest rates the authorities can try to manage the exchange rate by buying and selling pounds. When the pound rises near to two euros the authorities could sell pounds and add to the foreign currency reserves, and when the pound falls toward the lower value, the authorities buy pounds to nudge its value upwards. Should the authorities manipulate their currency in order to gain an advantage over their trading partners this is known as a **dirty float**.

The upper and lower levels are not publicised by the authorities, which means that it is difficult to speculate against the currency as it is not known how far the authorities will allow it to fall. An exchange rate that fluctuates between much wider bands can cope more easily than a fixed exchange rate with differential rates of inflation and economic growth. The idea is that by using a managed float the authorities can obtain the advantages of both floating and fixed exchange rates.

Key terms

Ceiling price: maximum price determined by the authorities.

Floor price: minimum price determined by the authorities.

Dirty float: manipulation of a floating rate to gain advantages over trading partners.

Activities

1 Why can a managed exchange rate be seen as a trade-off between a current account surplus and low imported inflation?

2 List the advantages of a managed float.

3 Why is the Monetary Policy Committee (MPC) role of targeting inflation important in stabilising the exchange rate?

After completing this chapter you should:

■ be able, with the aid of diagrams, to explain floating exchange rate systems

■ understand the operation of fixed rates and the diagrams required

■ appreciate why governments might choose a managed float.

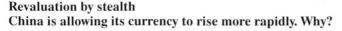

Revaluation by stealth
China is allowing its currency to rise more rapidly. Why?

IN 2005 two American senators introduced a bill into Congress that threatened to slap a tariff of 27.5 per cent on all Chinese imports unless the Yuan was revalued by the same amount (their estimate of how much the currency was undervalued). That legislation was dropped, but several other China-bashing bills are still working their way through Congress and accusations about 'unfair' Chinese competition will surely play a big role in this year's presidential election. Many American politicians and economists talk as if the Yuan was still fixed against the dollar. Yet on current trends, by the time the next president enters the White House the Yuan could be within spitting distance of the magic figure demanded in 2005.

Since the beginning of October the Yuan has climbed at an annual rate of 13 per cent against the dollar – its fastest pace since China stopped pegging to the dollar in July 2005 (see chart). Since 2005 it has appreciated by a total of 14 per cent.

While most business people are convinced that fixed rates have an advantage over floating rates it appears as if Beijing

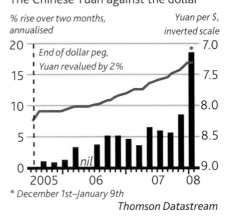

The great crawl of China
The Chinese Yuan against the dollar

*December 1st–January 9th

Thomson Datastream

Figure 1 *The great crawl of China*

has caved in to Washington's demands. But the main reason why China is allowing the Yuan to rise faster is because its policymakers believe the benefits to China from a rising currency now outweigh the costs. Beijing's top concern today is inflation, which rose to 6.9 per cent in November. On 9 January the Government announced tighter price controls on a range of products. The People's Bank of China (PBOC) increased interest rates six times in 2007, but this is unlikely to squeeze inflation, which has been driven largely by a jump in food prices caused by supply-side shocks. A faster pace of currency appreciation offers a more powerful weapon: it will help to reduce imported inflation, especially of food and raw materials. By reducing the need to intervene to hold down the currency, it will also curb the build-up of foreign-exchange reserves and hence monetary growth.

The Yuan's rise is unlikely to silence flag-waving American Congressmen or economists. The slide in the dollar since 2005 means the Yuan has risen by only 5 per cent in trade-weighted terms, according to the Bank for International Settlements. China's current-account surplus has risen from 4 per cent of GDP in 2004 to 11 per cent last year, so any gauge that defines the equilibrium exchange rate as the rate that would eliminate the surplus would suggest the Yuan is now even more undervalued. In 2005 Morris Goldstein and Nicholas Lardy at the Peterson Institute for International Economics estimated the Yuan was 20–25% undervalued. By late 2007 they thought it was at least 30–40% undervalued despite its gain over the previous two years.

But other economists say it is wrong to define the Yuan's correct value by the size of the current-account surplus.

A recent report from the Conference Board, an American business-research organisation, argued that: 'Although an undervalued currency contributes to China's trade surplus, it is not a primary cause of it and has very little to do with the bi-lateral United States–China trade deficit.'

Adapted from The Economist 10 January 2008

1 (a) Using the figures on the right-hand scale in the graph explain the effects on exporters and importers in the US economy. *(5 marks)*

(b) Using the data and your own knowledge discuss the various ways which changes in the external value of the Yuan might affect Chinese manufacturing industry. *(10 marks)*

(c) The extract states that 'most business people are convinced that fixed rates have an advantage over floating rates'. Explain why business people may take this view and discuss any difficulties that might prevent the reintroduction of fixed rates in the future. *(25 marks)*

2 (a) Why and how might the Government wish to influence the external value of its currency under an international system of floating exchange rates? *(15 marks)*

(b) Discuss the view that the same forces of supply and demand tend to correct a country's balance of payments deficit regardless of whether its exchange rate is fixed or fluctuating. *(25 marks)*

19   The European Union

In this chapter we will look at the United Kingdom (UK) in relation to the European Union (EU), an area that has grown more important to the country since it joined in 1973. After the end of the Second World War political leaders from the major protagonist nations realised that some way had to be found to keep the peace in Europe and increase the welfare of their populations. Out of such thoughts and meetings emerged what originally was known as the European Economic Community (EEC) and has now developed into the European Union (EU). The UK did not participate from the outset as it preferred freer trade and less government intervention and participated in the European Free Trade Area (EFTA) which allowed participants to trade freely among themselves and fix their own tariffs with non-members.

While the original six participants of the EEC (Belgium, Netherlands, Luxembourg, Germany, France and Italy) started by integrating their coal and steel production, in the Treaty of Rome 1958 they formalised their previous arrangements and created the European Economic Community which had the following characteristics:

■ the creation of a common market, an economic area within which there would be free movement of goods, services, persons, and capital

■ an emphasis on the progressive elimination of tariffs and quotas

■ provision made for an EEC competition policy

■ the creation of a common external tariff of 25 per cent

■ the putting in place of a Common Agricultural Policy.

Figure 19.1 *The EU flag; there are 12 stars because this number historically represents the symbol of perfection, completeness and unity*

The institutional structure of the EU

The Council of Ministers

This is the institution which decides on all major laws and policy changes and represents the individual nation's interests. The Council of Ministers is made up of ministers from each member state. Which government minister attends the meeting will depend on what is being discussed. If, for example, the discussion relates to monetary union or overall budgets it is most likely that the finance minister will attend.

The Commission

This institution represents the interests of the EU as a whole and is responsible for ensuring that EU laws and policies are carried out. The Commission is responsible for implementing the decisions of the Council of Ministers and the European Parliament. It is mainly responsible for proposing or starting new legislation and measures. All major proposals are finally decided on by the Council of Ministers before they can become law. There are, however, many minor areas of legislation over which the Commission has direct control. The major treaties often merely outline what changes need to be made and the Commission is then given responsibility for ensuring that the objectives of the treaties are brought into effect. The Commission has embraced a supply-side approach which is not always adopted willingly by the individual sovereign states. This can be seen in the difference in approach to the Stability and Growth Pact (SGP) where the Commission insists that public borrowing should be restrained to 3 per cent of Gross Domestic Product (GDP) while some of the major countries disregard this.

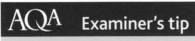

AQA   Examiner's tip

Remember that some aspect of the European Union may form the basis of a question in an A2 paper.

AQA   Examiner's tip

While detailed knowledge of the institutions of the EU is not required, candidates should have some idea of the functions of the institions outlined on p218–9.

The European Parliament

The European Parliament consists of 626 members directly elected by the people in each member state. The number of seats that each nation has reflects the size of the population.

The European Parliament has very little power to create new laws – it is responsible for discussing and making recommendations, but it cannot pass laws nor change them unless the Council of Ministers agrees.

The Court of Justice of the European Community

The European Court of Justice (ECJ) is the supreme court of justice for cases that involve community law. Cases come before the Court which interprets what the law means. The ruling becomes part of Community law and all EU countries, businesses and individuals will be bound by it. If Community law and national law conflict, Community law takes precedent.

The European Central Bank (ECB)

The ECB is the central bank for Europe's single currency, the **euro**, used by the 15 member countries of the Eurozone. The European Central Bank was established by the EU in 1998 with its headquarters in Frankfurt; its main task is to maintain the euro's purchasing power and thus price stability in the euro area. There is a president and an executive board made up of the governors of the National Central Banks which have adopted the euro.

The functions of the ECB are:

■ to maintain price stability – its target is to keep inflation below, but close to, 2 per cent

■ to define and implement monetary policy for the Eurozone

■ to support the economic policies of the Eurozone members

■ to conduct foreign exchange operations in terms of euros

■ to authorise the issue of bank notes

■ to ensure the smooth operation of the banking system.

In terms of monetary functions, including oversight and regulation of financial institutions, the ECB operates like any central bank. It has cooperated with the United States Federal Reserve to ensure that banks can obtain credit, as loan defaults – caused by lending to US borrowers (2007) with insufficient ability to repay their loans (sub-prime) – has caused a major shortage of credit in both the US and European banks.

The ECB is designed to be independent of political intervention, both from EU institutions and from member states. It also has financial independence as it has its own budget, separate from the EU budget. National governments are treaty bound not to seek to influence the decision-making bodies of the ECB.

In terms of accountability, the ECB publishes reports on its activities and has to address its annual report to the European parliament who can question and then issue its opinion to the executive board.

While in the UK system the inflation target is set by the government and the relevant interest rates are set by the Bank of England (BoE), the ECB decides both. This independence has been criticised by Nicolas Sarkozy, the French President, who wants to extend the mandate of the ECB to focus on growth and job creation rather than purely inflation. In response, the President of the European Commission and some national leaders have warned Sarkozy that he is undermining the principle of independence.

AQA Examiner's tip

From the viewpoint of an A2 economics student the ECB is a very important institution.

Key terms

The euro: the currency adopted by the members of the Economic and Monetary union (EMU).

AQA Examiner's tip

Make sure you keep up to date on the policies used by the ECB and Bank of England to deal with the macro-economic climate.

Key terms

Single market: removal of obstacles, such as customs checking, to allow the free movement of goods, services, capital and persons through the area.

European Monetary Union: a group of countries that have adopted the euro and have their monetary policy controlled by the European Central Bank.

The Lisbon Treaty (December 2007) will make the ECB a formal institution of the EU but does not include a written guarantee of the bank's independence, which may lead politicians to try to put political pressure on the bank's decisions. However at the time of writing (July 2008) the Irish referendum which has rejected the treaty has thrown its acceptance into question.

■ The single market

The Treaty of Rome 1957 set out four economic freedoms that it wanted to create in Europe: free movement of goods, free movement to provide services, free movement of capital and free movement of people. The **single market** came into operation in 1992 and removed barriers to movement of people and goods and since the Maastricht Treaty (February 1992), which created the **European Monetary Union**, the Commission has focused on liberalising the market for services and improving competitiveness through the Lisbon Strategy.

Benefits of the single market

■ Economies of scale – with 480 million consumers in 27 countries and almost 40 per cent of world trade there is scope for countries to exploit the economies of scale and the division of labour which leads to a rise in productivity. Freedom of movement for all the factors of production between the member countries should lead to a more efficient allocation, further increasing productivity.

■ Increased dynamic efficiency – the competitive environment should reduce monopoly power and increase innovation; inefficient companies will suffer a loss of market share and may have to exit the market. Consumers benefit from the competitive environment in terms of cheaper products and increased choice.

■ Increased liberalisation has led to the emergence of cheap airlines such as easyJet and Ryanair. Such developments would have been impossible without the single market. Lower electricity costs are available to both firms and consumers in states where the market has been opened to competition.

■ For business there has been a significant reduction in export bureaucracy as open borders cut delivery times and reduce costs. Consumers have full consumer rights when shopping in the single market and there are no restrictions on what they buy as long as it is for personal use. The single market is, in effect, a domestic market for European business.

■ UK citizens have the right to work, study or retire in all the other member states; there are around three-quarters of a million Britons living in other countries (National statistics, Total international migration tables 1991–2006).

Costs of a single market

■ There may be adverse impact on some sectors of a national economy as the increased international competition may mean that some firms are not able to compete. Some may lose their traditional markets to new entrants with a consequent loss of jobs.

■ The single market is still a work in progress, with gaps remaining in areas such as intellectual property rights, services, retail financial services and transport and energy.

■ The services sector has opened up more slowly than markets for goods and, although a new law was adopted in 2006 enabling companies to offer a range of cross-border services from their home base, it has not increased competition to the extent originally envisaged.

■ Delays have also affected financial services and transportation, where separate national markets still exist and the markets for both gas and electricity have not been completely opened up to competition as some countries are promoting national champions to the detriment of consumer interests. The fragmented nature of national tax systems also puts a brake on market integration and efficiency.

■ Most financial services have been liberalised and, in 2007, EU ministers agreed to unify national payments regimes which will make it easier for consumers to use credit or debit cards abroad and to transfer money to another EU country.

Case study

EU services package is approved, but delivery uncertain

European politicians approved legislation yesterday enabling service providers, from funeral directors to tour guides, to operate without hindrance across the 25-nation European Union.

But the package touted as the completion of the single market by allowing businesses to sell services across borders as easily as they sell goods is so broad that EU diplomats admit that they have no idea what the consequences will be.

It was passed in such a watered-down form that opponents and supporters expressed disappointment at the result. The so-called Services Directive has sparked huge battles between free-marketeers and trade unions across Europe. West European countries suffering high unemployment fear it could lead to 'social dumping', with unfair competition from cheaper workers from Eastern Europe who enjoy fewer social protections.

Although disappointed that the directive had been weakened, the European Commission was relieved that the legislation had been passed at all. The Internal Market Commissioner, said: 'This represents a real advance, it shows there is a willingness in the EU to pursue measures to promote more jobs and economic growth.'

Arlene McCarthy, a Labour Member of the European Parliament (MEP), who helped to steer through the legislation, called the vote historic, adding: 'This is the final piece in the jigsaw of establishing the single market. It has the potential to boost prosperity and lift Europe out of the economic doldrums.'

Services produce about 70 per cent of the EU's economic output, and employ roughly 116 million Europeans, but face countless restrictions on operating across borders.

A company wanting to start up in Germany may be required to join the local chamber of commerce, which has a five-year waiting list. Italy requires companies to employ a minimum number of people and put down a large deposit. In France, shops can usually open only with the approval of local businesses, who often object to foreign competition.

The new directive aims to sweep away such restrictions, giving service providers from accountants and computer programmers to plumbers and caterers the right to operate anywhere in Europe. Opening up the market in services could create 600,000 jobs.

However, after union protests about a 'race to the bottom', businesses will have to operate under the pay levels and conditions of the member state where they are selling their services, rather than those of their home country. Numerous sectors – from health

Activities

1 With the aid of an AD/AS diagram indicate the benefits of the single market on the UK economy.

2 Prepare a brief to defend the view that the single market has conferred more advantages than disadvantages on the UK.

AQA Examiner's tip

Do not confuse the single market and single currency.

Key terms

Trade deflection: redirection of international trade due to the formation of a free trade area.

Rules of origin: stipulation that a product must be manufactured from locally sourced components.

Intra-area trade: trade between the members of a trading agreement.

Trade creation: an increase in international trade that results from the reduction in tariff barriers.

and education to gambling and taxis – have also been excluded from the legislation.

The CBI (Confederation of British Industry) lamented a 'missed opportunity'. The deputy director-general, said: 'The likelihood of the EU achieving a free movement in services, one of its founding principles, in the near future has now seriously diminished.'

The British Government will try to beef it up. 'As in any long term negotiation, this is not the final text, and we will be working hard in the coming months to make the necessary improvements,' a British spokesman said yesterday.

Adapted from The Times *article by* **Anthony Browne,** *Brussels Correspondent, 17 February 2006*

■ From Free Trade area to Economic Union

We can determine a number of types of integration and they are indicated below in terms of increasing depth and commitment.

■ Performance areas where countries agree to give lower tariffs on certain trade, for example, the EU's association with certain African and Caribbean countries recently disallowed by the World Trade Organization (WTO).

■ Free trade area – members eliminate trade barriers between themselves but each continues to operate their own particular barriers against non-members.

■ Customs union – where members eliminate trade barriers between themselves and establish uniform barriers against non-members and a common external tariff.

■ A common market – a customs union that also provides for the free movement of labour and capital across national boundaries.

■ An economic union – a common market which also provides for the unification of members' general objectives in respect of economic growth and the harmonisation of monetary fiscal and other policies.

Trade deflection

Prior to joining the EU the UK was a member of EFTA, set up in 1960, which created free trade between the members but allowed individual countries to negotiate tariffs with non-members. A free trade area leads to a problem of **trade deflection** where traders will try to import goods to the member with the lowest tariff and then export them to the other members. This circumvents the policies of those that want higher tariffs as, once the goods are imported, trade inside the area is free. To avoid this, **rules of origin** are required to govern **intra-area trade** which ensures that free trade refers to partner's produce and not their imports.

Trade creation

Trade creation is said to take place when an increase in trade and economic welfare results from the reduction or elimination of trade barriers like tariffs and quotas which occurs when a country joins a customs union. The country moves from buying goods from a high cost country to buying them from a lower cost country inside the union. For example, a country might have imposed a 50 per cent tariff on imported machinery so most machinery sold would be domestically produced. If it joins a customs union there will be a common external tariff but intra-union trade means that machinery from member countries can be imported tariff free. Consumers in the country have benefited because they are able to buy machinery from a cheaper source.

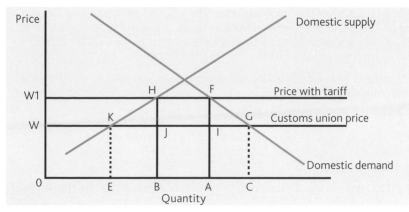

Figure 19.2 *Trade creation*

In Figure 19.2 W is the supply price for the product inside the customs union. Before entry the country has imposed a tariff on the product raising the price in the home market to W1. At price W1 domestic demand is 0A, while domestic supply is 0B, and imports are BA. Removal of the tariff reduces the price of the product in the market to W, domestic demand increases to 0C and domestic supply falls to 0E. Imports increase to EC. The difference between the original level of imports and the new level of import is trade creation: EB+AC. The welfare effect is shown by the area W, W1, F, G.

The government loses its revenue from import duty shown as HFIJ while the net gain to the country is the two triangles KHJ and FGI.

The supply curve reflects the domestic cost of production, so units produced in excess of E are produced at a cost above the price of which the product can be purchased from elsewhere, which is inefficient. The demand curve measures the marginal benefits of consuming the product, so cutting consumption to A means that consumers forgo consumption of units AC where benefits exceed costs.

Trade diversion

This occurs when, as a result of joining a union, a country has to buy goods from a higher cost producer inside the union due to the operation of the common external tariff. Prior to joining the union the UK had zero tariffs on imported food and purchased from low cost producers, such as New Zealand, Australia and the USA. After entry it was cheaper, due to the common external tariff for the UK to purchase food from less efficient producers inside the union like France and Spain.

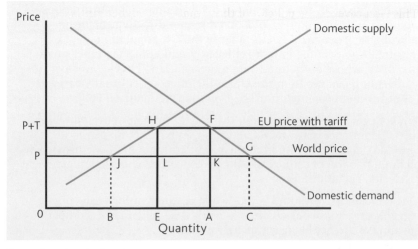

Figure 19.3 *Trade diversion*

AQA **Examiner's tip**

Make sure that you can construct
and explain these diagrams.

AQA **Examiner's tip**

Make sure you revise the earlier
material that you have studied in
the course, such as economies of
scale.

Figure 19.3 shows the food market in the UK. Before entry, the UK was
demanding 0C of food at world prices while UK farmers were producing
0B, so imports were BC. On entering the market price rises to the EU
level, which includes a tariff.

■ Demand in UK falls to 0A and domestic output rises to 0E. Imports
are now EA.

■ Total consumer welfare has fallen by P, P+T, F, G.

■ Domestic farmers have gained P, P+T, H, J at the expense of
consumers – gain from the higher price P, P+T multiplied by the
increased output E.

■ HFKL represents the revenue from the tariff multiplied by the amount
imported times the price.

■ The overall net loss is shown by the triangles JHL and FGK indicating
that the tariff has reduced welfare as a whole.

Economies of scale

The result of a customs union is usually both static and dynamic gains,
which may result from the economies of scale. A major reason for UK
entry to the union is the size of the potential market, which allows the
economies of scale to be exploited increasing intra-community trade.
The European Union has 480 million inhabitants compared to 60
million for the UK. Since the Single Market Act, 1992, a large number
of cross-boundary mergers have been taking place in order to exploit
the economies of scale. For example, in 2000 German conglomerate
Mannesmann and the British Vodafone AirTouch merged, creating the
world's largest mobile telephones group.

Competition

In a customs union, domestic industries will face greater intra-union
competition than before from firms in other member countries.
Competition will encourage dynamic efficiencies – research and
development, innovation, new products, new processes, new techniques
and reduced costs of production and prices. Competition will ensure
efficiency gains but the danger is that oligopolistic control may occur
through cross-border mergers, or collusion, which will reduce the benefits
of the increased competition. This means that competition authorities
will need to be vigilant, and in the EU the Competition Commissioner
has enforced competition policy, heavily fining companies that infringe
the competition rules.

Winners and losers

Membership of an economic union involves financial contributions,
which may be spent on an area that does not directly benefit the
contributor. The smaller percentage of the UK population employed
in agriculture resulted in more efficient production than other union
members, whose economies were more agrarian. This led to a net
transfer of resources from the UK to the more agriculturally based
countries that benefited from the Common Agricultural Policy.

While firms have benefited from the free movement of capital, witness
the large number of car manufacturers that have set up plants in
Slovakia; labour mobility from the recent entrants has been resisted by
all but a handful of countries, who are concerned about unemployment
levels and **social dumping.**

One point to bear in mind is that while customs unions can confer
benefits they are not as efficient as worldwide free trade as comparative
advantages are not being completely exploited.

Key terms

Social dumping: where goods are
produced by low wage labour
usually without expense by
employers on workers' social
benefits.

The Expansion of the EU

In 1993 at the Copenhagen European Council it was agreed that the Central and Eastern European countries could join, and since then 12 more countries, mainly from Central and Eastern Europe, have joined.

The UK sees these new entrants as beneficial as:

- The Single European market will be expanded and, even though at present their incomes are at best only 50 per cent of the EU average, the UK is in favour of increasing the available free-market size.

- They are free-market capitalist economies with very low rates of taxation or flat taxes and are natural allies of **Anglo-Saxon neo-liberalism**.

- They are seen by the UK as a powerful counterweight to the combined power of France and Germany within the EU.

Case study

Enlargement troubles

It might have been worse. On 11 December European Union foreign ministers agreed to suspend 8 out of 35 'chapters' in Turkey's negotiations to join the EU. This punishment was made only marginally more tolerable by the knowledge that Germany wanted a hefty 21 chapters frozen, and by the news that the EU had promised to re-examine (though not lift) its economic blockade of Turkish-controlled northern Cyprus. But the Turks were swift to rail at the EU's 'injustice'.

Turkey is not the only country in the south-eastern corner of Europe whose relations with the EU are now in limbo. Talks with Serbia over an association agreement were called off in May. There are specific reasons in each case. The Serbs are being punished for not handing over General Ratko Mladic to The Hague war-crimes tribunal; the Turks for not opening up ports and airports to traffic with Cyprus. But that there are troubles with enlargement across the board is more than just a coincidence. The assumptions and justifications that lie behind the policy are being challenged as never before.

For the past ten years these assumptions have run roughly as follows. There are gains for both applicants and existing members from expansion. The neighbours' wish to join is not a matter of partisan politics, so their populations will be ready to back EU membership even if sacrifices have to be made for it. The EU can thus shore up reformers in applicant countries. And any country that refuses to fit the mould (for example, Belarus) does not matter and can be ignored.

Meeting the conditions of membership is thus, in essence, a technical rather than a political or strategic issue. The strategic choice has been made by history: Poland (say) is obviously a European country and was always going to join the EU. Progress towards membership is therefore made by bureaucratic procedure, not political decision: you plug away at the details of, for example, drawing up national accounts, and all will be well. And once countries join, they are supposed to slot in seamlessly. That does not necessarily mean they will obey every item of EU law (even founder members do not do that). But there will be no significant backsliding, nor any unpleasant surprises.

Key terms

Anglo-Saxon neo-liberalism: economic reform aimed at boosting the dynamism of economies – in contrast to the 'social model' which stresses social objectives.

■ **Activities**

1 Find out the countries that have joined the EU since 1993.

2 With the aid of a diagram explain how joining the union could benefit Turkey.

3 Using the case study above and your own knowledge analyse the arguments for and against Turkey's entry.

For most of the past two decades, these assumptions held good. Enlargement was a stunning success. Bureaucratic plodding worked fine. The national consensus in favour of membership remained solid. But now all this is changing.

It has been clear for some time that popular support for enlargement is falling in both would-be and existing members. As a result, enlargement is no longer a subject of consensus, but rather an elite project (like the EU itself). So the old beneficial dynamic – Westernising elites apply for membership, Brussels supports them, they reap domestic benefits from accession – no longer works. Both Turkey and Serbia have pro-European governments. But the Turks do not want to open up to Cyprus, and the Serbs are unwilling to arrest their general, not least because both countries face elections next year – and in those elections the EU has become an electoral liability. Similarly, support for enlargement has become a liability in many existing members.

The EU has benefited hugely from its expansion, through larger markets and the creation of more efficient pan-European multinationals (among other things). It would be damaged by enlargement's failure, which could easily produce foreign-policy horrors in the eastern Mediterranean or in the western Balkans.

Adapted from The Economist, *13 December 2006*

How has the entry of the 'EU10' affected the EU?

There have been a number of consequences as a result of the 10 eastern European countries joining the EU:

- Increased the population by 100 million.

- Added only 5 per cent to the EU's GDP.

- Created in some existing members' fears about an influx of cheap labour and benefit tourists – the 'Polish' plumber!

- Led to a migration of capital from the West into the new entrants over the past 10 years – Slovakia is now the car producer of Europe.

- Required the attempt at drawing up of a constitution so that decision making did not become paralysed.

- Has led to migration into countries that did not restrict access.

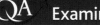

AQA **Examiner's tip**

Keep up with developments in Europe through the quality press and news.

Key terms

FOREX market: abbreviation of foreign exchange markets.

■ Monetary union

In order to move to an economic union which encompasses common policies for economic growth, monetary and fiscal policies, the EU needed to create a common currency. After experimenting with the exchange rate mechanism, where the member countries' currencies were fixed in value against each other, the full monetary union went ahead on 1 January 1999 for all those states which reached the convergence criteria.

There are a number of elements to the monetary union:

- A single currency used by all participants, the euro, which replaced all national currencies to facilitate business and commercial operations. The euro operates in the **FOREX market** as a managed float.

- An independent central bank, which regulates the rate of interest and monetary policy of members of the Eurozone.

- A Stability and Growth Pact that limits the public sector borrowing of the participating countries to 3 per cent of GDP, as a technique to stop countries frustrating monetary policy employed by the ECB. Many economists considered the pact as too restrictive in times of recession and Portugal, Italy, France and Germany have broached it. The pact was loosened by reforms in 2005 to allow extra spending on areas that would improve aggregate supply.

The potential benefits of a single currency

1 **Reduced transaction costs**. Transactions costs refer to the cost of changing from one currency to another. A single currency will eliminate the cost of foreign exchange transactions for firms. The European Commission suggested that elimination of transaction costs could boost the GDP of the countries concerned by an average of 0.4 per cent.

2 **Reduced exchange rate uncertainty**. Exchange rate uncertainty is reduced for intra-union trade but not eliminated as the euro floats against the rest of the world. Reduced uncertainty should increase trade between EU countries and lead to increased investment within EMU member countries, as it removes exchange rate uncertainty for foreign firms. Increased investment should lead to increasing rates of economic growth. The single currency has removed the possibility of devaluation, which some member countries have used in the past to increase their competitive position. Such devaluations may lead to increased inflationary pressure and competitive devaluations by other countries to restore their competitive position. It also adds to uncertainty, which reduces trade and growth.

3 **Increased intra-EMU competition**. While the operation of the single market led to greater trade within the EU, and greater choice for consumers, the euro increases price transparency as it allows consumers a more accurate comparison between markets than was available with different currencies. This increases pressure on higher cost firms to reduce their prices and improve efficiency.

4 **Increased foreign direct investment**. Up to the present the UK has received the 'lion's share' of direct investment from the rest of the world. However, if the UK remains outside, foreign firms may choose continental Europe, as the UK is geographically on the fringes of the area and the possibility of pound/euro rate variations add to uncertainty for firms. Changes in the rate would change the profitability of plants situated in the UK and, to combat such problems, some multinationals in the UK invoice in euros.

5 **Lower interest rates**. One of the major benefits of a single monetary policy run by an independent central bank is that government failure is less likely as interest rate changes will be made on economic rather than political grounds. The ECB is committed to low inflation which affects expectations and this has allowed lower interest rates than would otherwise occur. Lower rates are one of the factors which should allow increasing economic growth.

While there are substantial benefits to having a single currency there are also some disadvantages.

The potential costs of a single currency

Loss of an independent monetary policy. If the UK adopted the single currency the control of UK monetary policy would pass to the European Central Bank, which sets interest rates to achieve monetary objectives for the single currency area as a whole rather than for any one country within the EMU. This common monetary policy or 'one size fits all' policy has several implications:

■ At present the speed at which the Bank of England (BoE) changes the interest rate has an effect on the labour market and its 'tightness' is one of the indicators taken into account. While in the long run there is no trade-off between inflation and unemployment, in the short run it is possible to choose an inflation/unemployment trade-off on the short-run Phillips curve. It is unlikely that the ECB would attach the same importance to UK unemployment levels as the BoE, which may decide to choose an interest rate which reduces inflation slowly, giving time for the unemployed to find jobs, that is, trading off.

■ European economies have labour markets that are inflexible, labour mobility is low, and a demand-side economic shock creating structural unemployment could be met by adjusting monetary policy so that the exchange rate fell in value. But with a single currency this response is less likely unless the problem affects all countries in the Eurozone as the ECB is unlikely to react to the plight of a single country. A further difficulty is that the Stability and Growth Pact limits government's fiscal intervention to 3 per cent of GDP. The country may have to resort to a fall in real wages and consequently increased unemployment to restore its competitive position.

■ Asymmetric policy sensitivity. A single policy adopted by the ECB might affect some member countries more than others, for example, an increase in the rate of interest. In the UK, a relatively high proportion of borrowing for mortgage purposes is at floating rates but in Germany it is at fixed rates and in Europe renting is more popular than in the UK. As a result the UK will be more sensitive than Germany to an interest rate change and aggregate demand could be far more affected by the central bank tightening monetary policy.

■ Too deflationary. Some economists and politicians have suggested that the ECB is too concerned about 'burnishing its anti-inflationary credentials' at the expense of economic growth, and that the target inflation rate of a maximum of 2 per cent is too deflationary and leading to higher levels of unemployment. Such a monetary policy combined with the Stability and Growth Pact may lead to slow rates of economic growth. Experience so far suggests that the ECB is slower to react to falling growth rates than the BoE or the Federal Reserve.

The UK's stance on the single currency

The government has made no formal commitment ever to participate in the economic and monetary union. When Chancellor of the Exchequer, Gordon Brown argued that Britain should join the EMU only if the single currency proved successful, and the economic case for joining was clear and unambiguous. A Treasury paper, which accompanied Mr Brown's statement, sets out five specific economic tests that Britain would have to pass before joining the EMU:

■ the degree of alignment of British and continental business cycles

■ the flexibility of European markets to cope with economic shocks

■ the effect of monetary union on investment in Britain

■ its effect on the financial-services industry

■ its implications for British employment and growth.

Economic convergence. Possibly the most difficult problem is that the UK's economic cycle is not aligned with Europe's. The Treasury paper points out that Britain has more non-EU trade, more home loans made at variable interest rates than its partners, and that it is the only oil exporter. These factors make it hard for Britain's economic cycle to match Europe's, and hard for its interest rates to be the same. Figure 19.4 shows the economic activity in Euroland and the UK. The straight line shows desired economic convergence. The trade cycles are shown as horizontally opposed. The UK is in a recession while Euroland is recovering, which means that different monetary policies are appropriate – one size will not fit all!

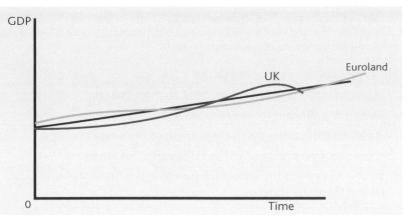

Figure 19.4 *Economic convergence*

Some economists argue that convergence should occur for a period of years before we join, while others argue that convergence will occur as increased trade will lead to similar aggregate demand in UK and Euroland and this in turn will lead to similar economic cycles. The UK authorities could promote convergence but this would require:

- The Bank of England changing its monetary stance from targeting inflation to adjusting the interest rate to promote convergence between the euro and sterling.

- A reduction in short-term interest rates which on the continent are lower than Britain. But, as the Monetary Policy Committee set interest rates to achieve the government's inflation target, they will be unlikely to cut rates unless the government makes corresponding increases in taxation.

Flexibility to cope with economic shocks. This requires labour flexibility, which means that to rejoin the labour market unemployed workers will accept lower levels of wages. Temporary contracts and part-time jobs are an acceptable form of employment and firms can hire and fire easily. Trade unions are not militant and perform a limited role in the economy where workers are both occupationally and geographically mobile. The UK economy is closer to this example than those of Euroland and is well placed to cope with economic shocks as firms in the UK are able to hire and fire more easily than their European counterparts. However, once a member, UK's responses are more limited by the loss of monetary policy and the **eurosclerosis** that still affects Euroland.

Investment in the UK. The UK has had the greatest amount of investment into the EU over the past two decades. The fear is that if the UK stays out, firms within the UK will suffer if the value of sterling increases and will then be more likely to base themselves in Europe instead. On the other hand, if sterling became exceptionally cheap the Eurozone might decide to discriminate against the UK's cheap exports.

Effect on the financial services industry. Initially, when the UK did not join in the 'first wave' it was confidently expected that financial business would move out of London to either Paris or Frankfurt. But this situation did not materialise and the London market has grown. However, joining would mean reduced interest rates, which should benefit traders as share prices would increase.

Key terms

Eurosclerosis: high unemployment and slow job creation despite economic growth.

Effect on UK employment and growth. The reduction in the rate of interest would lead to an increase in aggregate demand and an increase specifically in demand in the housing market. Under existing conditions the Monetary Policy Committee would adjust interest rates to compensate for the increased aggregate demand. Without such restriction inflation could increase and the government would have to use fiscal measures to reduce it. Tax increases are not only unpopular but have a disincentive effect on both workers and entreprezneurs which would not bode well for either employment or growth.

After completing this chapter you should:

■ appreciate the role and implication of EU institutions

■ understand different types of economic union

■ understand the strengths and limitations of the single market

■ appreciate how expansion of the EU has affected the UK

■ be able to appraise the arguments for and against and implications of joining the single currency.

A turning point?

For the four founding members, Argentina, Brazil, Paraguay and Uruguay, Mercosur was an engine of economic growth and trade creation. Then came traumatic devaluations and economic stagnation. Total trade within the block recently overhauled its previous peak, but it is dwarfed by the growth of the members' exports to the rest of the world.

One reason for that is the surge in world prices for South American soya, grains and minerals. The second reason is that Mercosur is drifting. It has failed to implement a pledge to create a genuine customs union, and it has allowed its rule book to be riddled with exceptions.

The upshot is that barriers have multiplied. For example, Argentina's government has tacitly backed the protestors who have blocked the main road bridge to Uruguay for months on end, and has recently backed banana growers who object to the import of cheaper Paraguayan fruit. Rather than use Mercosur's dispute-settlement machinery, it has filed complaints against Brazil at the World Trade Organization. Paraguay has failed to clamp down on widespread smuggling of Chinese-made electronic goods. And Brazil's partners object to the tax breaks given by its state governments to attract investment.

Chile and Bolivia became associate members in the 1990s, entering into free-trade agreements with Mercosur but not accepting its common external tariff. Last year Venezuela was accepted as a full member, at the urging of Argentina's president. Now the presidents of Bolivia and Ecuador want their countries to join too.

Mercosur has plenty of problems. They start with the big difference in size and government policies among members. Argentina's priority has been to protect inefficient but labour-intensive industries as it recovers from socio-economic collapse in 2001–02. Smaller Uruguay and Paraguay complain that the group has done little for them.

Brazil's diplomats say they want fewer trade restrictions and, at last, a common customs code as at present each country collects its own customs revenue, and tariffs are levied on goods from outside the block each time they cross a border.

Mercosur's paralysis is beginning to exasperate business people. Though long protectionist, Brazil's industrialists are nowadays keen to seek new markets – although Brazil exports raw materials to China, 70 per cent of its manufactured exports are sold within the Americas. Industrialists complain that Brazil is losing markets because the United States has struck preferential trade deals in the region.

Adapted from The Economist, 5 July 2007

1 (a) Using the text and your own knowledge outline the requirements of a common market. *(5 marks)*

   (b) With the aid of a diagram explain what is meant by trade creation and the benefits that it may confer. *(10 marks)*

   (c) Evaluate the view that unions such as Mercosur assist world trade in accordance with the principle of comparative advantage. *(25 marks)*

2 (a) Explain the economic arguments for and against the UK adopting the single currency. *(15 marks)*

   (b) Discuss the view that the UK cannot adopt the single currency until the economy converges with the other Eurozone members. *(25 marks)*

Examination skills

Preparing for and taking the A2 examination

The key to exam success is to understand the material that the question requires and good old-fashioned, thorough revision. Hopefully you will have revised the material as you have gone through the course, but it is still a good plan to start revision early in order to reduce the stress of trying to cram at the last minute.

- If you have a revision technique which has proven successful, then continue with it.

- If not, get a copy of the syllabus, which will indicate the main areas, concepts and terminology with which you must be familiar (you can find this at www.aqa.org.uk).

- Get your notes organised and work out a revision plan. Break the syllabus down into manageable bits – the chapters in this book are a good example.

- When you start revision you are unlikely to be able to concentrate for long periods of time, so it is a good plan to revise a particular topic initially for about one hour, then have a 10 minute break before starting again. As you get more accustomed to revision you will be able to concentrate for a longer period of time.

- Use past papers and check that you can recall the correct material to answer them. Plan out your response and then check it against the mark scheme. Some answers require diagrams, asked for or not. Practise drawing the diagrams until you are fluent. Check the website for the correct build up of the diagrams and exercises that you can practise.

- Don't forget that A2 is synoptic, so AS material must be revised as well, especially areas like elasticity and economies of scale which regularly appear at A2.

- Make sure that you can recall the major theories and diagrams without your notes and can apply your knowledge to all situations. Don't waste time trying to memorise model answers as you must answer the question that the Chief Examiner sets, not the question that you would have liked set!

- Revising with friends can be useful as you can explain ideas to each other, plan and write answers to questions and then compare your answers. It may also help to reduce your stress levels as it can help you to see the progress you are making and will show you that you are not alone.

- Throughout this book we have provided you with examiner's tips, which should assist you with the examination and the knowledge that you require in order to be successful.

Link

See the examination skills section in *AQA Economics AS* (p236) for advice on setting and marking the exam.

Mark schemes

All examinations are marked on the basis of a mark scheme that is drawn up by the Chief Examiner when the papers are set. The mark scheme is not rigid but will be adapted to account for the way that candidates have answered the questions.

The format of the A2 paper for Units 3 and 4 is as follows:

- Time allowed: two hours

- Two sections – A and B – each worth 40 marks

- Section A – one data response question from a choice of two – you are advised to spend one hour on each section – each piece of data has three questions to it – the mark allocation is 5, 10 and 25

- Section B – answer one extended writing, essay-type question from a choice of three. Each question is in two parts: part (a) carries 15 marks and is marked on the issues-based mark scheme, and (b) carries 25 marks and is marked on the levels mark scheme

- Unit 4 has an almost identical format; the only difference is that one of the section A data questions will be on The Global Context and the other on the European Union Context

Two approaches have been used in the construction of the mark scheme.

1 An issue-based approach

The mark scheme for parts (a) and (b) of the data response questions and part (a) of the essay questions adopts this approach. The mark scheme lists the marks that can be awarded for particular issues (and associated development) that the candidate might include in the answer. An example from the specimen paper for Unit 3 specification is given below:

Extract D (lines 21–24) suggests that immigration has helped keep interest rates at low levels which 'inevitably may have an impact on consumer credit, savings and the exchange rate, and hence on aggregate demand'. Explain the concept of aggregate demand **and** analyse

two ways in which lower interest rates might raise the level of aggregate demand. *(10 marks)*

Marks are awarded as follows:

Explain aggregate demand, for example, the total spending on goods and services in an economy per time period, and explain the components of aggregate demand. *(Up to 2 marks)*

Explain the ways in which lower interest rates raise the level of aggregate demand, for example:

- lower interest rates make consumer credit cheaper *(1 mark)*, as well as bank loans to consumers *(1 mark)*, leading to greater willingness of consumers to borrow *(1 mark)*, in order to spend more on consumer durable goods which cannot be afforded from current income *(1 mark)*
- investment
- savings
- the exchange rate
- it becomes cheaper for the Government to borrow to finance more spending

Award up to *4 marks* per consequence explained.

Make relevant use of diagrams – up to *2 marks* per diagram to a maximum of 3 marks.

Reward references to the UK economy.

Maximum for part (b): 10 marks.

2 A levels approach

This approach is used for part (c) of the data response questions and part (b) of the essay questions. The Levels Mark Scheme identifies five levels representing differences in the quality of work. A range of marks is allocated to each level. Examiners decide the level into which an answer falls. The level chosen should be the one which best fits the answer provided by the candidate. Candidates do not have to write an answer that satisfies every statement in the level description. Examiners then choose the mid-point mark which has been identified for that level and then fine tune by considering the extent to which the answer meets the level description overall.

The levels and their descriptors are as follows:

In part (c) of the data response questions and part (b) of the essay questions, 40 per cent of the marks are available to award to candidates who demonstrate that they can evaluate economic arguments and evidence, and make informed judgements. An answer showing no evidence of evaluation, however good the analysis, should be awarded a maximum of 15 marks (in Level 3). The quality of evaluation should be the sole distinction between a Level 4 and Level 5 answer. As indicated below, the quality of written communication used should be taken into account when awarding marks.

> ### Link
> *AQA Economics AS* contains advice on the quality of written communication.

Level 1: A very weak answer

Few, if any, relevant issues are recognised. Descriptions and explanations lack clarity. Economic concepts and principles are not adequately understood or applied to the question and its context. No satisfactory analysis or evaluation. Little, if any, appreciation of the inter-relatedness of economic issues, problems and institutions. There might be some evidence of organisation in the answer but generally it fails to answer the question. Spelling, punctuation and grammar may be poor. There is little use of specialist vocabulary.

0 to 6 marks *Mid-point 4 marks*

Level 2: A poor answer but some understanding is shown

A few issues are recognised but there is only limited evidence of the candidate's ability to apply relevant economic concepts. Descriptions and explanations are sometimes hard to follow. An attempt is made to answer the question but there is little satisfactory analysis or evaluation. There is some very limited appreciation of the inter-relatedness of economic issues, problems and institutions. There is some limited logic and coherence in the organisation of the answer. The candidate demonstrates some ability to spell commonly used words and to follow the standard conventions of punctuation and grammar. Some use of specialist vocabulary is made but this is not always applied appropriately.

7 to 11 marks *Mid-point 9 marks*

Level 3: An adequate answer with some correct analysis but very limited evaluation

A few issues are recognised. The candidate has attempted to apply relevant economic concepts and ideas to the question and its context. A reasonable understanding of some concepts and theories is demonstrated. However, the evaluation of the issues, arguments and evidence is limited or superficial. There is some understanding of the inter-relatedness of economic issues, problems and institutions. There is some logic and coherence in the organisation of the answer. The candidate is generally able to spell commonly used words and usually follows the standard conventions of punctuation and grammar. Some descriptions and explanations are easy to understand but the answer may not be expressed clearly throughout. There is some use of specialist vocabulary which is applied appropriately.

12 to 16 marks *Mid-point 14 marks*

Level 4: Good analysis but limited evaluation

Several relevant issues are identified. Good understanding of economic concepts and principles is demonstrated throughout. The candidate is able to apply these concepts and principles to the context to answer the question. A clear understanding of the inter-relatedness of economic issues, problems and institutions is demonstrated. The candidate shows the ability to think as an economist making effective use of the economist's 'tool kit' of concepts, theories and techniques. There is some appreciation of alternative points of view. Satisfactory use is made of evidence and/or theoretical analysis to evaluate the issues/arguments/models identified. The candidate demonstrates some ability to synthesise the arguments presented and come to some relevant conclusions, although these might not always be based on evidence presented. Spelling is generally accurate and the standard conventions of punctuation and grammar are usually followed. The answer is well organised. Descriptions and explanations are clearly expressed. A wide range of specialist vocabulary is used with facility.

17 to 21 marks *Mid-point 19 marks*

Level 5: Good analysis and evaluation

Several relevant issues are identified. Good understanding of economic concepts and principles is demonstrated throughout. The candidate is able to apply these concepts and principles to the context to answer the question. A clear understanding of the inter-relatedness of economic issues, problems and institutions is demonstrated. The candidate shows the ability to think as an economist making effective use of the economist's 'tool kit' of concepts, theories and techniques. There is an appreciation of alternative points of view. Good use is made of evidence and/or theoretical analysis to evaluate the issues/arguments/models identified. The candidate demonstrates the ability to synthesise the arguments presented and come to conclusions which are based on the evidence presented. A clear final judgement is made. Spelling is generally accurate and the standard conventions of punctuation and grammar are usually followed. The answer is well organised. Descriptions and explanations are clearly expressed. A wide range of specialist vocabulary is used with facility.

22 to 25 marks *Mid-point 24 marks*

Synoptic Assessment

All questions in Units 3 and 4 are synoptic and as a result you need to demonstrate that you are able to think as an economist and to use effectively the economist's 'tool kit' of concepts, theories and techniques.

You should demonstrate that you:

■ understand the inter-relatedness of many economic issues, problems and institutions

■ understand how certain economic concepts, theories and techniques may be relevant to a range of different contexts

■ can apply concepts, theories and techniques in analysing economic issues and problems and in evaluating arguments and evidence.

Stretch and challenge

As the advanced extension paper is no longer available for the most able candidates, 'stretch and challenge' has been included in A2 and is met by all the questions that require extended writing, and level 5 of the Levels Mark Scheme indicates the high expectations candidates are required to meet in order to achieve top marks.

What skills do you require?

You will have noted from the mark scheme that certain skills are being tested by the specification:

■ Knowledge of the subject

■ Application of knowledge to the problem set

■ Analysis of the problem or issues

■ Evaluating the evidence and making judgements.

Knowledge

Knowledge requires candidates to show that they can understand what is meant by the question, can choose the relevant areas to discuss and use the correct economic terms to explain it. A question that asks you to explain the possible causes of deficits in an economy's balance of payments will expect you to have knowledge of the likely causes and develop some of them, for example:

■ an overvalued exchange rate

■ high marginal propensity to import

■ a productivity gap

■ excessive inflation.

Application

Knowledge is essential for any economist, but the knowledge must be applied to economic problems to be of use. For instance, knowledge of how government policies overcome market failure may need to be applied to an unexpected question. Candidates would be expected to apply and adapt their knowledge to the circumstances and possibly suggest how a specific policy would affect the economy. Chief Examiners set wide-ranging questions and candidates are expected to be able to apply their knowledge to a wide range of different contexts, two of which are mentioned in the specification. The country referred to in the question may be unfamiliar but a student who has understood how government intervention affects the economy would be expected to be able to use this knowledge. Similarly, in terms of a diagram, the student may be familiar with a marginal social costs and benefits diagram and may have understood the analysis in terms of, say, car usage. Application of this knowledge in a different context, such as an industry disposing of toxic waste, would be an example of application.

Analysis

By analysis we mean dissecting information and using it to explain a problem or issue.

Quite often Chief Examiners ask you to explain data trends from information provided and then link it with other information. Analysis can also be shown graphically where a diagram is used to explain a situation or the result of a particular economic policy. An example could be 'With the help of a cost curve diagram explain how both a firm and its customers may be affected by the economies of scale'.

Your diagram would show what you expected to happen and the text would analyse the likely outcomes for both firms and customers.

In economics analysis is usually:

■ written explanation of a theory

■ a diagram to enhance explanation

■ some equation or use of mathematics when, for example, analysing elasticity.

Evaluation

Evaluation requires candidates to draw conclusions from what they have previously explained or to suggest a particular course of action and argue which courses of action might be most appropriate in a situation. While drawing a simple conclusion a candidate may show some degree of judgement, at A2 level examiners expect more involved evaluation and explanation of the likely effects, drawing on the analysis. The specification makes it quite clear as it states that 'in part (c) of the data response questions and part (b) of the essay questions, 40% of the marks are available to award to candidates who demonstrate that they can evaluate economic arguments and evidence, and make informed judgements'. This can be seen in the essays of students who read widely and are knowledgeable about current economic affairs. Often, economic columnists in the quality newspapers will evaluate a particular course of action that the government is taking and reading such comments assists students in making more valid judgements. There are a number of ways in which evaluation can be undertaken:

■ Any essay question in economics will require a number of issues to be discussed, for example, for the question 'Outline the main disadvantages of the price mechanism as a means of allocating resources', some of the issues that might be discussed are:

– that no account is taken of external costs or benefits

– might lead to the development of monopolies

– uneven distribution of income.

■ If each of these issues is discussed, the drawing of a conclusion or evaluation of the importance of the point needs to take place. While this can be written at the end of the essay, candidates are more likely to be successful if the evaluation occurs after the relevant issue has been discussed and analysed. This does not preclude a final conclusion at the end of the essay. Leaving all evaluation until the end of the essay may result in the student forgetting what has previously been analysed, leading to a lower level of evaluation than would have occurred had it been continuous. Many years' experience as an examiner suggests to me that the more organised and focused candidates, who achieve high marks, tend to evaluate throughout and as a final conclusion.

■ For evaluation to be sound it must be based on the theory or material that you have previously analysed. The marks will be for the quality of the evaluation and not for a statement of personal opinions.

■ Evaluation is what is described as a higher order skill and can be seen at a number of different levels. At a basic level the student may just draw a conclusion from the analysis. In terms of the example given above the student may decide that, as no account of external costs takes place, pollution will result. A more sophisticated conclusion may be that pollution will result but the authorities will deal with this by other methods because the overall advantages of the price system greatly outweigh the disadvantage that it ignores external costs.

■ Evaluation may require the student to consider the importance of competing theories where assumptions are likely to be stated and considered. For example, a candidate might discuss both the benefits and the disadvantages of economic growth to an economy and then evaluate the outcome. The student might decide that growth is beneficial but it will cause certain problems, but the problems can be overcome by the increasing wealth that is generated by the growth. On the other hand, evaluation could consist of the student stating that growth impacts unfavorably on the environment and that growth should be slowed. A further conclusion might be that, at present, it is too early to tell as there is still a large amount of disagreement among experts. Any of these responses would count as evaluation and be rewarded by examiners.

■ Evaluation may occur when considering the likely results of policies and their wider ramifications on the economy. For example, an increase in the levels of income tax is likely to reduce disposable income, which may lead to a fall in aggregate demand. It may also cause a fall in the demand for imports and lead to less effort and participation supplied by the working population; a disincentive effect. Discussion of these and drawing conclusions about them as a result of a change in policy would count as evaluation.

■ Empirical evidence may also be considered and evaluated. At the risk of repetition, knowledge of what is currently going on in the economy and the world will improve your evaluation of policies and their effects.

Glossary

Absolute advantage: where a country using a given resource input is able to produce more than other countries with the same input.

Absolute poverty: when an individual or household's income is insufficient for them to afford basic shelter, food and clothing.

Accelerator theory: the theory that the level of investment is related to past changes in national income.

Activist shareholders: shareholders that will clamour for greater dividends and may mobilise other shareholders to oppose the management.

Activity rate/participation rate: the proportion of the population of working age in a job or actively seeking work.

Actual growth: an increase in the productive potential of the economy matched by an increase in demand.

Ad-volorem: a tax which is a percentage of the price of the unit.

Adaptive expectations: where decisions about the future are based upon past information.

Adjustable peg: value of the fixed exchange rate can be changed as circumstances require.

Allocative efficiency: the optimum allocation of scarce resources that best accords with the consumers' pattern of demand.

Allocative inefficiency: when resources are not used to produce the goods and services wanted by consumers.

Anglo-Saxon neo-liberalism: economic reform aimed at boosting the dynamism of economies – in contrast to the 'social model' which stresses social objectives.

Annual General Meeting: annual meeting where shareholders can discuss the accounts and elect directors.

Anticipated inflation: where economic agents correctly predict the future rate of inflation.

Appreciated: when a floating currency increases in value.

Appreciation: increasing the value of a currency in a free-floating exchange rate system.

Automatic stabilisers: features of government spending and taxation that minimise fluctuations in the economic cycle.

Average cost pricing: setting the price at the level of average cost.

Average fixed cost: total fixed costs divided by the number produced.

Average product: the total product divided by the number of workers.

Average revenue: total revenue ÷ number sold.

Average total cost: total cost divided by the number produced.

Average variable cost: total variable costs divided by the number produced.

Backward-bending supply curve for labour: the individual labour supply curve is thought to be this shape because it is assumed workers will prefer to work fewer hours as their income increases above a certain level.

Balance of payments: a record of the financial transactions over a period of time between a country and its trading partners.

Balance of trade in goods: visible exports minus visible imports.

Balance of trade in services: invisible exports minus invisible imports.

Balanced budget: where government receipts equal government spending in a financial year.

Barometric price leadership: a firm whose price changes are accepted as they are adroit at interpreting market conditions.

Barriers to entry: obstacles that stop new firms entering a market.

Base rate: the interest rate a bank sets to determine its lending and borrowing rates. It will tend to offer interest rates below the base rate to savers, whilst charging rates above the base rate for borrowers.

Benefit principle: the argument that taxes should be linked to the benefits received by taxpayers.

Benign deflation: falling prices resulting from technological advances across the economy.

Brand loyalty: a measure indicating the degree to which consumers will purchase a firm's product rather than a competing firm's product.

Broad money: money held in banks and building societies that is not immediately accessible. This money is held in accounts for which notice is required to make withdrawals, for example, some types of savings accounts.

Budget deficit: where government spending exceeds government receipts in a financial year.

Budget surplus: where government receipts exceed government spending in a financial year.

C

Canons of taxation: the characteristics of a 'good tax', after Adam Smith.

Capital account and **financial account**: the part of the balance of payments that records capital flows in and out of the country.

Capital expenditure: government spending to improve the productive capacity of the nation, for example, on schools and hospitals.

Capital market discipline: where firms may be taken over by other firms if they appear to be making lower profits than their assets would suggest.

Carbon footprint: the amount of greenhouse gases produced measured in terms of carbon dioxide.

Cartel: a group of firms working together, or colluding.

Casual unemployment: a kind of frictional unemployment occurring when workers are laid off on a short-term basis.

Ceiling price: maximum price determined by the authorities.

Classical or real-wage unemployment: results from real wages being above their market-clearing level, creating an excess supply of labour.

Collusion: where firms cooperate in their pricing and output policies.

Comparative advantage: where a country can produce a good with a lower resource cost input than other countries.

Competition Commission: a government organisation responsible for implementing policy in relation to monopolies.

Competition policy: methods that the UK government and EU authorities use in order to make markets more efficient.

Concentration ratio: the proportion of the market share held by the dominant firms.

Conglomerate merger: where firms with no obvious connection combine.

Constant returns to scale: where an increase in factor inputs leads to a proportional increase in factor outputs.

Consumer price index (CPI): the headline measure of inflation, derived from movements in a weighted basket of consumer goods over a 12-month period.

Contestable market: where there is free entry and free exit of other firms.

Contractionary or **deflationary fiscal policy**: where the government runs a large budget surplus.

Copyright: ownership of rights, for example, to a book, giving redress at law for copying by a third party.

Corporate citizenship: indicates that organisations embrace sustainable development.

Corporation: a private enterprise firm incorporated with The Registrar of Companies.

Cost-benefit analysis (CBA): an investment appraisal technique that takes into account all the private and external costs and benefits of an economic decision.

Cost-push inflation: inflation caused by economy-wide increases in production costs.

Crawling peg: frequent changes in the value of a fixed exchange rate.

Credit crunch: a recently coined term used to refer to the reduced willingness of financial institutions to lend to households and to one another.

Crowding out: where a public sector deficit deters private sector investment and consumption.

Current account: the part of the balance of payments that primarily records trade in goods and services.

Current account deficit: when imports of goods and services exceed exports.

Current account surplus: when exports of goods and services exceed imports.

Current expenditure: government spending on the day-to-day running of the public sector, including raw materials and wages of public sector workers.

Cyclical budget deficit: a budget deficit resulting from fluctuations in the economic cycle.

Cyclical or **demand-deficient unemployment**: unemployment due to a lack of aggregate demand.

D

Dead-weight loss: reduction in consumer and producer surplus when output is restricted to less than the optimum level.

Decreasing returns to scale: where an increase in factor inputs leads to a less than proportionate increase in factor outputs.

Deflation: a fall in the general price level.

Deindustrialisation: a fall in the proportion of national output accounted for by the manufacturing sector of the economy.

Delisting: refers to the practice of removing the stock of a company from a stock exchange so that investors can no longer trade shares of the stock on that exchange.

Demand-pull inflation: inflation resulting from too much demand in the economy, relative to supply capacity.

Department of Trade and Industry: the government department responsible for British industry.

Depreciated: when a floating currency decreases in value.

Depreciation: in relation to currencies, reducing the value of a currency in a free-floating exchange rate system.

Depreciation: in relation to fixed assets, a fall in the value of an asset during its working life.

Deregulation: the process of removing government controls from markets.

Derived demand: occurs when the demand for a factor of production arises from the demand for the output it produces.

Devaluation: reducing the value of a currency in a fixed or semi-fixed exchange rate system.

Devalued: when the authorities decrease the value of their currency against others.

Direct controls: controls on imports, such as tariffs and quotas.

Direct investment: the acquisition of productive assets, for example, factories and offices.

Direct taxes: taxes levied directly on the income of an individual or organisation.

Director: an individual elected by a company's shareholders to set corporate policies.

Dirty float: manipulation of a floating rate to gain advantages over trading partners.

Discontinuous marginal revenue curve: region over which a change in marginal costs will not lead to a change in the firm's price and output levels.

Discrimination: where groups of workers are treated differently to other workers in the same job regarding pay and employment.

Distribution of income: how income is shared out between the factors of production.

Distribution of wealth: how wealth is shared out between the population.

Dividends: financial return from the ownership of shares (equities) in a firm.

Dominant market position: where a firm, or group of firms working together, have a market share of 40 per cent.

Dynamic efficiency: efficiency over time – new products, techniques and processes which increase economic growth.

E

Economically inactive: the percentage of the population who are either not in work nor seeking it.

Economic cycle: the cyclical pattern of short-term fluctuations in GDP from year to year.

Economic growth: an increase in the real output of the economy.

Economic rent: the payment received by a factor of production over and above that which is needed to keep it in its present occupation.

Elasticity of demand for labour: the responsiveness of quantity demanded of labour to a change in the wage rate.

Elasticity of supply of labour: the responsiveness of quantity of labour supplied to a change in wage rate.

Enterprise culture: A way of life that emphasises the importance of individuals who create their own businesses and create wealth.

Entrepreneur: individual who organises the factors of production in order to make a profit.

Equilibrium unemployment: when aggregate demand for labour equals aggregate supply of labour.

euro: the currency adopted by the members of the Economic and Monetary union (EMU).

European Monetary Union: a group of countries that have adopted the euro and have their monetary policy controlled by the European Central Bank.

Eurosclerosis: high unemployment and slow job creation despite economic growth.

Eurozone: the countries in the EU that have adopted the single currency.

Exchange controls: restrictions on the ability to trade foreign currencies by a country's central bank.

Expansionary fiscal policy: where the government runs a large budget deficit.

Expenditure-reducing policies: policies used to correct current account imbalances by reducing consumer spending power.

Expenditure-switching policies: policies used to correct current account imbalances by encouraging consumers to buy domestically produced output rather than imports.

F

Family Expenditure Survey: a representative monthly survey of UK household expenditure used to derive changes in the consumer price index (CPI).

First degree price discrimination: when the discriminating firm can charge a separate price to each individual customer.

Fiscal drag: increases in the burden of taxation when tax allowances are not increased in line with inflation.

Fiscal policy: the use of government spending and taxation to meet economic objectives.

Fiscal stance: whether the government is seeking to increase or decrease aggregate demand through its fiscal policy measures.

Fisher equation or **equation of exchange**: the mathematical identity $MV \equiv PY$ (or $MV \equiv PT$), where M is the money supply, V is the velocity of circulation of money, P is the price level and Y is real output (T is the number of transactions in a year, also equivalent to output).

Fixed costs: costs of production that do not vary as output changes.

Floor price: minimum price determined by the authorities.

Foreign direct investment: investments in the domestic economy in new manufacturing plants by foreign multinational companies.

FOREX market: abbreviation of foreign exchange markets.

Frictional unemployment: workers moving between jobs.

G

Game theory: an analysis of how games players react to changing circumstances and plan their response.

Geographical immobility: the inability of a factor of production, usually labour, to move to where jobs exist.

Gini coefficient: a statistical measure of the degree of inequality of income or wealth.

Globalisation: worldwide growth of multinational companies, international integration, the spread of free markets and policies of liberalisation and free trade.

Golden rule: the UK government's fiscal rule that net government borrowing should only be to fund infrastructure projects.

Goodwill: the value of a firm in excess of its asset value including reputation, brand name, trade contacts and general expertise.

Government failure: when government intervention to correct market failure does not improve the allocation of resources or leads to a worsening of the situation.

Gross domestic product (GDP): output produced by resources within the UK.

Gross national product (GNP): output produced by resources within the UK, plus net property income from abroad.

H

Hit and run entry: where new firms enter the industry, cream off some of the supernormal profits of the incumbents and then exit.

Homogeneous: all products are the same irrespective of who makes them.

Horizontal equity: when people or firms with the same income and financial circumstances pay the same amount of tax.

Horizontal integration: where two firms at the same stage of production combine.

Hostile bid: a bid to buy shares in an attempt to gain control of the firm which is opposed by the firm's directors who fear job loss.

'Hot money': volatile capital movements which take place in the foreign exchange markets due to interest rate changes.

Human Development Index: a measure of economic welfare based on the average of three indicators – standard of living, life expectancy and educational attainment.

Human Poverty Index: a measure of economic welfare based on four basic dimensions of human life: longevity, knowledge, economic provisioning and social inclusion.

Hyperinflation: very large, rapid increases in the general price level.

Hypothecation: when taxes are earmarked for a specific purpose.

Hysteresis: the tendency for a variable not to return to its original value or state when changed; for example, unemployment can lead to higher unemployment.

I

Income: a flow of money to a factor of production. An individual's income may include wages and state benefits.

Income effect (of a wage increase): depending upon an individual's target level of income, he or she can work fewer hours for the same overall pay.

Increasing marginal returns: where the addition of an extra variable factor adds more output than the previous variable factor.

Increasing returns to scale: where an increase in factor inputs leads to a more than proportionate increase in outputs.

Incumbent: existing firm(s) in the industry.

Indirect taxes: taxes levied on spending on goods and services.

Inflation: a sustained increase in the general price level.

Innovation: turning invention into commercial use; introducing a new product or process.

Integration: combining with other firms.

Interdependent: where actions by one firm will have an effect on the sales and revenue of other large firms in the market.

International Monetary Fund: a multinational institution set up in 1947 to operate the adjustable peg exchange rate system.

Intra-area trade: trade between the members of a trading agreement.

Inventory investment/stock-building: investment by firms in stocks of raw materials and stocks of finished goods ready to be sold.

Involuntary unemployment: when a worker is willing to accept a job at the going wage rate but is not offered one.

J

J-curve effect: in the short term, a devaluation or depreciation will lead to a deterioration of the current account before it starts to improve.

Joint profits: where firms agree to maximise shared rather than their individual profits.

K

Kinked demand curve: a theoretical approach that endeavours to analyse the reasons for price stability in oligopoly.

Kyoto Protocol: an agreement made at a global summit meeting in Kyoto, Japan, to cut world carbon emissions.

L

Labour market failure: where the free market fails to achieve an efficient allocation of resources in the labour market.

Labour productivity: output per worker per hour.

Laffer curve: a model that shows the theoretical relationship between tax rates and tax revenues.

Lateral merger: a particular type of horizontal merger.

Law of diminishing marginal returns: where increasing amounts of a variable factor are added to a fixed factor and the amount added to total product by each additional unit of the variable factor eventually decreases.

Legal monopoly: a firm with 25 per cent or more of the market share.

Limit pricing: setting a price so low that other firms will not enter the industry.

Liquidity: the degree to which financial assets can be easily converted into money.

Long run: period of time during which all factors become variable and the scale of output can change.

Long-term growth rate: the average rate of economic growth sustained over a period of time.

Lorenz curve: a diagrammatic representation of the distribution of income and wealth.

M

Malevolent deflation: falling prices resulting from a significant downturn in economic activity.

Marginal cost: the cost of the extra unit of output.

Marginal cost pricing: setting the price at the level of marginal cost.

Marginal product: the output added by the extra worker or unit of a factor.

Marginal product of labour: the change in total output arising from hiring one more worker.

Marginal propensity to import: the proportion of an increase in income that is spent on imports.

Marginal revenue: the addition to total revenue from the production of one extra unit.

Marginal revenue product (MRP): the value of the physical addition to output arising from hiring one extra unit of a factor of production.

Market failure: where the free market fails to achieve an efficient allocation of resources.

Market power: when a firm has the ability to exert significant influence over the quantity of goods traded or the price at which they are sold.

Market share: percentage of the total market held by the company.

Marketable wealth: wealth that can be transferred to others.

Marshall-Lerner condition: devaluation or depreciation of a currency will lead to an overall improvement in the current account as long as the combined price elasticities of demand of exports and imports exceed one.

Measure of Domestic Progress: a measure of economic welfare designed to reflect progress in quality of life and progress towards a sustainable economy by factoring in the social and environmental costs of growth, and benefits of unpaid work such as household labour.

Menu costs: the time and money spent by businesses in changing their prices in line with inflation.

Minimum efficient scale: this corresponds to the lowest point on the long-run average total cost curve and is also known as the output of long-run productive efficiency.

Misery Index: a measure of economic welfare constructed by adding the unemployment rate to the inflation rate.

Monetary base control and reserve asset ratios: restrictions imposed by the Bank of England on the ability of high street banks to supply credit and bank deposits.

Monetary factors: the financial rewards to a particular occupation, for example, wage, commission, bonus.

Monetary policy objective: a target or goal that the Bank of England aims to meet.

Money illusion: when economic agents fail to realise that changes in money values are not the same as changes in real values.

Monopsonist: a single, dominant buyer.

Multiplier/accelerator model: a model which describes how the interaction of the accelerator theory and multiplier effect lead to changes in national income.

Multiplier effect: a change in one of the components of aggregate demand leads to a greater overall change in national income.

N

NAIRU: the non-accelerating inflation rate of unemployment, that is, the level of unemployment at which there is no tendency for inflation to accelerate.

Narrow money: notes, coins and balances available for normal financial transactions.

Nash equilibrium: where the optimum strategy is to maintain current behaviour.

National debt: borrowings of government over successive years.

National income: output produced by resources within the UK, plus net property income from abroad, minus depreciation of the nation's capital equipment.

National minimum wage: a statutory minimum wage introduced to boost the earnings of the low paid.

Nationalisation: state control of firms.

Nationalised: taking a firm/industry into public ownership – ownership by the state.

Natural monopoly: a firm that can theoretically gain continuous economies of scale and where it is thus uneconomic for more than one firm to supply the market.

Natural rate of unemployment: the unemployment that exists when aggregate demand for labour equals aggregate supply, that is, voluntary, frictional unemployment.

Negative discrimination: when a group of workers is treated less favourably than others.

Negative externalities: negative spillover effects to third parties not involved with the consumption or production of the good. Social costs exceed private costs.

Net advantage: the overall rewards to a particular occupation, taking into account both monetary and non-monetary factors.

Net current transfers: mainly government transfers to and from overseas organisations.

Net income flows: the difference between inward and outward flows of interest, profits and dividends.

Neutral fiscal stance: where the government runs a balanced budget.

Nominal interest rates: interest rates not adjusted for inflation.

Non-marketable wealth: wealth specific to a person, which cannot be transferred.

Non-monetary factors: the non-financial rewards to a particular occupation, for example, holidays, leisure time and convenience.

Non-monetised sector: valuable economic activity where no money changes hands.

Normal profit: the amount required to keep a factor employed in its present activity in the long run.

O

Occupational immobility: the difficulties faced by workers wishing to change occupations due to not having the required skills or qualifications.

Office of Fair Trading: a government organisation responsible for implementing aspects of competition policy.

Oligopoly: where a few large firms have the majority of the market share.

Open market operations (OMOs): the buying and selling of government bonds in exchange for money to either increase or decrease the money supply.

Optimal output: the ideal combination of fixed and variable factors to produce the lowest average cost.

Optimum output: the optimum combination of fixed and variable factors.

Output gap: the difference between the actual level of GDP and the productive potential of the economy.

P

Parallel pricing: where firms charge identical prices.

Participation rate/activity rate: the percentage of the population of working age currently in work or actively seeking work.

Patent laws: a grant of temporary monopoly rights over a new product.

Perks: non-monetary benefits like an expensive car provided by the firm.

Phillips curve: an economic model that shows a trade-off between inflation and unemployment.

Public Limited Company (PLC): a firm owned by a group of shareholders whose shares can be traded on the London Stock Exchange.

Policy instrument: a tool or method of control used to try to achieve an objective.

Pollution permit: a right to emit a given volume of waste or pollution into the environment.

Portfolio investment: the acquisition of financial assets, for example, shares and financial derivatives.

Positive discrimination: when a group of workers are treated more favourably than others.

Potential growth: an increase in the productive potential of the economy, not necessarily matched by demand.

Poverty audit: assessment of the government's performance in eradicating poverty.

Poverty trap: when individuals or households are no better off following a pay increase because tax paid increases and benefits are withdrawn.

Predatory pricing: setting a price that may bankrupt a competitor firm in order to try to take it over.

Price agreements: where firms collude to fix a price at which a product will be sold.

Price discrimination: where an identical good/service is sold to different customers at different prices for reasons not associated with costs.

Price leader: a firm that establishes the market price that all other firms in the agreement follow.

Price taker: a firm that has to accept the price ruling in the market.

Price war: where firms competitively lower prices to increase their market share.

Principles of taxation: a modern list of characteristics of a 'good tax' system.

Prisoners' Dilemma: where prisoners both choose the worst option.

Private finance initiative (PFI): a form of public–private partnership in which private sector firms undertake the bulk of the work.

Privatisation: sales of government-owned assets to the private sector.

Product differentiation: a way of distinguishing a product from that of competitors.

Productive efficiency: when a firm operates at minimum average total cost, producing the maximum possible output from inputs into the production process.

Productive inefficiency: when firms are not producing at minimum possible average total cost.

Production possibility boundary: diagram of a simplified economy showing the maximum combination of products that can be produced given maximum productive efficiency.

Profit maximisation: where a firm chooses a level of output where marginal revenue equals marginal costs.

Profits: when total income or revenue for a firm is greater than total costs.

Progressive tax: where the proportion of a person's income paid in tax increases as income increases.

Proportional tax: where the proportion of income paid in tax stays the same as income increases.

Public interest: a term used broadly to cover the public's right not to be exploited by firms abusing monopoly power.

Public sector net cash requirement (PSNCR): the difference between government spending and revenue.

Public–private partnerships (PPPs): partnerships between the private and public sectors to provide public services.

Purchasing power parity: exchange rates that take into account how much a typical basket of goods in one country costs compared to another country.

Q

Quantity theory of money: the theory that increases in the money supply will lead to increases in the price level.

R

Rational choice theory: where all costs and benefits are considered before a decision is taken.

Reactive behaviour: the action taken by firms in response to a change in behaviour of a competitor.

Real Gross Domestic Product (GDP) per capita: the total output of the economy in a year, divide by the size of the population, adjusted for inflation.

Real interest rate: the nominal rate of interest minus the rate of inflation.

Recession: negative economic growth over two successive quarters.

Regressive tax: where the proportion paid in tax falls as income increases.

Regulation: setting rules and controls that restrict market freedom.

Regulatory capture: where agencies set up to regulate industries or firms can be 'captured' or influenced by the firms they are intended to oversee.

Relative poverty: when people are poor in comparison to others.

Replacement ratio: unemployment benefits divided by the income an unemployed worker could receive if in work.

Repo rate: the interest rate set by the Monetary Policy Committee of the Bank of England in order to influence inflation. Short for 'sale and repurchase' rate.

Restrictive agreements: where firms collude to indulge in anti-competitive policy.

Restrictive trade practices: methods used by firms to reduce competition in a market.

Revaluation: increasing the value of a currency in a fixed or semi-fixed exchange rate system.

Revalued: when the authorities increase the value of their currency against others.

Ricardian Theory: David Ricardo was a UK economist 1772–1823; outlined the theory of comparative advantage.

Risk averse: where one party does not take any action that might promote retaliatory activity by another party.

Rules of origin: stipulation that a product must be manufactured from locally sourced components.

S

Satisficing: the firm is producing satisfactory but not maximum profit.

Seasonal unemployment: casual unemployment resulting from seasonal fluctuations in demand.

Semi-variable costs: costs which have both a fixed and a variable element e.g. landline telephone usage.

Second degree price discrimination: when the discriminating firm can charge a separate price to different groups of customer.

Semi-manufactures: products beyond the raw material stage that are used in the production of finished products, for example, chemicals, stone, metals.

Shadow price: a price calculated to more accurately reflect the costs and benefits to society of a good, particularly where no market price has previously been calculated.

Share options: the right to buy or sell stock at an agreed price.

Shoe-leather costs: the time and money spent 'shopping around' by consumers to find the best deals when prices are rising throughout the economy.

Short run: period during which fixed costs and the scale of production remain fixed.

Single market: removal of obstacles, such as customs checking, to allow the free movement of goods, services, capital and persons through the area.

Social dumping: where goods are produced by low wage labour usually without expense by employers on workers' social benefits.

Specific tax: a tax levied at a fixed rate per unit.

Stagflation: the coexistence of high levels of inflation and unemployment.

Stakeholders: firms, organisations or individuals with an interest in the firm.

Static efficiency: efficiency at a point in time – includes allocative and productive efficiency.

Strategic value: of extreme importance to a country – may be required in circumstances like war.

'Stealth' taxes: a negative term coined by government critics to describe taxes designed to go unnoticed.

Structural budget deficit: a budget deficit resulting from fundamental changes in the structure of the economy.

Structural performance and conduct model: individual performance depends ultimately on the industry structure where variables in the model are structure, conduct and performance.

Structural unemployment: unemployment due to a change in the pattern of demand and production.

Structural unemployment: unemployment due to a change in the pattern of demand and production.

Sub-normal profit: profit below normal which should lead to firms leaving the industry.

Sunk costs: irretrievable costs that occur when a firm exits an industry.

Supernormal profit: a return above normal profit – a surplus payment.

Supply-side policies: a range of measures designed to increase aggregate supply.

Sustainable investment rule: the fiscal rule that over the economic cycle, public sector debt should not exceed 40 per cent of GDP.

Sustainability (of economic growth): economic growth which does not impose costs on future generations.

T

Tacit collusion: where firms have reached an 'agreement' as to each other's behaviour as a result of repeated observations over time.

Technological unemployment: unemployment due to the introduction of labour-saving technology.

The Budget: the governments' annual announcement of changes to its planned levels of spending and taxation.

Theory of marginal productivity: key theory underpinning the demand for labour.

Third degree price discrimination: when the discriminating firm can charge a different price in each country.

Total costs: fixed costs + variable costs.

Total profit: total revenue minus total costs.

Total revenue: what the firm receives for the sale of its product = price × number sold.

Trade creation: an increase in international trade that results from the reduction in tariff barriers.

Trade deflection: redirection of international trade due to the formation of a free trade area.

Trade embargoes: prohibition of the export and import of certain types of products.

Trade union: an organisation of workers who join together to further their own interests.

Trade union mark-up: the addition to wages secured by members of a trade union, compared to what they would earn if there were no union.

'Tragedy of the commons': the over-exploitation of natural resources that are not owned by single individuals or organisations.

Transfer earnings: the minimum payment needed to keep a factor of production in its present use.

Transfer payments: government payments to individuals for which no service is given in return, for example, state benefits.

Transmission mechanism of monetary policy: the process by which a change in interest rates affects aggregate demand and inflation.

Trend rate of economic growth: the long-run average increase in GDP.

U

Unanticipated inflation: where economic agents do not accurately predict the future rate of inflation.

Unemployment: the number of people of working age who do not currently have a job but are actively seeking work at existing wage rates.

Unemployment trap: where the income tax and benefit system reduces the net increase in income people can expect from taking paid work. Thus many people would not choose to take a job.

V

Variable costs: costs of production that vary with output.

Velocity of circulation: the number of times the money supply changes hands in a year.

Vertical equity: when the amount that people and firms pay is based on their ability to pay.

Vertical integration: where firms at different stages of production combine.

Voluntary unemployment: when a worker chooses not to accept a job at the going wage rate.

W

Wage differentials: differences in wages arising between individuals, occupations, industries, firms and regions.

Wage-price spiral: the process whereby increases in costs, such as wages, lead to increases in prices, which in turn leads to firms' costs increasing, and so on.

Wealth: a stock of valuable assets.

'Welfare to work': a series of policies designed to increase incentives to gain employment.

X

X-inefficient: sometimes called organisational slack, not reducing costs to their lowest level – the gap between the actual and lowest possible cost.

Z

Zero sum game: where a gain by one player is matched by a loss by another player.

Index

Note: key terms are in **bold**